The Mystery of the Trapped Light

The Mystery of the Trapped Light

Mystical Thoughts in the Dark Age of Scientism

JAMES TUNNEY

James Tunney is the author of this book and owns all copyright ©
in this work and assert all moral rights thereto 2020.

Cover image copyright © James Tunney.
Based on an original oil painting by the author.
Above image 'Mystical Spirits of Science,' pastel on roof-paper.

ISBN: 9798644288533

To Jeffrey Mishlove

A charismatic champion of the best version of us.

Also by James Tunney

Mysticism & Spiritual Consciousness

The Mystical Accord – Sutras to Suit Our Times,
Lines for Spiritual Evolution

Fiction

Blue Lies September

Ireland I Don't Recognise Who She Is

Contents

1. **Lightgate** 11
   1.1 Identifying Light: Natural, Physical, Spiritual, Magical 11
   1.2 Darkness: Physical and Spiritual 19
   1.3 The Mystical Path for Spirit 35
   1.4 Perennial Spiritual Consciousness and
       the Challenge of Scientism 41
   1.5 Ghosts of St. Pancras 49
   1.6 The Contested Prometheus 52
   1.7 Light in Spirit and Science: Glowing Birds
       and Precious Stones 62
   1.8 Trapped Light Today 74
   1.9 The Fork 78
   1.10 The Nature, Art and Metaphysics of Light 83
   1.11 Light v. Heavy 101
   1.12 Light of the Flame 103
   1.13 The Omnipresence of the Spiritual Light 110
   1.14 From Stars to Astral Light and Beyond 140
   1.15 Can Insights on Light Be Unified? 150
   1.16 Trapped in Matter of Mystery 166
   1.17 Mystery Schools 173
   1.18 Approach and the Five Illuminations 184
   1.19 Shattered Experience of Light 189
   1.20 Conclusion: Mystic Prescience of Threats and Traps 195

2. **Origin of Mystic Light** 208

3. **Perchance Trapped Light are We in a Way** 216

4. **The Light Within. Inwards** 224
   4.1 We are Light of Spirit Consciousness 224
   4.2 Find Your First Light so Spirit Grows 229

5. Light and Heavy 233
   5.1 Seek Lightness of Spirit Letting Go 233
   5.2 Relinquish to Allow Spirit Be Light 237
   5.3 Relinquishment: Mind How Everything
       is Enfolded Even in Words 240
   5.4 Lightened We are Liberated. Upwards 244

6. False and Artificial Light 249
   6.1 Tending to Light Misled. Astray 249
   6.2 Machine Light May Destroy Spirit 252
   6.3 Knowing is the Second Light 256

7. Dark Night 259
   7.1 Spiritual Darkness Seeks Second Light 259
   7.2 Second Light Seeks to Settle 263

8. Celestial Light 266

9. Journey Towards the Other Light 269
   9.1 Spirit Journeys to Third Light. Up 269
   9.2 Third Light Descends if You Ascend 274

10. Lamp and Lighthouse 279

11. The Influx of Light 284
   11.1 Fourth Illumination. Down-Across 284
   11.2 Create a Nexus to Numinous Light. Up-down 286

12. Pillar of Light 288

13. Mystic Light 289

14. From This Light to the Next 290

15. Mystic Path of Light 295

16. Lesson of Light 299

Glossary 302

About the Author 357

"…take heed, as unto a lamp shining in a dark place…"

King James Bible, 2 Peter 1:19

"The true light that enlightened everybody was coming into the world."

King James Bible, John 1:9

"But all things that are reproved are made manifest by the light; for whatsoever doth make manifest is light."

King James Bible, Ephesians 5:13

"The power which is a reflected beam of pure Consciousness, called the understanding, is a mode of abstract Nature; it possesses wisdom and creative power."

"This is the self-luminous, witness of all, ever shining through the veil of the soul; making the one aim this Self, that is the contrary of all things unreal, realise it by identification with its partless nature."

The Crest Jewel of Wisdom, Sankaracharya

"Then the Lord of Death will say 'I will consult the mirror of karma'."

Tibetan Book of the Dead

"…walk thou only in the right way properly, which is called the way of light…"

"…draw thy spirit into that majestic light, wherein the original patterns and forms of things visible are to be seen."

"Wherefore seek the fountain of life, waiting in the deep ground of thy soul for the rising there of the sun of righteousness, whereby the light of nature in thee, with the properties thereof, will be made to shine seven times brighter than ordinary."

Signature of All Things, Jacob Boehme

"For when I say darkness, I mean a lack of knowing; as all that thing that thou knowest not, or else that thou has forgotten, it is dark to thee, for thou seest it not with thy ghostly eye."

"Ghostly, the eyes of thy soul is thy reason, thy conscience is thy visage ghostly."

"…and my spirit would brood upon ways of escape and ascent to its native regions…"

"And then we shall be made so subtle in body and in soul together, that we should be then as swiftly where us list bodily as we be now in our thought ghostly."

The Cloud of Unknowing

"The inner light doctrine is that there is something of the Divine Source of God in the human soul."

Social Law in the Spiritual World, Rufus Jones

"For in and out, above, about, below,
'Tis nothing but a Magic Shadow-show,
Play'd in a Box whose Candle is the Sun,
Round which we Phantom Figures come and go."

The Rubaiyat of Omar Khayyam, Fitzgerald Translation

"In essence, we are all the same. The principle of light shines within each and all. Pure consciousness is our abiding nature."

The Gift of Consciousness, Gitte Bechsgaard

"Without going out of my door I can know all things on earth."

The Inner Light, Song by the Beatles

1. Lightgate

> "Wherever the traces of mystical experience are to be found in past history, they are associated with the imagery of light..."
>
> **William Anderson**, *The Face of Glory*.

1.1 Identifying Light: Natural, Physical, Spiritual, Magical

Throughout the history and pre-history of humankind, there has been a consistent sense in diverse spiritual traditions that we are spirits somehow trapped in flesh or matter. A remarkably persistent perennial insight is that while we were created, evolved, placed, imprisoned, beguiled or fallen into flesh - we are essentially and obviously something else. Perennial vision suggests we come from light, possess it still and ought to return there pursuing an illumined way through present incarnation. This spiral of light appears to describe mystic paths to spiritual destiny. However, it may be misrepresented to become a denial and rejection of the material world and body in a manner inconsistent with spiritual evolution. Even the word 'cell,' basis of all life, referred to a small room for a monk or imprisoned miscreant. Despite mystical truth in metaphors or reality of being trapped light, extreme left and right sneer. Other writers such as Rosemary Ruether warn against such falsehoods,

> "The Big Lie tells us that we are strangers and sojourners on this planet, that our flesh, our blood, our instincts for survival are our enemies. Originally we lived as discarnate orbs of light in the heavenly light. We have fallen to this earth and into this clay through accident or sin. We must spend our lives suppressing our hungers and thirsts and shunning our fellow beings, so that we can dematerialise and fly away to the stars."

If a unifying religion evolves in future, it will be based on light. To understand it, we must accept darkness, especially within ourselves. The universe provided this ostensible duality as contrast to allow us perceive reality, know, be and evolve. But like all dualities, like inside and outside, it is illusory and deceptive at times and will be non-dual in the end. Mystics seek unification of poles above and people's split-mind and spilt energy below. Perceptual unity is not Romantic moral relativism however. While such a new theology may be based on light there are very distinct conceptions that might be used as we shall see. Contemplation and experience of the phenomenon of light help us understand life, mysticism, magic, religion, art, psychology, parapsychology, science and technology. Individuals must evolve spiritually in an integrated way so a whole, holy worldview can emerge. To be the best version of ourselves we use mystical insights to alter disintegrative elements in our perilous psychic state. I advocate holistic, individual, spiritual evolution through experience and imagination whilst retaining sovereignty, steered by basic principles of compassion from perennial wisdom and committed to growth and increased comprehension. If recurrent spiritual insights of light being entangled or entrapped in matter, so evident in perennial wisdom, leads to a negative view of flesh, body and nature, I reject such pessimism but not the basic intuition. While we seek transcendence, it is a mistake to reject great glories of earth. Indeed wisdom of ancient and indigenous people, mother goddess and Divine feminine is needed to find a new relationship with our sole homeland. We should appreciate forest, flowers, animals, mountains. If you can safely swim in the sea, lakes, climb mountains or trees, run, walk, walk barefoot, feel sunlight on skin, grapple, move, tumble, hop, talk with friends, family and strangers, greet, appreciate what you eat, paint, enjoy art, have a massage, do yoga or whatever, to celebrate your body on earth, you are participating in an incredible world, helping yourself be a whole person. Indeed, technological alienation of humans from earth and their body is part of the greatest danger we face. So let us examine actual and spiritual light and darkness in the context of mysticism, science and scientism, examining the interplay and especially the mystery of being trapped in matter.

Natural light has a narrow, ordinary, common sense meaning that refers to how, and sources whereby, we see or how visual receptors are activated. The source by which we see is light and is thus related to visibility. We can make life complicated by nuances such as the fact that we do not see light but objects which reflect it, that colour is the non-absorbed part of the spectrum, that there may be infra-red elements of sound or what we are seeing is really in our brain. But that gets too far away from my simple purpose of proposing some way of thinking about how we can discuss wider perceptions of it. Seeing is not just about physical light in the eye but also about how it interacts with perception in the mind. Light also has a wider definition or meaning. Light in physics really refers to the electro-magnetic spectrum and all waves and rays thereon, with visible light being but a sliver. Light involves waves classified by frequency or rays that do not need a medium although there are others types beyond that do. Quasars emit the full range it seems. Here we will focus particularly on visible light with occasional considerations beyond in the penumbra. If one equates visual evidence of scientific representation of the spectrum with ostensible relative insignificance of visible light, we misrepresent the depth and importance of colour for us, as an existential, psychological, psychic and public phenomenon. But when we think of light remember the various ways you might subjectively encounter, experience or apparently perceive it, apart from purely metaphorical illumination and before we fully conceive what might be termed 'spiritual light' or in Latin *lux spiritualis*. This ancient description is sometimes contrasted with natural light which is often *lumen*. Sometimes corporeal and incorporeal light are unified. Natural light does not cover all encountered waves such as certain types in the brain or mechanical ones like sound or infrasound (that some believe may cause certain psychic phenomena). Bear in mind that some perception, although real to the beholder, may be regarded as some type of optical effect whereby eye or brain is deceived and produces 'illusions' through contrast, brightness, shadows, scintillations, parallax or mirages. Something exists to cause such illusions. Rainbows are not there in one sense but are in another. Similarly 'disruptive colouration' exists in nature and was mimicked in camouflage. Beings can create illusions. Diseases of the mind may delude perceptions and make distortions. But if we think of the presumed source as external or internal and type as visible or invisible, we get a simple, classification of light, in its widest sense from the viewer's, subjective perspective to begin with.

1. **External visible light** - The light we see from the sun, fire, other beings, plants and things including perception of certain, extraordinary phenomena.

2. **External invisible light** - The waves on the spectrum we cannot see, but may potentially feel or not or may be ultimately affected by, through say radiation sickness if subjected to them. Thus examples might be x-rays, infra-red, ultraviolet or gamma rays.

3. **Internal visible light** - Light that may be perceived in brain or body apparently visible or perceptible even when our eyes are shut in the dark. Thus we might think of phosphenes, hypnagogic experiences, meditation images, visualisation, dreams or memory.

4. **Internal invisible light** - Light operating within the body or mind that is not visible, whether perceptible or imperceptible. This could be electromagnetic energy with reference to say emotional states in the heart's electromagnetic energy, by analogy and actually to light, by sensations such as deep feelings of radiant emotion.

5. **Combined light** - Perceptions of experiences that may embody all or some of the above perhaps with external-internal, visible-invisible and subjective-objective blurring and even illusion. The UFO experience may combine all types of light phenomena for some people.

The fourth category is the most difficult to pin down, but has to be a valid category or type. A dichotomy used elsewhere is of 'spiritual' and 'sensible' light. However spiritual light is sensible in the sense of acting on senses in the widest sense. The ghost word 'spectre' comes from spectrum, meaning image or apparition from a root 'to see' or observe. When people like David Hume talked of senses, they had an extremely narrow conception which undermined the integrity of their conclusions. Likewise there are many particular visual phenomena that may occur in the eye of the beholder that are difficult to categorise such as floaters, visual snow, blue fields and Purkinje images. Some of these are 'entoptic' which means they come from within eye or brain, but are related to light or its absence. Such sights are distinguished from hallucinations which may involve more than visual images but are still internal. However there is still some perceived light. We could complicate it more by debates about whether the outside exists or everything is in our mind, but we descend quickly into philosophical quicksand. What is inside and what is outside is not easy to explain with light. So even how we personally encounter light and what we see, without considering confusion, illusion or mental imbalance, is complicated.

We might consider what 'light' used specifically in spiritual discourse means and how to define it, similarly based on perception of phenomena from reports of subjective experience. *Spiritual light phenomena might be defined as perception or recognition of light that has a significant, spiritual or profound psychological effect involving an actual alteration or enhancement of consciousness through some unique, extraordinary or elevating quality thereof that may occur as an unexpected event or recur through encouragement and engagement with practices calculated to engender them.* It could be termed 'mystical light' and distinguished from physical light because of its extraordinary form, important personal impact or actualising effect. The definition immediately raises the question of whether another form of light exists, or light from another space or dimension can be encountered or if it's all in the mind. Spiritual light may involve all five possible, experiential phenomena of subjective experience, where existence is not controversial but explanation is controvertible. In the context of internal invisible and combined light, there is already a penumbra of subtler but significant manifestations or sensations known to the spiritually evolving but strange or alien to many contemporary scientists and people. But the accepted notion of actual light, even with fuzzy edges, excludes what may be higher or subtler perception of it. Perception of unique light effects that impact psychologically cannot be regarded merely as an aberrant or anomalous reaction to explicable events. In spiritual discussion, visible light is often a reflection of higher form. This pervasive light is source of all in certain spiritual traditions and physical light is a correspondence or copy or lesser manifestation of a more perfect form. We see great medieval Catholic cathedrals (increasingly under threat) as symphonies in stone, masterworks in masonry, but this is inside-out. Cathedrals were meant to be poetic homages in stone to light in my view. We became fascinated with shell and forgot the pearl. Movement of light in Chartres or Lincoln Cathedral represented a lesson about spiritual light, whose orchestration was material reverence to higher immaterial forces, through channelling and diffusion of natural light. In much perennial wisdom, spirit is described as a type of light that comes from a greater source into flesh or matter by which we should orientate and return to. Light is central in most religions but reduced to meaninglessness by ritual, priesthoods and institutional capture. Science dismisses much experience and rejects what it cannot explain. Human perception is capable of operating on a plane beyond scientific comprehension. Light in spiritual consciousness is a comprehensive tradition precisely because it is a consistent perceived reality. However use of the word 'light' is often like the word 'nature' or 'natural' and needs to be examined to clarify.

Study of physical light might be the universe's way to allow slow spiritual learners a last chance. Humankind can learn the hard way through microscopic knowledge of what once was available to it through macrocosmic, balanced awareness and spiritually-based endeavour. Alternatively it tears itself apart with madness of a nature-alienated world serving machines. Even if one cannot accept the idea of any supernatural dimension, an understanding of light's magic provides a great focus for wonder. In mystical study, true light is the *lux spiritualis* which led to scientific research of light. No intellectual revelation of physical light will ever surpass intuitions of spiritual light for mystics. Solar cults based on light have dominated many spiritual systems and have often been seen to be masculine with feminine lunar cults. Even so, my suspicions is that if you dig a bit deeper you will find a feminine, goddess aspect, lost or suppressed which say recognises sun consciousness as feminine manifesting in a masculine ray in the form of a 'son.' Perhaps, dual masculine-feminine may be indicated by a non-dual, combined masculine beam of light particles and a feminine wave. Another concept is 'light of nature,' (*lumen naturae*) which represented light manifest or trapped in matter in nature. There is a critique principally of scientism to follow. Some problems with scientism do come from science itself and its philosophy. Increasingly, historians are showing how the Enlightenment and rise of atheism came out of Christian theology and not from a tradition of free thought. Techniques of disputation facilitated the antithesis of the religion. Likewise many Catholics had a profound impact on it. Reason was one sort of light. The metaphor of light as knowledge was taken by Francis Bacon to represent scientific method.

If we have a conception of a range of light experiences we have a foundation to look at relevant scientific knowledge. It is clear that we react to sunlight or heat in a sauna and how health is dependent on light. Most sea creatures live in the 'photic zone' where sunlight shines. Spiritual health needs light as well. Spiritual descriptions, both metaphorical and actual, create a range of light experiences that may be physical, psychological or psychic. Phenomenology means we can pay attention to personal experiences and give credence to them particularly with consistent recurrence. There are many who will deny perennial phenomena of spiritual experiences ignoring significance of light-based perceptions, dismissing them as 'pseudo-science.' Parapsychology, spiritual and folk history struggle with scientism but unless threats of scientocracy prevail, mystical significance of light will persist for anyone on a quest to evolve spiritually. Let us explore ideas of light and tension between scientism and spirituality, bearing in mind subjective and objective evidence and how the former can become the latter in certain circumstances. The best scientists have great gaps in their understanding. Unfortunately, if we look to philosophers instead, we see a love of wisdom withered and they appear like sales people in a shoe shop whose main job is to return discards to correct compartments. Often they are ideological and not open about it. Pragmatists oppose ideology to avoid narrowing the terrain. Let us examine light to understand ultimate facts intimately. I have stated elsewhere that we do not need gurus, not that we cannot be taught by true teachers wherever they arise from, humble but not humiliated. But spiritual evolution is what every individual should do in their own way. The hidden mystic path should be brought to light and while esoteric restrictions may have been necessary at times, it should be open. The individual who evolves spiritually is the greatest protection of genuine liberty. An underestimated danger facing the individual is scientism and we may be entering a dark age led by it. Let us consider what darkness means as supposed antithesis of light. Then it is worth considering what mystic paths of spiritual evolution suggest before examining what scientism involves and how these forces interact in debates about who we are. This provides the framework for poetic lines to approach truth more obliquely. Imagery and description of spiritual experience mirrors physical vision, perception and light and often involves them.

I am not trying to be a moralist here but present distinctions to distinguish forces, but I am not a relativist or neutral about collective control. There is another type of light which could be called 'magical light,' to distinguish from spiritual light, addressed to the mind and emotions. *Magical light is the use of light primarily to achieve altered states of consciousness through remarkable, overwhelming physiological or psychological force usually through dramatic, technological, chemical or physical means, often in groups or on other people, so that illusion, suggestibility and hypnosis can override the will of the observer to achieve some objective.* Magic is about enforcing will and may be benign or not. Magical light is not induced by the percipient and is not mystical light although they overlap, particularly in the context of healing, shamanic, initiation or mystery school ceremonies. Discos, mass rallies, concerts, tv, advertising and sports events use magic light.

1.2 Darkness: Physical and Spiritual

At the Nuremburg Rallies, the *Lichtdom* or Cathedral of Light was a formidable spectacle of sorcery produced by searchlights that had the most powerful impact on spectators to the benefit of the Nazis. Technology and paganism were united in a cold heart of darkness. Here was will rising in light form with might to the heavens, uniting primitive, pagan sorcery with power of technological enlightenment calculated to mesmerise and hypnotise in a magical way. Use of light at night-time was very deliberate. Magical light was used to harness mass psychic power in a pseudo-spiritual way. Related books have been written about 'dark charisma.' Mass rallies have mass. Likewise humankind can re-define principles of behaviour to create alternative conceptions of right and wrong, dark and light. Suggested use of holograms in intelligence operations indicates other possible uses of magical light. Light and dark oscillate.

Illumination presumes possibility of its absence. As light emerges into darkness, let us begin briefly with the idea of the dark. Remember the eye changes at twilight to see a slightly different colour range. Interestingly, that is when fairies and other beings appear most. Sometimes we can see what we could not hitherto. Artists and mystics are often just using natural abilities to see properly. Whistler would train himself and others to look at a scene and memorise it to be reproduced later. People use devices now. Memory and systems were critical in magic. Many phenomena associated with parapsychology occur in the dark. Sometimes people say they had a dark mood or are in a dark place and that seems inevitably negative in our light-filled world. But darkness is also a metaphor or context. The idea that darkness is to be avoided at all costs is somewhere between silly and dangerous, even about temporary feelings and states. Natural darkness is beautiful and no mere emptiness. Indeed science seems to have elevated darkness through concepts such as dark matter, black body and black holes. In science, darkness is equally complex, elusive and certainly no mere absence. Darkness is often a clue in science, sometimes suggesting some other phenomenon is at play such as with Crooke's Dark Space. The eye's pupil is dark, as we need darkness to see.

In Praise of Shadows is a famous work by Tanizaki on traditional Japanese and Zen aesthetics, appreciating beauty of subdued light and shade in space and gleaming on things like candlelit lacquer. Mystical darkness involves impressions. For example, 'dazzling' or 'Divine darkness' are recurrent descriptions in mystical experiences. Intellectually, lack of knowledge is equated with darkness and meaning is distorted by what Nietzsche called the 'black art of obscurantism.' This word comes from the Latin verb meaning 'to make dark.' Academics equate incomprehensibility with depth. Metaphorical darkness within us is necessary to know before we see contrast. Different types of darkness may operate together. Some native groups, such as the Kogi in Colombia, still use darkness in significant spiritual ways as ancestors have done everywhere. Pagans, witches, shamans, hermits, anchorites and anchoresses and mystery schools have long embraced darkness. Orpheus descends into the underworld where blackness in the spiritual womb incubates. Mithraism was practiced in underground rooms. Dante goes to the underworld. Plato uses the cave in a negative sense. A theatre means a place to behold or see. When we go to a cinema we come from bright reality outside into a dark cave lit by dreams, illusion, fantasy and nightmare. Unfortunately, we have difficulty in disentangling illusion and reality in the theatre of our own psyche. Outside may become inside, often to our detriment. Lightness and darkness is part of the whole and hence what is holy. Healing needs wholeness. It is a mistake to assume that because physical or mystical darkness is involved in a practice it is negative. Enlightened 'model prisons' in Australia put prisoners into solitary confinement in darkness for weeks paradoxically. Bentham's *Panopticon,* although not really implemented, was a planned Enlightenment, utilitarian, light-filled way to see imprisoned people all the time. Evil done by the State was a tool against other evil for him. Ironically science denies invisible omnipresence but seeks to re-create it with control tools. Believing you know what is good for others is a sure path to evil. Alternatively, when you cannot tell Voldemort is the bad guy, you have taken it too far. It is stranger still when classic principles are rejected and new thought crimes invented and even applied retrospectively.

A reflection on deceptive duality may help. The paradox of polarity of light and dark is that an appearance of illumination may involve another form of darkness and likewise its semblance may mask a dimension of light. It might even be said that every light creates a contrasting darkness and every sort of darkness allows light manifest. Like Taoists understand, we seek a centre of dynamic balance aware of contrast. Even knowledge comes at a price, so some notional intellectual darkness may be preferable to too much of it. Often the moon goddess or earth was worshipped at night. The word 'occult' really refers to that which is hidden or secret. When groups are persecuted they will perform in secret, in woods or underground in cool catacombs like early Christians, more conducive to holy concentration. Caves and dark places have always been used in pre-historic rituals and practices of initiation because they were associated with the feminine, yin force and because darkness allows light phenomena appear or manifest, letting light work in a more pronounced way, sometimes combined with other factors such as drumbeats or substance use. That is how certain mystery traditions worked, being essentially shamanic. Like the astronomers who loved the night dearly we should not fear mere darkness and we need it. Light all day and all night, as in the Arctic Circle, is disorientating as I found. In Greek legends or as expressed in literature, we will become 'shades' or ghosts, we are shadows. The Latin word 'umbra' was an Elizabethan name for a ghost. As I 'adumbrate' these meanings I foreshadow or outline. Phantoms often appear as light figures in illustrations perhaps because darkness is not the current, natural domain of representation. 'Illustration' was used to mean spiritual illumination at times and refers to the Latin word illustrare which means to light up or illuminate. Paradoxically, we see that all politic propaganda uses illustration to promote dark plans, suggesting the deeper level of possession in the potent magic of psychological manipulation. Illumination presumes darkness as the ground. It is hard to film darkness properly. Mystery needs obscurity. As the Irish poet Kavanagh wrote,

"Through a chink too wide there comes in no wonder."

Shade and shadow are related to the word and concept of shelter and protection. Shadow is conducive to enhanced perception. Edmund Burke in 1757 wrote *A Philosophical Enquiry into our Ideas of the Sublime and the Beautiful*. This work on aesthetics defined Romantic conceptions of the sublime for people who wanted revolutionary social change. Burke understood that we are moved by forces which are not pleasant as such. There are feelings of astonishment based on a sense of awe, horror or even terror from beholding say a mountain or waterfall which offend classic proportionality, creating a sense of extraordinary power and danger in imagination to engender the extraordinary or sublime. Things can be made 'very terrible' by obscurity or darkness until we adjust our vision or light is increased and that is why ghosts and goblins affect us so. Uncertainty or lack of form increases fear. This obscurity can be seen in Milton's depiction of Satan. The Romantic was manifested in Gothic fascination with darkness and horror reacting against the Enlightenment light of rationalism after the destructiveness of Reformation stripping of altars. A certain split persona and a Protestant sense of damnation emerges which is not merely intellectual or sensational but really about soul or spirit.

Spiritual darkness is a more serious concern. Underneath the Gothic novels was the Faustian pact, especially after Goethe. Perhaps the link is suggested in the names *Goethe-Gothic-Goetia*. Goethe wrote Faust. He contains influential Gothic elements. Goetia is about conjuring of demons and sorcery. You sell your soul for sensuality but go to the devil. Wilde may have felt hell on earth with his own double life after his fall. Novels like *The Monk* were admired by De Sade. Lucifer (a daemon, devil or fiend) appears as a dark figure in lightning, summoned by desperate sorcery and secures the once pious monk's soul with a signed contract. This story has clarity of moral consequence long obscured by modern writers. Some see a certain Romantic and Gothic quality through Marx and Freud to heavy metal music. Another Dubliner, Bram Stoker crafted *Dracula*, an archetypal creature of the night. Yet another Dubliner, Charles Maturin, also exemplifies the Protestant Gothic tradition with the influential tale, *Melmoth the Wanderer*. Oscar Wilde wrote *The Picture of Dorian Grey* and the signed pact is reduced to a mere deeply expressed desire and statement that 'he would give everything.' This is modern selling of soul, in a shallow world of appearances, a public statement that you would give everything (including your soul) for some material or mundane reward. Heaven and hell are inside you, paths look the same, it depends on your intention whether you seek poison or perfection for soul or spirit. The Faust tale reflects Job in the Bible where Satan and God speculate about his faith. To add to a cast of Irish-inspired villains we might add in Professor Moriarty from the writer of Sherlock Holmes. Sir Arthur Conan Doyle was also interested in the spirit world and was an unsuccessful eye-doctor. This is not an insignificant connection as we will see.

There is another idea of the Apollonian and Dionysian where the former is about sun, light and order and the latter is irrationality and emotions. Paglia says it is about light on one side versus dark, wild and underground nature. Kant disagreed with Burke, who made an impact through the clarity of his thought. The great event which moved Burke was the French Revolution which evoked ideas of light and darkness. In a famous essay he talked of darkness and false lights from love of reason in his defence of the ancient order. He believed that ancient rights would be lost in revolution. The Reign of Terror indicated how the aims of reason were followed with a primitive violence suggesting that rationality was not enough. More realistically, the appeal to rationality is a trick to overcome conservative forces from competing claimants to control. Darkness deserves attention in terms of its nature, form, aesthetic, metaphorical and mystical dimensions. Darkness of mood of an author and their time often unleashed trapped creative light. We will see that with a famous mother and daughter combination in the same era of the best of times and worst of times.

The dark side in *Star Wars* is represented by the Sith and the Dark Lord who employ anger, fear, hate and suffering. Darkness is absence of light and reflects the Zoroastrian duality of black and white, evil and good. The 'Prince of Darkness' and associated minions emerges in studies of Mani and Gnosticism. Spiritual darkness in many religions and traditions refers to an absence of spiritual or Divine light and a propensity to destructiveness as well as a dark presence. Darkness may be in the individual or outside or both. In certain esoteric schools, this darkness is caused by distance from original light. Darkness is associated with sin and spiritual ignorance. Spiritual darkness represents evil which usually hides and does not want to operate in light. The *Gospel of John* tells of Jesus bringing light, representing light and providing the example of light so others would not be in darkness. In *Genesis*, God created light, not least so people could see creation. Light represented spiritual life against spiritual darkness. Darkness is disorder, ignorance and destruction in the spiritual and worldly domain. But as indicated, darkness has another stream in mystical Christianity. Writings purporting to come from first century Athenian Dionysius appeared in the sixth century and are now attributed to 'Pseudo-Dionysius.' It is clear he was a Neo-Platonist. This work was influential for presenting a 'negative theology' that might fit into Hindu non-dual thinking. This means that you say what the Divine is not. He inspired many Christian mystics. One aspect of his writings was emphasis on darkness as Divine. Eriugena translated the work of Dionysius. An idea of interpenetration of darkness and light emerges in both. Two words for darkness are used in Latin, *tenebrae* which sometimes represents spiritual darkness and *caligo* which was more related to Divine darkness at times. Looking at the mystical journey of subsequent Catholics, darkness appears significant for luminaries like St. John of the Cross. Mystics may also encounter demons which are creatures of darkness to them. Mystics know the journey involves light and darkness to the end and beyond, so they get used to it. So for the Christian mystic there is a spiritual perception of darkness related to ability to adhere to rules or not and a mystical element related to perceived places in imagination related to seeking communion with Divine or angelic beings. In those dominions demons may represent darkness because they are distant from the Divine light and destructive towards codes of conduct. Demons may also personify archetypal temptations or be projections of internal struggle when flesh resists the path indicated by prophets. It is a mistake to ignore the belief that they are real entities and one may be possessed. Many Christians insist on the reality of demons and dangers of possession and point to original sources and hundreds of years of experience. Certain psychologists like Van Dusen took this seriously. Parapsychology is closer to religious practice insofar as it is open to study such phenomena. This tradition about possession emphasises the importance of spiritual sovereignty. New religious movements of the left-hand path and bodies that are Satanic apparently emphasise ideas of the prince of darkness, black flames, dark gods and black books. So it is ignorance of contemporary Satanism to suggest such ideas were merely constructions of Christian fantasy in a moral panic. Similarly, the distinction between black and white types of magic existed in relation to Mongolian shamanism and traditional ideas. Again, the 'black faith' related to shamans using bad spirits. Such terminology changes, but it was used. It appears intellectually inconsistent to allow extra-terrestrials, fairies and the astral domain and deny the possibility of existence of demons or the fact of possession. In that, sorcerers and religious are together.

Exploration of our shadow side, as suggested by Jung, indicates how our archetypal aspects need to be appreciated. Maybe every person internalises an archetype of day and night in their psyche independent of the external. Many popular spiritual writers, such as Debbie Ford, emphasise embrace of the dark side. Even the mystic going towards God has the 'dark night of the soul' or 'the night of initiation' whereby darkness is a necessary prelude to entering light. The abyss found by some philosophers may be mystic black light of the Sufis, according to Corbin, or night of light or luminous blackness. 'Black world' is a description that emerges from the Shamanic tradition. Some people may have been led to believe that such darkness or abyss is inevitably a desperate, demonic plain too frightening to navigate. In contemporary medicine, the person in pain possibly undergoing profound psychic change is likely to get some pills. Pageants that helped with passages in spiritual life have been parked. To some extent the hero must take the risky journey. The shaman's job is to go to such places for the good of community. If one is unconvinced and needs to look at a lowest, rational common denominator they might investigate emerging neurological studies of altered states of consciousness in relation to specific shamanic states which suggest the left to right brain shifting process and front to back. Such experiences are well-known to facilitate visitor presence sensations and ability to dislocate from the rational, fixed but limited perspective. Such experiential evidence is not merely attributable to disease although it is very common for such special individuals to have had some predisposing factors or propensities.

It is foolish for Christians to ignore demons when their history is replete with them. The torment, torture or temptation of St. Anthony has been one of the great themes in Western painting. Some philosophers who deny these things want to torture us instead with their infernal concepts. The story told by early church fathers of this mystic who lived in the Egyptian desert, has Divine intervention with light as well as darkness. The accepted stories are full of demons and strange creatures in his dwelling place and the sky. Anthony seems to get on with his prayers even though demons inflict damage. However it is important to note that these creatures, which could be anything, terrestrial or extra-terrestrial, outside or inside, were accepted as real in some way by the Church and artists. Mystics encounter beings out of the ordinary and often not of this world. St. Anthony supposedly encountered a being who wished to be saved by God, unlike the people thereabouts. This happens too in Islam. Far from ignoring them, mystics may rejoice with the creature's faith. This reflects a long-held view that the highly spiritually evolved may have to engage with demons or 'ultra-terrestrials' at times because of their powers, not least on the basis that they must have been created by God and if fallen must be re-converted. And Jesus did. God did. Darkness within or without has demons. Mystics say there are beings that exist beyond normal perception. That does not mean they are inevitably bad however. Bear in mind also that darkness or shadow may be relative in that we judge things visually by contrast. There is a spiritual principle here to learn. This might be termed the principle of contrast. *Spiritual contrast suggests that making something too pure or puritan, will create a sharper, misleading ostensible contrary thus making it easier to find the apparently impure to react against even though the latter luminosity is constant when seen without contrast.*

That is where Goethe understood something Newton did not about colour. I found it hard to understand the fascination with Satanism until I began to see how indulgent, condemnatory, self-righteous people acting inconsistently with compassion can zealously create its ostensible opposite. When Satanism is supposed to exist in martial arts, yoga and innocuous activity, it serves to promote disbelief and perhaps allow genuinely dark activity thrive away from normality. Similarly, Aghori in India could only arise in a society structured on ritual purity and a caste system. The left hand path may have come because of strictness. I could not understand why there were Maoists in Nepal till I went there and talked to some of the politicians. Aghori seek darkness in order to come to the light. The pendulum swings, see-saw's descent requires compensatory movement. Yin moves to yang and vice versa. In Northern Ireland all sides that turned to violence claimed they were re-acting. Certainly, 'dark arts' are descriptions of occult practices. Likewise, extrapolation from notions of purity and associations with light created a sense of darkness as bad as used in relation to Africa in the 'dark continent' or as employed by Freud in relation to women's sexuality to suggest an unknown or unexplored domain. Too much focus on light, brightness, purity, hygiene and inoffensiveness will create its opposite. Balance, middle path, fulcrum, foreshore may yield more than confrontation. There is a danger that mysticism serves spiritual darkness if it is merely escapism or becomes confused with vindictive magic. However, such notions of contrast should not suggest that everything is relative, that one cannot identify any quality, that quantum physics suggests impossibility of analysis. Mystics point to certain higher order values. Magicians may appear to be mystics but, unless they are of the divine type, they may be more interested in controlling the physical world as super-materialists seeking to be superhuman. The critique of materialism is not inconsistent with higher worship of it. The mystic warns against control and opts for persuasion and thus non-use of violence. That is not to say that one should not resist evil. If you cannot have a conception of evil, you will not oppose it and will willingly participate in its production rather than seek to prevent its manifestation. Sometimes force is necessary.

So darkness is a simple physical phenomenon with particular characteristics, apparently. That is before one considers what darkness contains and whether it is an illusion or not. Taoists see the yin dark side of the hill and presume different properties on the bright side. Both are duality manifest everywhere in dynamic balance. Even in the spiritual realm, Christians accept a dark side, to be dealt with. The exorcist does so because they have authority. Individuals seek to minimise darkness within. God speaks to Satan. Evil is associated with darkness although the figure of Lucifer is associated with light and Satan with hellfire. In-between is not clear. This may be seen in conjuring and the idea of a demon. Grey areas come. Federico Garcia Lorca, the great Spanish poet wrote about the 'duende' spirit of inspiration found in flamenco which he identified with darkness. Artistic daemons or muses may be confused with demons. In esoteric studies, darkness is complex. In Blavatsky's theosophy, darkness is seen as a source of light in some ways and in certain streams of elusive Rosicrucianism, light and dark are identical save in the human mind. A non-dual instinct suggests that there is a dynamic balance within a whole and manifestations are mutable in dynamic balance. That does not mean that everything is morally relative. Mystics insist on inter-relationship which mandates compassion not a unity which makes it seem pointless. The implication is of a process of spiritual elevation not merely sitting on a spectacular couch watching cosmic tv with more interesting characters to pass the time as a participant perceiving they are observers and not players in a theatre slightly more engaging than other nihilism on offer interspersed with occasional intellectual bingo to while away the ennui. We are spiritual agents. Likewise, magicians may be materialists who seem to see limitations of concentrations on matter but sometimes merely seek to employ psychological and psychic forces in order to exercise control of the material world and people. It was Miranda who Huxley took his title from with her inexperienced enthusiasm,

> "How many goodly creatures are there here!
> How beauteous mankind is! O brave new world,
> That has such people in't."

When Jung let go and went inside himself he encountered great archetypal shadows. When mystics go inside they go to dark places to find light but may encounter entities. Ambiguity exists. In such twilight zones we need principles like the idea of spiritual sovereignty. Thus you do not relinquish spirit to any higher, dark or apparently luminous figure. You do not make a 'pact with the devil' or a Faustian pact with your soul. Conjuring comes from Latin con (with) and jurare (to swear an oath). Usually it meant summoning demons. However, conspiracy is also conjuring. Joining an esoteric secret society whereby you submit to rules and procedures is conjuring. Apparently benign actions beneath cloaks of secrecy, motivated by a claim to beneficial purposes could represent the opposite because one volunteered to be 'in the dark.' A corporate being is an entity with real world effects which even in law will have separate legal personality. Under oaths the most nefarious demons within humankind can be summoned. The line is between retaining spiritual sovereignty and legitimately exploring one's shadow side. An oath to an ideological group is conjuring. So being kept in the dark is accepting moral or psychic responsibility. Similarly a direction through the Buddha or Christ or Zarathustra or Mani or messengers of light maintains focus, but over-zealousness may make light darken. Light and dark are equally encountered on the mystic path and by the magus. Black magic is deepest darkness.

Mistleberger points out that even Crowley distinguished the *Knowledge and Conversation of the Holy Guardian Angel Ritual* from black magic. Manly Hall writes about black magic in *Secret Teachings of All Ages*. He identifies the main idea. There are higher planes of good spirits and lower planes of dark and evil spirits under the Fallen Angel and his ten princes. Good spirits help people but evil spirits serve people with evil intents who seek them through ceremonial magic, allowing an individual to master an elemental being. But 'true black magic' involves the sorcerer summoning a demon that will serve them in return for their soul which they forfeit on death. Such people will want to stay alive as long as possible. But then he makes a bold claim,

"The most dangerous form of black magic is the scientific perversion of occult power for the gratification of personal desire. Its less complex and more universal form is human selfishness, for selfishness is the fundamental cause of all worldly evil. A man will barter his eternal soul for temporal power, and down through the ages a mysterious process has been evolved which actually enables him to make this exchange. In its various branches the black art includes nearly all forms of ceremonial magic, necromancy, witchcraft, sorcery and vampiricism."

There were a number of characters that seem to recur in any attempt to discuss the nature of evil, magic, moral choice and darkness. Dr. Faust and Dr. Frankenstein bring us to others such as Lucifer and Satan. Faust and Frankenstein are about power and technology including magic. Prospero is a good magician at the border and another useful one for discussion is *The PK Man*. Underlying these is the protean figure of Prometheus. The 'left-hand path' is difficult to define but the adjective that emerges most is darkness. The Children of Loki are cited by occultists, as are Lucifer, Leviathan, Lilith, Satan and Kali. The Dragon Rouge seems to have sacraments of black masses and follows the path in an antinomian way. Black flames are a common theme emphasising a type of basic energy like Kundalini. These organisations are often highly informed on esoteric matters. They argue that they create light through exploring darkness and that the objective is to reach illumination and divinity. Similarly, like mystics they argue that they receive inspiration from the forces they represent. The mystic and the dark occultist share the belief that they are dealing with something which is not fantasy.

But there are no simple answers. I have no wish to add to the feeding frenzy on the reputation of the Catholic Church but nevertheless I use this example. One presumes that such an institution is dedicated to good. Then we have a litany of charges of sadism and cruelty against the institution. Then we have to bear in mind that some opponents are also deserving of caution. For example, it is clear that after Gramsci, the Trotskyist approach was to destroy such institutions. So some opponents do not come with clean hands. Similarly if you compared allegations of sexual offences of DJ's or people in the UK music industry and priests, the figures might surprise but no one wants the former shut down. Then we see an exaltation of Protestant reason and a 'work ethic' which followed on from 'stripping of the altars.' But within the tradition itself, we see an ancient prophecy such as St. Malachy suggesting the 112th Pope would be the last one and this one is that. We might also consider another Malachi Martin, a Jesuit priest who worked in the Vatican and wrote novels about it. He believed the Popes erred in not acting on the secrets of Fatima and not honouring Divine instruction. He believed Satanic masses were conducted in the Vatican. He believed Cardinal Siri had been elected Pope in conclave but was not allowed take the role. Then Martin is accused of being a foreign agent. And so it goes. There has been a long tradition that the idea of 'black masses' derive their power from the inversion of sacredness and thus require participation of consecrated forces. I do not report these statements to cause scandal. I believe that if the Church declines (as it seems to be doing) there will be a price to pay for the good elements and a new tyranny will emerge. But within the Catholic Church itself we see similar fears. The best example is the mysterious story of 'St. Michael's Prayer.' This was recited after mass from 1886-1964. It implores St. Michael to protect us from Satan. St. Michael was the traditional opponent of dark forces. There are allegedly lines linking Skellig Michael (which made an appearance in Star Wars recently) to Jerusalem. Rudolf Steiner believed that St. Michael became a critical figure in the late 19th century because of a 'war in heaven' and incarnation of evil spirits as a result. The prayer was added by Pope Leo XIII after a vision in the Vatican. There are also prayers to St. Michael in the context of exorcism and against 'the spirit of evil in high places.' The story goes that Leo had a vision of Satan challenging God for control of the Church and deciding on the twentieth century to take over. Why is this relevant? The idea of spiritual darkness is a constant one. Evidence suggests that institutions dedicated to good may be captured. Priests may disown and become enemies of prophets. Fetishisation of ritual and legalism may displace underlying spirit. Like an ounce of gold can be stretched for fifty miles so can mystical charisma in ritual till we can hardly see it. The individual must retain responsibility for their own spiritual evolution, even if happily in a Church that offers more advantages than disadvantages. Relinquishing spiritual sovereignty to someone who appears good involves a huge risk. You must interpret that which appears to be filled with light through use of reason. Similarly when people criticise parapsychology on religious grounds they appear to ignore the history of spiritual traditions. Visions of light and darkness dominate spirituality as far back as can be intelligibly realised and those phenomena have demonstrable real world consequences. Every individual has responsibility for their own spiritual evolution and that is why mysticism is relevant. Enlightened people who laugh at demons within or without or scoff at aliens, should look back at the history of religions, spirituality, art and politics. Spiritual sovereignty is complemented by good conduct which reduces darkness. Likewise Jesus and Buddha or St. Michael are perceived as protective forces. Using Jesus or Buddha or The Prophet as role models is believed to create spiritual protection against darkness, on a principle of like to like. But then one must look at diversity of beliefs and figures that are difficult to interpret like Rasputin. Similarly Crowley was a reaction to strict Christianity, equally pious in his unique way. When I suggest a dark age of scientism, it borrows the concept from European history.

In summary 'darkness' is what exists when no light source dominates. In the absence of light certain types of activities arise. Darkness may be associated with a negative, low or destructive feeling of psychological state. Darkness is a complex concept or analogy in science. In spiritual terms, darkness may be a lack of knowledge of Divinely-inspired work in an intellectual or spiritual sense. Darkness may be failure to follow rules and associated states or perceptions of guilt, regret or fear. Darkness may indicate certain stages on the path of illumination. Darkness may even be part of highest experience of Divinity. It may be an illusion or false contrary to unduly pure light. Darkness may represent the negligent, reckless or deliberate actions of institutions acting with authority in an illegitimate, distorted and evil way.

Mystics and prophets are often killed. On the mystic path, darkness is nuanced. Mystics emphasise self-actualisation. Mystics are sceptical about institutions. Mystics emphasise basic principle and personal experience instead of sophisticated doctrine. Mystics may embrace physical darkness. Mystics allow a certain intellectual shadow distrustful of legalism, undue rationalism and microscopic thinking. Mystics accept and engage their own archetypal darkness. They are most interested in the reality of spiritual light. When we examine dualities, we see non-dual, dynamic balance. Now mundane doctrines invent new 'darknesses' with correct behaviour, utterances, confessions, punishments and a kaleidoscopic range of moral analysis that shifts to create confusion. Even Iris Murdoch, the Irish-born novelist philosopher who tried to construct metaphysics for morals without theology or God, talked in terms of light and dark and was convinced of the existence of good and evil. We do not see certain people and hence they are in darkness or not in the light of acceptance. Hence Sojourner Truth asked if she was not a woman because she had been a slave? What we physically see can by ignored in perceptual darkness. While mystics emphasise non-duality, we cannot ignore all signal in the noise. Consciousness is calculated to enhance empathy, not to deny there is compassionate conduct. Darkness cannot non-exist and matter may be darkness. In Bhagavad Gita, matter is dark in a field of luminosity. Light insinuated into flesh. The substantia nigra or 'black substance' in the brain contains neuromelanin. This dark neural material is sensitive to light and significant for ideas of 'Dark Light Consciousness' for Edward Bruce Bynum. Similarly, when we see the scientists investigating light, they often need darkness. Native American 'medicine' was once deemed devilish but is gaining the respect it deserves. The ancient *I Ching* sets out 64 hexagrams. Number 36, *The Darkening of the Light* suggests there may be an appropriate time to hide your light under a bushel and maintain inner light. Dark and absences indicate that actions depend on circumstances. While Confucians might see a sharper delineation between good and evil, Taoists might see it more subtly. However, even for flexible people it never meant that evil tyranny does not exist. Just as magic became a rebellious counter-balance to religious rationalism and facilitated some science, the rebel-outsider will always turn something upside down with a book or even a bomb.

What seems light may be dark. David Kennedy worked in international humanitarianism and wrote *The Dark Sides of Virtue*. He wondered whether noble intervention might be counter-productive. Whether it is human rights, religion, politics or Prometheanism, there is certain danger of intervening because you know best and are doing it for 'good' reasons with a group behind you, especially when you need to destroy another one. Science has explained many things about light and dark that we know already. With little light in winter, people feel differently. Light and darkness impact on body rhythms. Adaptations create also something not there previously. However native people and mystics understood visionary potential of darkness, underground or in a cave. Absence of technology is optimum. Letting go of control opens a new dimension of experience. Release of light allows us scry our subconscious and encounter archetypal forces and symbols, opening up channels of perception. Darkness fulfils a cleansing function by peering into a dark mirror. Many people like lucid dreaming. Everyone explores in their own way. Sometimes more control is not what we need, because conscious mind is at times inferior to other consciousness. Relentless focus on lucidity can create darkness in the same way as failing to fall asleep over a long period impairs judgment. Native peoples and ancient cultures facilitated these experiences within the community. Beyond individual mystic practice, the danger arises from creating collectivist systems where psyche of a few concentrated in institutions are projected back onto waking consciousness of the group. Relinquishment of control by the individual facilitates such concentrations. If we embrace our sovereignty and explore, we might be reluctant to make a sacrifice to others' warped fantasies based on essentially psychic preoccupations of control. It is not escape from community for the mystic. We must bring something back, but not force it on anyone. From where I lived in Dublin you could just make out the ruins of the Hellfire Club in the hills. This involved occultism among 'Enlightened' aristocrats. Swift thought them monsters. One can always examine the evidence.

1.3 The Mystical Path for Spirit

When we think of vision we can contemplate it from the perspective of the viewer, looking and seeing in light and usually less in darkness. The mystic asks who is it that is looking? Then they ask how can we know who is looking? This looking is not for your eyes only. We can look with the body and spiritual eyes. Many would say that when the veil is lifted we see ourselves looking back and hence we should treat others like ourself. Spiritual evolution must involve an individual journey of heart, mind and spirit or it is merely mummery and mimesis. Mystical experience is the true original of all religion and necessary vital energy for sustenance of personal belief. It is supremely subjective in some ways while enabling great objectivity in a balanced way as well. Religion may make a poor imitation of the original mystic insight leading some to project that simulacrum onto their worldview. It is important to identify what mysticism represents in order to understand the idea of spiritual evolution. It is self-evident that you are conscious. The mystic believes you are spirit and spiritual consciousness is your primary nature. With the inverted 'Enlightenment,' spirit was cast out of intellectual debate and has not been replaced. The scientific attempt to substitute consciousness constructed by the brain has failed. Widespread evidence suggests specific mystical events or practices may lead to an individual epiphany or a realisation through an altered state that may transcend senses of time, space and reality. Mystical experiences create a virtuous spiral of spiritual evolution perceiving limitations of physicalist, materialist or mechanistic worldviews. An escape from straitjacket of ego and even a sense of corporality at times, may lead to a profound sense of peace that banishes existential despair, creating a new sense of meaning, loss of death fear and a sense of actualising purpose. Consciousness of inter-relationship or union with the cosmos or Divine with particular respect for relationships grows. Mystical experience often results in a sense the percipient has been transformed by a download of knowledge or sudden understanding which may create a sense of turbulence. People may find it difficult to explain the exact nature of mystical experience. Study of mysticism involves a claim that practices or extraordinary events experienced, result in an alternative perception of reality with profound implications. Puncturing limitations of reality with arrows of perception creates an aperture in the matrix. While the mystically inclined do not fear death but claim present meaning, transhumanists and cryogenics companies want to mechanise, freeze life, upload or re-animate it, such is their abhorrence of engaging fully with existence. Bentham was stuffed to go on display as an 'auto-icon.' Reductionist, materialistic mind-sets with cultivated despair of some existentialists and postmodernists, promoted by certain ideologies calculated to displace established notions in the West, will inflict a new empire of mind. Granted there are some fringe religions like the Raëlians who promote cloning but the end of physical life is the accepted spiritual norm. There have been many materialists committed to extending life and even bringing it back or re-animating it. This has been consistent whether in Russia or the US, from Alexander Bogdanov to Peter Thiel. There has also been a consistent idea of collectivising consciousness which is manifesting as a real threat with neural interfaces.

I believe there is a general process of mystical development that goes as follows.

1. **Search** - A person seeks answers to the meaning of life or a suppressed part within them does.

2. **Engagement** - A set of practices or an event opens the doors of perception seeking the true or higher self.

3. **Transformation** - The perception of reality, purpose, relationships and worldview is altered through focus.

4. **Crafting** - The person seeks to preserve the framework, fashion a nexus to the numinous and give some gift to the community.

The Mystical Accord laid out a mystical path as follows. The individual starts off as a spiralling growth of ego and self and through a process of purification at a certain stage of maturity approach their true self, representing a greater proximity to such pure consciousness in us as is fundamental in the universe and insufflated as our spirit. Our spirit must evolve through its journey discerning the real from illusory and identification of true knowledge. Spirit on a quest aims to open a 'nexus to the numinous' to combat existential despair. Aligning ourselves to be in accord with the highest of our potential and universe is a way to describe what has been a perennial concern. An examination of mystical traditions reveals some parallel features that reflect the idea of perennial wisdom. True self is as close to pure consciousness as we can be and enhances our lives, reduces existential despair and increases certain powers of an intuitive parapsychological or perceptive nature.

Engagement with lessons of light and concentration and contemplation provide a glittering way that may assist some who find it difficult to make sense of apparent diversity of experience alien to their own. It is my belief that everyone should seek peace and purpose within, not for some programme of pacification but rather for some push towards exploration of human spiritual potential. There are a wide range of profound experiences which involve light which are spiritual. These are more common for spiritually committed people or mystics. For example, Evelyn Underhill in her classic book *Mysticism* wrote about the 'Illuminative path' in mysticism. She saw light as being part of a particular stage of illumination on the mystical path just as there is a dark stage. Many of her examples in Christianity refer to the Divine as the 'Uncreated Light.' Illumination for her was a phase on the way to a higher unitive state. Illumination related to an individual spiritual and intellectual realisation preceding a subsequent higher, unitive stage that may unfold later. Still, even at the most advanced stage with experience of proximity to the Divine, light plays a critical role. She cites descriptions by St. Teresa of her Divine dazzling, white, brilliant visions. Teresa distinguishes spiritual and physical light being delightful and appearing whether eyes are closed or shut. Nevertheless there are a whole range of experiences that people who are not disciplined mystics report that sound suspiciously like what the established ones say. The idea that shines through spiritual literature suggests a path of light which can aid a person in their own evolution consistent with existing religious practices or for people of no adherence. Those who have been affected by profound events such as Near Death Experiences, UFO encounters, apprehensions of otherworldly beings, certain dissociative traumatic experiences, peculiar or precognitive dreams or engaged in intense practices such as prayer, contemplation, concentration, painting, meditation, yoga, visualisation, tantra, breath-work or entheogenic drugs may experience spiritual light phenomena. I am sceptical about the promotion of psychedelics as a first port of call particularly if that represents a political policy of pacification calculated to continue a condition of blissful servitude. But recurrent light experiences of mystics paralleling profound events that affect non-mystics, suggest a perennial phenomenon. Evidence through mystic commitment or circumstance indicates that light is the medium of spiritual evolution. The medium may indeed be the message. Even when you investigate this idea of Marshall McLuhan that became important in Silicon Valley and his prediction of the global village, there is a strange conclusion. As Tom Wolfe pointed out, McLuhan thought the global village might be a bloodbath as well as a utopia. Influenced by Teilhard de Chardin, McLuhan suggested that the global village might allow creation of 'the mystical body' where people become united technologically under electronic conditions in the 'body of Christ.' This is dangerous and I disagree with the idea. Nevertheless it is impossible to underestimate the impact of mystical thinking. Mystical thinking, spiritual evolution and the idea of spirit itself are under threat from scientism. Scientism is simply the illusion that science and scientific thinking can explain, know and solve all riddles of the meaning and purpose of life and an associated arrogance. One threat will be the attempted takeover of mystical and spiritual domains through commercial exploitation of technological means to induce altered states of consciousness made available as spiritual experience simulacra or simulation without 'dogma.'

Perhaps this is as Baudrillard anticipated with a need for hyper-reality in banality through sorcery of simulation and the 'perfect crime' of abolishing transcendent reality where all become objects and no longer subjects.

There is often a difference between scientist and mystic. Mystics deny final authority of others to explain all personal experience. Scientists insist on final authority of others to explain all personal experience. Mystics seek experience of knowledge addressing the mystery of life. Scientists seem to seek knowledge of experiences denying the mystery of life. Scientists insist on validity of repeatability of experiments they never actually repeat. Mystics insist on validity of repeatability of experience they regularly seek to repeat. Scientists in the last couple of centuries have discovered invisible waves, fields, particles, energy, vibrations. Mystics have indicated them for millennia. Mysticism has responsibility for cults, charismatic leaders, psychosis and pseudo-science but science has no responsibility for secret medical experiments, weapons of mass destruction, military-industrial complexes, pollution nor mass pharmaceutical pacification of the populace. Mysticism is an individual pursuit of a meaningful way separate from religion. Nevertheless, critiques of religion are also disproportionate, often in disregard of facts and not applied to science itself. But there are good scientists and good mystics, bad scientists and bad mystics. The middle way is needed for balance. If mystics desert religion to beg benediction with a crown of thorns made from electrodes of science, they move from frying pan to fire. Informed, evolved spiritual beings acting independently will be a formidable force. Conscientious scientists and mystics are threatened by scientism.

C.S. Lewis appears very rational and not mystical in his approach to Christianity despite fantasy in his novels. Because he knew Tolkien and other myth experts and could distinguish professionally between legend and reported fact, he committed to Christianity convinced the events reported happened. In the original preface to *The Screwtape Letters,* which is about devils, he says there cannot be 'The Devil' who opposes God but there can be devils who are angels who rebel. The chief devil is Satan and he is opposed by Michael. He thinks these beings are poorly represented in art and that Goethe's human character Faust was worse than the devil he presented. Hell is a place of envy and resentment. But the greatest evil,

> "...is conceived and ordered... in clean, carpeted, warmed, and well-lighted offices, by quiet men with white collars and cut fingernails and smooth-shaven cheeks who do not need to raise their voice. Hence, naturally enough, my symbol for Hell is something like the bureaucracy of a police state or the offices of a thoroughly nasty business concern."

Likewise, Camille Paglia argues that banal managerialism is responsible for the influx of destructive French post-structuralism thought she says destroyed US universities and real radicalism. She suggests that there is a disease of 'presentism' and a 'failure of a universal vision in scholarship.'

At the other end of the scale, projection of barrenness and infertility of some places loved by ascetics onto the entire world is not useful. Retreat to wilderness or withdrawal are part of the hero's journey on a mystic path. Without seeking to return with something of benefit it may fail, although example may be the teacher. Mystics bring something back. It is interesting whether certain Gnostic and ascetic strands were influenced significantly by parched landscapes they emerged from. A lusher land may create more benevolent views of the material world. That does not invalidate mystical truths from bright beautiful deserts but is just a factor in consideration of emphasis on ideas of materiality and mother earth.

Mystics generally go towards a certain light recognising darkness. However, science and technology have literally created a mass of new, artificial light and a philosophy which lit up public mind and space. This builds on science, commerce and scientism. All that light of emphasis creates darkness. Progress contains darkness in the sense of a negative intellectual force. Success of the scientific model has created a military-industrial complex combined with surveillance state and an impoverished environment while capturing institutions so the religion of science, commerce and worship through scientism creates a new dark age. This dark age is characterised by destruction by rapacious forces, the desire to control people and reduce the scope of legitimate freedom of expression and privacy. Militant atheism with other forces of control, both extreme left and right ultra-materialist, want now to dispirit us with manipulation of magic light to substitute spirit with a simulacrum. Mysticism was suppressed and self-imposed restrictions were imposed by communities and esoteric bodies that drifted more into magic and were captured like all institutions are. If mystics independently evolve utilising some intellectual discipline but guided by higher values of compassion and engaging reflexively within society, they will be a saving force. Mysticism is like water, people confuse its lowliness for weakness.

1.4 Perennial Spiritual Consciousness and the Challenge of Scientism

Let me begin by defining scientism (or simply science gone wrong) in my own way. Scientism is the ideology, philosophy, disposition or attitude that claims that scientific method is the exclusive method of examining all reality and thus elevates or extends scientific conclusions beyond the evidence, extrapolates without justification or applies such evidence to inappropriate contexts, assumes that the unexplained does not exist, that existing limits of scientific knowledge necessarily excludes alternative explanations and that certain endeavours must fail because they do not fit expectations of the dominant, materialist paradigm.

The subjective experience of light has been undermined by the shift to objectivity which goes beyond method. This shift has created objects where subjects once were. All life, science, art and spirituality come from original light. Spiritual study of light has been instrumental in evolution of great scientific endeavour. Nevertheless, the very idea of existence of spirit is under threat. Convince someone they have no spirit, one can convince them of anything. Most groundwork in scientific study of light came from spiritual quests scientists now seem blind to. Reformation science took intellectual achievements of religious experimenters (as well as buildings and wealth) and claimed everything had come about through their own diligence and later even gave their booty as evidence of their superior work ethic. The Enlightenment claimed all scientific advances came about in spite of religion. Relentless extrapolation from the theory of evolution sought to dispirit us through reduction to haphazardness, luck and chemicals. Philosophies that materialist dogmatists spawned culminated in certain streams of post-modernism that helped create conditions for what may be literal, human slavery by a tyranny of mesmerised masses and mini sects of scientism.

Approaching the spiritual path means we cross a scientific minefield. Science seems to be the great enlightening force of illuminated ones bringing light to darkness, filling heavens and minds with light actually and archetypally. Science brings things to light and brings light to things. In doing so, science seems to have struck at the heart of spiritual meaning. Science is very successful when it remains within appropriate realms. It fails when it claims exclusivity of knowledge beyond boundaries of the discipline or forgets assumptions it makes and wisdom of caution and humility. The history of science is often a process of hagiography and supposed martyrdom without any self-criticism. Certain writers are ideological and others merely repeat ahistorical simplification of the past. Science is based on beliefs and some disbelief is labelled 'pathological' by other eminent scientists. As Huston Smith put it, we have made metaphysics out of method. Smith and others have identified how values, purposes, qualities and existential meanings of the whole do not emerge from science. Indeed qualities must be excised for method to operate successfully with empirical concentration. If we deal with dimensions beyond senses, claims to knowledge resting on their superiority cannot solve them. When we deal with first principles about being and knowing, metaphysics and meaning, words are inadequate at times. As a mathematician uses symbols, so do spiritual teachers use parable, metaphor and analogy. Spiritual experience is mirrored in language but is not it. Models of macrocosms and microcosms are not reality. Propositions are fingers pointing at the moon but are not the moon itself. Masters in spiritual tradition often transcend detail and communicate in a manner deceptively simple whose allusive truth is a higher level of reality requiring participation, projection of imagination and perception above fragmented facts. Spiritual reason should resonate to facilitate spiritual evolution. Such evolution is also part of our relationship to earth. We are spirits wonderfully embodied in a magnificent, magical place and we might wander differently and protect more effectively if we appreciated what is being sacrificed presently.

The nature of knowledge and ideas such as *scientia* and *sapentia* suggest distinct forces. Subjective phenomena of spiritual experience include deeply perceived and felt realities that transcend scientifically delineated ideas and cannot be dismissed. We can state our foundations and proceed tentatively towards truth rather than promoting absolute certainty. It is not intended to make the 'category error' of mixing science and spirituality inappropriately. However, I urge people to reclaim spirit and reject denying claims of poor philosophy, idiotic ideology and scarifying scientism by simple recognition of their instantiated spiritual nature. When neuroscience cannot say what consciousness is nor how it arises, nor where memory is located nor how our sense of self and higher faculties operate, we have no reason to be defensive about a belief existing from time immemorial asserting that we are spiritual beings in physical vessels or have form within our spiritual one. Furthermore, forces mutilating the natural world seem intent on destroying identity of spirit in us. Dispiritingly it appears there is conspiracy to dispirit us that should inspire reclamation of spirit in ourselves first, and then others, so we can aspire to flourish. To summarise, science has inherent limitations. Those who resort to scientism which goes beyond methods of science to make claims and draw conclusions without adequate basis in evidence, driven by over-confidence and disregard for opposing epistemologies and ontologies, need to be challenged. All hypotheses have postulates, foundations or axioms on which they are based. My hypothesis is that there is a perennial mystical path based on the nature, understanding and experience of light that has enough consistency to suggest reality, and is available to all to renew their existing beliefs or create a new one. While we can examine some analytic contours, poetic lines may point to experienced reality more than mere model. As technology owned by elite groups threatens to become our masters, it is time to wake up. Worship of science and the religious doctrine of scientism threaten all. In the endgame, one of the only defences will be a commitment by the universal spiritual commonwealth of individuals to seek commonalities to combat enslavement. We must do it ourselves. No group will save us. Individuals evolving with sovereignty will create stronger informed networks of agency impossible to destroy through institutional capture, creating what Swedenborg termed secret agents of the Holy Spirit. This is not about secret societies but what Eckartshausen explained as the invisible congregation of light.

My postulate simply states that we are spiritual beings with spiritual consciousness, part of a creative cosmic or Divine consciousness fundamental in the universe we know and whatever others we discover. Spirits are meant to evolve and on that spiral path people should not sacrifice spiritual sovereignty. Believing in God makes it easier to believe you are spirit but the former is not necessary for the latter. Atheism has become an agenda which will attack the spirit, because much of it never was free thinking. Likewise, specific attempts to comprehend the nature of creative force, beyond comprehension, are not as important as apprehension of immanence or transcendence. Insofar as creative consciousness manifests in us, we can gain a sense of who we are, by proper exploration of our essential nature. Human dignity, much ethics and legal principle derive largely from this exploration. Our efforts to extend compassion and care for others come principally from this recognition. The primary mystic argument is based on recognising reality of spiritual experiences without dictating specific doctrines. Being spiritual beings, our major purpose is to evolve spiritually and that necessarily must involve a consistent individual engagement irrespective of external forces. Discovering or developing our spirit is consistent with meaningful motive that is itself creative of realities which militate against ennui, pointlessness, nihilism, disorientation and despair that inevitably follow the dispiriting process. When we go back to key English Enlightenment groups that promoted the Industrial Revolution (such as The Lunar Society for example) we see arguments for 'reason' combined with manufacturing and machine-love that suggests relegation of people in the new secular religion. One also sees the light-image associated with meetings at the time of full moon. The assault on religion in the West has been fierce. Some critiques are justified, many not. The attack on God was one strategy and the existence of spirit will be just as intense. Many are not honest brokers exploring issues, such as 'entryist' Trotskyists who wish to de-stabilise existing institutions.

The contested core of perennial philosophy is consonant with the view expressed in this work. Perennial wisdom is believed to be ancient, recurrent and largely consistent in its central concentration on inner, mystic knowing. To some it always existed as an idea. To others it is inherent in the structure of spiritual belief. These ideas suggest commonality despite disparity. Such wisdom or philosophy flowers because it is planted in our nature. It is cultivated by those who follow mystic ways. Mysticism indicates a path to evolve spiritually. It permeates philosophies and practices and suggests that great cosmic good generated and manifested in nature, concentrated as creativity in us, is meant to evolve to rise back home like a swooping kingfisher skimming water. Whilst religion is defined by its collective nature, mysticism is individual. Values that direct the mystic will be compassion, courage and conscientiousness that are found in most spiritual traditions.

The individual who evolves spiritually will contribute to welfare of their fellow beings as they recognise dignity of others through such awareness and assist in enhancing human consciousness. Indeed as C.S. Lewis argues, lack of a higher order basis for morality and law (such as God for him) will lead to totalitarianism or despotism lacking in moral restraints. The phenomenon of spiritual perception and subjectivity are often beyond reach of scientific, neuroscientific, mathematical and philosophical methods. Nevertheless, spirituality is under severe attack. There has been an unending war on spiritual modes, sometimes by dominating spiritual traditions. Today, positivists and materialists often promoting political ideology, seek to uproot spirit. While spirit is being denied, derided and denigrated, the effort to define consciousness has failed quite miserably. The rare but more convincing explanations seem to suggest some kind of spiritual inhabitation of matter manifesting as a dynamic, embodied and extended agency. But mostly the dominant idea is to reduce, split and control. Pending some marvellous explanation in future, it is hard to see why simple explanation of spirit is not better than any other. I think people should explore religious traditions they are most familiar with first but it is hard to go anywhere without an inner inkling of spirit. It has been a long held instinct. It is no surprise we have a longing to find it again, particularly if one sees clear consequences of contemporary deconstruction of spirit as part of physicalist, naturalist, materialist, reductionist worldviews. In addition, the field of parapsychology and specific examples of phenomena of persistent subjective experience of a spiritual nature such as Near Death Experiences (NDEs) and After Death Communications (ADCs) suggest potential of life after death. The onus of proof lies with proponents of spirit's non-existence while we wait for explanation of consciousness (and while we are at it why we dream and how anaesthetics work). Mathematics may make many magical models but they only reflect reality and must inevitably present an incomplete picture.

Scientism, as promoted by oligarchical forces that congregate to utilise materialist ideology, whether in extreme right or left forms, seems to have fashioned an absurd, reductionist and ultimately dispiriting Enlightenment idea through literalistic interpretations of Darwinian evolutionary determinism to fundamentalist *The Selfish Gene*, meme-machine. Raymond Tallis, philosopher and neuroscientist, criticised 'biologism,' 'neuromania' and 'Darwinitis.' Restrictive functionalist and computational analogy between mind and computer and ideas of 'eliminative materialism' cut away mind and consciousness. Still within science we see thinkers such as Robert Rosen in biology, who sought to emphasise how function dictates structure and that we cannot understand life or how an organism behaves and interacts without a view that transcends matter. Cause and effect may not operate so easily in life systems which anticipate states and have a sense of inner time. Nevertheless we are ceding power and sovereignty to machines, robots and AI daily, seduced by scientism, mesmerised by machines, acquiescent as farm animals.

Scientism and pseudo-scientific projections in political, psychological and social sciences have engaged in a cannibalistic, deconstruction of spiritual consciousness and endeavoured instead to promote a constellation of kaleidoscopic identities as a strange substitute to deconstructed spirit and self. Battering rams that thinkers (such as Gramsci) released are often based on promotion of straw-men and over-simplification of history. Scientism and certain streams in post-modernist thought that are ideological serve short-terms goals of technocrats. Scientocracy or technocracy desired by Francis Bacon and anticipated by Zamyatin, C.S. Lewis, Huxley and Orwell and promoted by H.G. Wells, seek now to secure servitude and slavery of individuals by sacrificing them to collectivisation and control processes in a new, replacement religion of techno-romanticism. Ayn Rand wrote about dystopian futures in books like *Anthem*. While she did promote individuals against the collective, she saw technology as cure rather than cause of collective oppression. I disagree with her attack on spirituality through her wide definition of mysticism. Machine worship occurs in an increasingly disenchanted environment whose despoliation, from Blake's Satanic mills onwards, supposedly has no connection with the new paradise claimed to inhere in obsessive curiosity and single-mindedness of scientists who create monsters they deny or claim they provided another solution to problems they have no sense of having caused. Ultimate machine-love involves departure from natural selection and evolution that technophiles supposedly love. That was a feint for artificial selection, transhumanism and oligarchical scientism long-intended despite ostensibly enlightened claims of useful idiots willing to gull masses succumbing to servitude, inexorably manifesting before our eyes through contemporary crisis betraying dangers of forces they champion.

Science itself acts as if it is an amoral force which merely observes and only acknowledges it is participant when fruit of the endeavour are overwhelmingly positive. It points to cure without identifying its role in creating the problem that necessitated it. It purports to ridicule mystery mystics recognise and then announces with great sense of achievement it has discovered a new mysterious particle that overthrows beliefs, they confidently established. It asserts about human origins until the next fragment is found somewhere, ostensibly oblivious to the process randomness and with disregard for caution it urges elsewhere. Nowhere has it been more unimpressive than in the attempt to eliminate the idea of consciousness, personality, selfhood, free will and morality as illusions that impede entirely objective third-person analysis. We are not mere third persons, objects without irreducible, subjective experience, qualities and inherent dignity. Be careful when you subscribe to some of these theories that you comprehend implications of their utility. It is vital to challenge them. It is why spiritual beings should not shy away from belief or knowledge without good cause as counterweight to deadly, dispiriting forces permeating the disenchanted, destructive society of scientism. The literalist in science can be as destructive as that in religion. Individual spirituality and collectivist religious institutions are not the same thing. Remember many mathematicians seem to believe in an ideal world whose reality reflects something more akin to mysticism. Reflect also that the models of mathematics that make science that makes technology that makes the world, grew because mathematical preoccupations lead there. Maybe unsolvable mathematics that could not be done or comprehended combined with incompleteness and constrained by limited choices based on principles of elegance, actually define some mystic domains. Mystics claim some things are discernible but inexpressible with our limited minds calculated to comprehend and survive peculiarities of physical life evolved on this planet. The ideal reflection of maths may be out there but there is much more than matter and that does matter. As Brian Josephson indicates, scientists may be guilty of 'pathological disbelief.'

The universe's beginning and our inevitable end and concerns for life on earth are consistent preoccupations. While some are linked to notions of Armageddon or Millenarianism and thus with influential religious views, a predominantly rational, reasonable mind is more troubled by perception of imminent demise of natural infrastructure of existence. In that lies an irony as rational forces promote disenchantment of nature and sacrifice sacred guardianship to new gods of science. The machine worldview consecrates instruments of reduction, utility and exploitation of the material. Similarly, proponents of whizzing worlds of things fail to mention the price we have to pay. We must develop individually because we are always faced with those who force us into their world sometimes motivated by noble ideas. Finding your way I recommend the potential of perennial wisdom. We are unique beings who must begin with our spiritual consciousness before we seek to influence others. If not careful we will be mere material objects in a mechanised world. As we evolve spiritually we need to be wise and heed warnings others have made. Anti-capitalists now argue that mindfulness is a western disease associated with privileged individualism and should be replaced with social mindfulness. Romanticisation of machines run by elites who know better than you and clockwork collective control without inherent dignity is worrisome whether from left or right. That is where Mary Shelley's vision came to assist me. Her spirit sensed that glorification of Prometheus by her Romantic friends and embrace of power instead of love was a dangerous direction.

1.5 Ghosts of St. Pancras

Writing another book, I visited an area I know well beside a bustling railway terminus. In the north-west London church yard they said the young girl from nearby Somers Town sat and traced letters on her mother's grave. Her mother had only stayed alive for a few days after her daughter's birth. It felt as if her mother was there, a ghostly stranger through the medium of writing she left, of a radical who wanted strong, independent women. Perhaps the young daughter learned to read here as her fingers spelt the inscription of the mother whose name she then shared.

MARY WOLLSTONECRAFT

GODWIN

Author of A Vindication of the Rights of Women.

Her mother Mary had written on rights of women balancing the writing of Tom Paine's *Rights of Man* that would influence the founding of the US. She also wrote about a governess in 1788 called Mrs. Mason which reminds one of Mary Poppins. The author of the former had gone to Ireland as a governess and the author of the latter would also go there on a voyage of mystical discovery. She would also live up the road later. Travers had been influenced by AE. Russell, the Irish mystic. The *Mary Poppins* film has esoteric references as does the character, from Sufism some say to Freemasonry. Wollstonecraft always emphasised the need to develop as an individual overcoming sensuality to have one's unique sensibility grow. Blake illustrated her children's stories, emphasising light in the effort to facilitate children in an era of repression. Mary Wollstonecraft is more recently celebrated for her refutation of Burke's view of the French Revolution in her *A Vindication of the Rights of Men*. Young Mary would often read these and other writings here. Inky spirit whispered fervent beliefs to her flesh and blood remaining in mortal realms to silently shape the unique individualism of her daughter.

Young Mary's mother, father, lover and friends were all concerned with the nature of life and how we negotiate it, personally and on a public level. Later young Mary would meet her poet lover Percy here and their trysts began at this spot where the River Fleet once flowed by the old church that went back to Roman times. The cosy church was where her mother celebrated her marriage to a fellow radical only a few months before her death in giving Mary life. Young Mary grew up here in the Regency period among beautiful forms that stood in stark contrast to rookeries fed with inflow of revolutionary refugees and impoverished people, near to where the mad King was being treated. She would see great experiments of empire with electricity that could re-animate corpses beloved by scientists wanting to become godlike to win God back to mankind with fire and light of unencumbered reason shifting from alchemy to chemistry. Young Mary's spirit whispers to us now still to suggest we face an eternal choice that must make us decide who we are. She discovered in her mother's letters that Mother Mary knew in her heart and mind that we were not 'organised dust.' Her mother seemed to know some Creator or consciousness had set this wonderful natural world in motion. She wanted women to be free, not by having power over men but over themselves. Her mother saw imprisoned life in matter and old structures that was exacerbated in a society which imprisoned women. Young Mary was very aware of how we could be trapped by surges of ideas and machines not just of rapacious commerce but also by the empire of mind that would grow without the great sensibility her mother urged. Her mother had radicalism precisely because of her spiritual and super-sensible disposition and not because of its rejection. Thwarted when she had projected her love onto mere mortals she began to find deeper, immanent manifestation in the natural world of a divinity that transcended religious denomination and disappointment. Mary would follow her mother and courageously rely on her own inward powers to find the highest in herself. She knew people, their beliefs and blind obedience could make one miserable such that light of day would be 'wretched to them.' Her mother wanted women to attain strength of body, mind and soul and not weakness. Education was a 'false light' if it did not tend to perfection nor aim for love higher than mere romantic illusions attached to people or principles that could never bear the weight of those pretentious projections. Though her mother mixed with Thomas Paine and those rebel luminaries, it seems for the older Mary there was love and for both Marys that love had to start off with individuals unencumbered. The father of the young girl was William Godwin. Some see him as the father of anarchism. Some see him as father of progressivism and liberalism of the type that grew up in the US. He seems to have been over-simplified. But it is clear these parents were uncommonly influential. The young girl, who became Mary Shelley after marriage to the celebrated Romantic poet Percy Bysshe Shelley, would use her love and dreams to show dark figures that lurked in minds possessed by doctrines of infallibility of material progress and superiority of human creativity enhanced with technology. This new romance, seeking to displace other discredited institutions, sometimes threatened to destroy the sap and essence of *sapentia* and originating impulse that yielded fruits which seeded their seeking. They would be tempted to attack the tree roots in a passion for rejection of control by one branch. Rousseau, the father of Romanticism warned against the model of Prometheus. Rousseau went into reveries in nature away from authority towards mysterious darkness of night and psyche where magical mystic revelation and poetry occurs away from dull Enlightenment. However there is balance. As Burke indicated, Romantics may have such over-sensibility for themselves and over-indulgence of their own desires that they abandon good and evil and will sacrifice others for what has been termed an 'indiscriminate sympathy' or attachment which paradoxically fails to respect other particular individuals if blinded by certainty of its own feeling. While we can be careful about how we react to perceived evil, we should not deny it. Intellectual magnanimity which stands aloof from direct sadism, infliction of pain, destruction and war-mongering contributes to dangerous banality of evil. Likewise, I do not enter kaleidoscope literary arguments about Prometheus but merely suggest that Mary Shelley apprehended a truth in a mystic way which warns against reliance thereon. This is relevant today as transhumanists seek myth sources to sell machine-people to us. Light is also about illumination of minds and how ideas affect us.

1.6 The Contested Prometheus

Prometheanism and Prometheism have specific meanings that I am not going to explore. But I need to define what I mean when the term is used and it is, in a way, consistent with Mary Shelley. She believed that choice of evil was a mistake in seeking happiness and that hubris leads to nemesis. Victor Frankenstein was interested in magicians like Agrippa and Paracelsus and then in science. The destructive power of lightning was a key event for him. The parallel made by some is with the Manhattan Project. Science created a monster without moral direction, focused on devastating details without concern. This has been called 'government in the dark' by Neil J. Sullivan. Prometheus is associated with forethought, because of his Greek name, but it is not of the type which includes risk-analysis and, if it does, will be disregarded through recklessness. So the definition of the type of Prometheanism I mean is as follows. *Prometheanism is a protean purpose based on rebelliousness against caution and restraint which sees acquisition of technological power by any means as the ultimate and necessary function of the apotheosis of humans to assimilate into the divine realm by becoming unconstrained creators.* It is not mere inventiveness and it makes a commitment to technological advance particularly through elite management of the collective by the enlightened and bold few. It is essentially materialist and not ultimately spiritual. It is akin or allied to some types of Luciferianism and Satanism. Magic becomes scientific and science becomes magic. This type of Prometheanism is hostile to mysticism, save as an instrument to commandeer to master the material.

Prometheus is associated with fire and being skillful in its application. He is a daring figure who will defy the gods and becomes a symbol of reason and defiance. He may have created humans out of clay. Prometheus stole fire from the gods of Olympia, or back from them, ruled over by Zeus and we supposedly got illumination and metalwork from the daring theft of this Titan. He was forced to steal it back in response to a failed trick by him on Zeus. He did so by hiding fire in a hollow fennel stalk. The deception involved getting Zeus to eat bones and fat instead of more edible meat at a meal. Maybe he should be linked with the contemporary meaning of 'backfire.' Alternatively, backfire also indicates a strategy to prevent bigger fire by lesser fire. Anyway, he was punished by being chained to a rock and having his liver pecked daily by a bird of prey. His classic theft was out of pity for humankind. Pandora came as a result with a jar that contained evils when let out. There are versions of the story. It is a story. There are inconsistencies because it is unclear what the moral is or even what type of myth it was.

Some of my best friends are, or may be, Prometheans so I am not seeking to create a polarising perspective but rather one of parallax and precaution. Neither am I rejecting Romanticism which I have been accused of. Rather it is about dynamic balance suggested by Taoists. Certain anthropologists argue that there is no true version of a myth. This is not about postmodernism but indicating the impossibility of finding one definite meaning from a mutable general story with multiple possible interpretations from a culture far removed, manifesting competing contexts inconsistent therewith where the same canon presents alternative options with apparently contrary morals. The myth of the Titan Prometheus is used by Neo-liberals, Marxists, Anarchists, Supremacists, Symbolist painters, musicians and 'freedom fighters.' Even the 'Mystic Chord' of Scriabin is called the Prometheus Chord. Scriabin interestingly wanted to convey the idea of light in music. The myth is incapable of yielding a single fixed meaning. Still, I take issue with the belief that unrestrained acquisition of technology by any means against the gods of moral scruples is a great symbol and inspiration irrespective of harm caused thereby. As studies of Prometheus in literature indicate, the figure means different things at different times and stands for both unethical transgression and courage. Indeed it may be that the idea of unethical transgression is equated with courage. Titans were disintegrating forces in mysteries of Greece. Some see Prometheus as a trickster figure, but Lewis Hyde argues he is not because he is too serious, his brother Epimetheus is left out and he failed in tricking Zeus so that humans suffered.

The simple point is that Prometheus is sometimes used to support the move towards transhumanism and merging of human and machine. Mechanisation of humankind and nature makes mystic spirit hard to develop, and that might be the purpose. If conditions for spiritual evolution deteriorate then much of the next generation will lose spiritual potential. The myth or symbol does not convey any clear moral. Romantics such as Novalis, were mystics aware of the impact of techno-rationalism and that is why he sought to promote what has been termed 'magic idealism.' Despite the sophisticated world we live in, scientists cannot fully agree on some basic definitions such as what is life? While we may point to Schrödinger's attempt, there are still shortcomings. When it is impossible to define life, what can we expect from people who believe matter is all that matters when we ask about the meaning of life?

By the time she was 18, Mary attempted to answer these questions in a book published in 1818, begun after a vision. She reflected on the conflict between the organic and mechanical. While she loved the essential Romantic (Percy) and was inspired to write her great book by Lord Byron, she reacted against Romantic passion for the mechanical. Academics increasingly acknowledge that in Britain and in France, Romantics contributed to the love affair with invisible forces of electricity, magnetism, light and machines. Inventors like John Tyndall went on journeys to understand light but realised that matter would not explain the mystery. Mary Shelley's myth is a metaphor of Enlightenment's darkness and displays prescience of problems unleashed by the new order. Romantics loved machines and science from that time onwards. The sense of Romanticism can be seen in other clusters of creativity perhaps such as depicted in *How the Hippies Saved Physics*. Therein, understanding the light of quantum cryptography and quantum information science is traced with some irony to New Age scientists often in California, specifically in Berkeley. Interested in Eastern Mysticism relegated to the fringes as they were no longer necessary to the Cold War, the Hippies re-examined Einstein, Schrödinger, Heisenberg, Böhr and were not content to 'just do the calculations' for institutions. Philosophical speculation and cosmopolitanism were needed again especially in the micro-world where alternative realities existed. Telepathy, remote-viewing, meditation, Tarot, psychedelics, Esalen, Timothy Leary, Ken Kesey, Buckminster Fuller, physics and psychics, New Age, Hippie, Human Potential and the Orient influenced physics by opening it up to a wider panorama based on a re-interpretation of Bell's Theorem. Bell seemed to ring a great invisible bowl of Eastern mysticism through non-locality in spite of Einstein's ideas about the limitations of light, allowing re-examination of ideas abandoned beyond the margin to forgotten pastures of pseudo-science. Bear in mind it has always been Romantics who were open to what is now the domain of parapsychology in their quest for re-enchantment and transcendentalism. Early Romantics wanted to synthesise reason and feeling, science and spirituality, not reject the intellect. They had hoped thereby to create a revolution of mind through archetypes such as the poet-magician. Yeats would later manifest that figure as today perhaps the novelist Whitley Strieber does. However there is always a danger that Romanticism could turn into something else with manifestation of narcissism and technological worship in the 'society of the spectacle.' Others can come afterwards, with less nobility, to use the strategy without the original compassion.

Mary Shelley, aged 8, was allowed stay up late after being caught behind a sofa when Samuel Taylor Coleridge visited her father. She heard him recite *The Rime of the Ancient Mariner* and that would influence her as would his story *Christabel*. In this poem the old sailor is released from punishment when he blesses sea snakes, seeing their beauty instead of the slimy things they had been to him. The suggestion is that all creatures are made by God. This anticipates the contemporary Romantic openness to alien contact. Coleridge was a central figure in the Romantic movement and influenced American Transcendentalism. *Kubla Khan* was written after taking opium in an altered state. As an addict he set a trend, and cast a shadow that could be seen in the Hippie counter-culture of the Romantic individual seeking the sublime, altered states and the transcendent. However, few will look for the deeper commitment in him to spirit and the individual and may fall for some superficial elements that appear consonant but in reality are opposite. Romantics rejected organised religion and had a lasting effect but arguably failed to create conditions that would prevent a far more pervasive threat to the individual by assumption that my enemies' enemy must be my friend and sometimes arguably contributed unintentionally to success of scientism by failing to see how forces they opposed and undermined could have been a possible balancing counter-weight. Duality creates imbalance even if claimed to be non-dual.

It is a mistake to make simplistic extrapolations. Romantics may be more interested in science than people assume. Romantics may contribute to science in a significant way and may love machines. In poetry and literature, Romantics, radicals and revolutionaries sometimes made Satan a hero, through writers such as Milton, Godwin and Percy Bysshe Shelley, as a symbol of the oppressed before a restrictive controlling force. People presumed to love the sublime in nature were often led to counter-cultural pre-occupation. The actual body-snatchers thrived in Shelley's age. I suspect certain Romantics love power or force whether it comes through nature or nuts and bolts. At the time, William Lawrence promoted the now standard idea that consciousness emerges and was unjustly condemned by the religious establishment for his honest endeavours. Mary Shelley consulted him. The same debate is with us. We are all participants. On the threshold of a new era of AI, genetic engineering, robotics, nanotechnology, quantum computing and post-quantum mechanics, we face the same issues. Some false lights beckon, not least new versions of Prometheus that provoked great work by both Shelleys to entirely different ends. Remember too that there is a strong, silent stream of esoteric tradition that is very influential back to Roger Bacon, which seeks to deny higher light by focusing on a dominating, scientific, occult and sometimes Luciferian tradition. Mary Shelley saw the advances, achievements and how Romantics embraced Prometheus as a symbol. She saw the danger and that operated in her subconscious and manifested in a vision of the modern Prometheus, Dr. Frankenstein.

Prometheus is conceived as being godlike, enhancing consciousness, demonstrating foresight in various depictions of this Titan in Greek legend and art. He is partly a recurrent trickster reflecting archetypal concerns from even more ancient examples. I understand uses of the myth to promote individuality and courageous invention. I accept dangers of citizens ceding control. I applaud creativity and endeavour. Ayn Rand made most use of the myth. However she also promoted a very repressive view of human spirituality. Facing the same issues brings us back to the central issue of individual, spirit and notion of evolution. But the nature of light we seek is not the same. As the shaman may go through a spiritual dismemberment and reconstitution in a different dimension we must cohere and choose the path. Prometheus promotes magic rather than mysticism although there are mystical readings also.

Reasonable capitalists know that market concentrations destroy benefits available through the invisible hand Adam Smith explained. Communists understand dangers of concentration of power. Anarchists oppose the whirlpool of power away from people. Libertarians fight against undue control of the individual by institutions. Institutions grow like monsters. Institutions can be captured. Neo-Marxists say Stalin captured the Bolshevik party. Christians are worried about Illuminati. All curiously agree there is a great danger posed by oligarchy and history proves this justified. Small groups impose structures to rule others and the collective generally triumphs over the individual. Even with Christianity, the slight differences create bitter divisions that dwarf shared doctrines. Instead of concentration and the collective, an axiom here is that individuals matter. Individual scientists, artists, writers and poets, philosophers and mystics indicate the way to individuals. We got into great difficulties anytime we ceded power to groups or collectives operating on the basis of noble principles. Individuals allowed to develop their spirit and power can contribute with courage. Spiritual flourishing in an age driven by groups and collectives, with barely disguised disdain for both spirit and individual, requires inspiration with recognition of threats posed not least by deconstruction of the very idea of the individual, spirit, free will and even consciousness.

Coming home in a buggy one night in London, Bucke had a great experience of light which changed his life. This led him to formulate his concept of cosmic consciousness.

> "Finally the basic fact in cosmic consciousness is implied in its name- that fact is consciousness of the cosmos- this is what is called in the East the "Brahmic Splendor," which is in Dante's phrase capable of transhumanizing a man into a god. Whitman, who has an immense deal to say about it, speaks of it in one place as "ineffable light- light rare, untellable, lighting the very light-beyond all signs, descriptions, languages." This consciousness shows the cosmos to consist not of dead matter governed by unconscious, rigid, and unintending law; it shows it on the contrary as entirely immaterial, entirely spiritual and entirely alive; it shows that death is an absurdity, that everyone and everything has eternal life; it shows that the universe is God and that God is the universe."

Bucke had been reading Percy Shelley and others beforehand. This aspect of Shelley is the real value, more than scientific instruments he carried or vital energy that intrigued him. Shelley sought to open those portals that allow spirit triumph. Commitment to reality and force of spiritual light are perennial inspiration. It is critically important we are not misled nor talked out of our inheritance. That does not mean we have to believe we will become gods but perhaps we can encounter divinity now. Cosmic consciousness is not seen to be the highest state for some albeit higher than normal.

Champions of materialist, mechanist, naturalist, scientistic, scientocratic and technocratic worldviews who seek to impose elite control over unenlightened masses eventually will seek to create a loose pseudo-religious, collective or constellation of cults that present approximations based on persuasive, magic but false experiences, as substitutes to persistent reality of genuine spiritual evolution so the one true religion of scientism and evolution though artificial selection can triumph over superstitious remnants amongst those not succumbed yet to sweet servitude suggested by masters. That is if the mission laid out clearly by people such as H.G. Wells has not been achieved. The most probable means is controlling us by AI and enslaving our consciousness with neural links facilitated by some scientists that see themselves as enlightened in rational and even spiritual terms. Contours of control were laid out by researchers such as John C. Lilly in his work during the Cold War in the context of study of brainwashing as has been identified by Williams. Mary Shelley discerned a danger in use of the Prometheus myth and sought to restrain this Romantic tendency. She foresaw that bringing fire down from the sky might not be so desirable. A great arms manufacturer might be a hero to Rand but others see restraint as heroic not least in relation to the natural world.

The use of the Satan symbol by Shelley must be taken for the poetry it was. Similarly avant-garde art uses Satanic figures to counteract often in a theatrical, shock and awe, cool, trickster, transgressive, ironic and often banal way with sometimes serious themes underneath. Nevertheless that does not mean that worship of demons and Satanism outside the public eye is the same, or that people do not engage in horrendous acts for such causes. But it is often the respectable, banal who commit evil acts as well as those using the power of corporate personality. While Burke criticised the French Revolution and those round Mary Shelley celebrated it, others lived it. Marat became a figure like Jesus for the revolutionaries. Murdered in his bath, trying to relieve his skin disease worsened from hiding in sewers, he became a hero for a while. His remains went to the Pantheon and he was a saint. He had a eulogy from the Marquis de Sade. One of Marat's main works was *Discoveries on Light*. It was not well-regarded by other scientists, such as the chemist Lavoisier. The 'father of chemistry' who dedicated his enlightened wisdom to ensuring acquisition of as much gunpowder as the State needed, had a tragic end when the other enlightened, reasonable ones chopped his head off. The principle of indestructibility of matter was his discovery. The science of light and the light of reason went together as manifested in the change to Temples of Reason and later Robespierre's Cult of the Supreme Being during the Reign of Terror. Any vehicle of collective good will have severe limitations. Authority can impose restraints but it is harder to generate good and certainly to impose goodness. Revolutions usually fail. The reality was best articulated by Juan Miranda in the film *Duck you Suckers*.

> "I know what I am talking about when I am talking about the revolutions. The people who read the books go to the people who can't read the books, the poor people, and say, "We have to have a change." So, the poor people make the change, wah? And then, the people who read the books, they all sit around the big polished tables, and they talk and talk and talk and eat and eat and eat, eh? But what has happened to the poor people? They're dead! That's your revolution."

Another revolutionary, born very near Newgrange was John Boyle O'Reilly. He was admired as a poet by Whitman and John F. Kennedy. He became a journalist and an English soldier before going over to the other side. He joined the main Irish Republican secret brotherhood, was captured and sent to Australia as a prisoner (after having been originally sentenced to death) and life imprisonment. On the long journey he and others established a handwritten newspaper with convict poetry and stories. His first view of a person in Australia was of a fellow Aboriginal prisoner in chains on the beach. O'Reilly escaped by ship and came to Philadelphia. Then he went to Boston. He was a writer and helped others escape. One poem he wrote was *Prometheus-Christ*. He argues that Prometheus is not the model we need and that those who claim to be Christians are not following Christ, as evidenced by their role in institutions of power. He suggests we make 'devils of our gods.' Man is half angel and half fiend and is ruled by greed and cant and not a real Christian power which loves nature and is dedicated to happiness and brotherhood of humankind. Christ was not where 'the ninety slave for ten' on the 'devil-built hill.' Thus again we see good and evil and the idea of solely material instead of soul progress. The real law seemed to be simple justice 'clad in light' between darknesses reflecting a certain Celtic Christianity. The only revolution that will work is the internal individual one but the opportunity to do so will reduce with collectivist technocracy.

The advocates of the inventive, creative, industrial types fail to acknowledge that the positive and triumphant aspects of the market system had a strong Judeo-Christian basis as well as a Greco-Roman one. There is no Adam Smith market theory without Christian theology. Look at the law of negligence. Without this principle, manufacturers would not have had the same incentive to improve their systems of production. The law of negligence requires a manufacturer to take reasonable care in production so damage will not ensue. Management accountancy principles came later and their statistical elaboration through TQM had profound effects. But the principle of negligence in the common law world came in the 1932 case of *Donoghue v. Stevenson*. The duty of reasonable care or neighbour principle was articulated specially on the basis of a legal reading of loving your neighbour. In law, you must not injure your neighbour, or someone who might be injured by your failure to take care. A similar approach in relation to science and the environment could have prevented many problems.

1.7 Light in Spirit and Science: Glowing Birds and Precious Stones

Science emphasises the objective study of light whilst dealing often with people who have unique subjective sensibilities. Light, optics, vision, sight and eyes manifest in the physical, philosophical, psychic, psychological, parapsychological, painted, photographic and plastic forces of all progress both material and spiritual. Walter Ong wrote that the *'philosophy of noetics'* is almost entirely based on the analogy of vision. How and what we see is the basis by which we express higher levels of understanding and inner wisdom. The mind's eye, spiritual eye, all-seeing eye and third eye are all receptors of spiritual light. There is a fundamental connection between study of physical and spiritual light which has been severed to our detriment. Before undue specialisation, scientists were often open to the supernatural. Newton studied alchemy as well as light and many other things. His rival Hooke worked for the great Irish-born scientist Robert Boyle. Boyle investigated a blue-green glow on a chicken glowing in his pantry in 1667. Such bioluminescence is caused by living organisms converting chemical energy into light. Boyle followed this line, looking at fungi and making important discoveries about oxygen. This path of study would later lead to knowledge of the enzyme luciferase. Such light is very useful in study of disease and in genetic contexts. Boyle endeavoured to show how science could corroborate divine order. He was also interested in second sight. He had connections with Robert Kirk. Kirk wrote *The Secret Commonwealth* in 1691, which should be regarded as a significant work in a number of ways, not least in parapsychology. As a Christian, Kirk wanted to show that the folk belief about fairies and strange phenomena were consistent with a belief in the Divine. So he recorded fairy lore and stories of second sight which corresponded remarkably well with Irish experiences. Fairies or Siths had 'light changeable bodies' best seen at twilight. Funny that *Star Trek* had Captain Kirk. *Star Wars* had Sith. Philip Pullman has *The Secret Commonwealth*.

Many parapsychologists were interested in light and spirit phenomena. This spirit-light curiosity connection is obvious in the work of certain scientists who contributed significantly to psychic research. The suggestion is often that such professionals were duped, gullible or just poor scientists. Certainly, there were unscrupulous and clever frauds but there was also good science. No great invention comes without many prototypes and evidence takes time. Sir William Crookes studied light. He was interested in cathode rays and phosphorescence. His interest in light helped him develop Crooke's radiometer or light mill. He discovered thallium through spectroscopy which is the study of interaction between light and matter. He developed sunglasses, protective eyewear and the spinthariscope for seeing scintillations. His Crooke's Tube was important in relation to cathode rays, electrons and x-rays. Curiously we see the form of the Maltese Cross in such tubes. All came about from thinking and looking at light phenomena as they occur. In some ways light beckons to the answer. It was no surprise he was interested in the supernatural. Being open-minded and curious, he investigated evidence worthy of study but was ridiculed because it questions the materialist paradigm. Sir William Barrett was an English Professor physicist with connections to Dublin who made important technical contributions. Having problems with his eyesight, he did what had been done by others before and investigated his eye. He went further to develop an entoptiscope. He developed ways to look inside his eye and record it. He also was critical in the development of psychical research. Observing internal vision is related to mystical endeavour. His detachment and observation are admirable. Those who studied the mysteries of eye, light and vision were often very open to studying the spiritual eye, light and vision. Some would argue it is the same with different emphases, maybe a reflection of the duality inherent in the brain. Perhaps one side tends to physics of the eye and the other the spiritual eye with parapsychology shimmering in between. Also John William Strutt (Baron Rayleigh) was a scientist who studied light and developed the theories called Rayleigh Scattering and Rayleigh Waves and contributed to theories that led to quantum mechanics. He was also interested in psychical research.

Another scientist who was a psychic investigator was Zöllner, the astrophysicist. He also had a technical interest in light and vision. Star light was studied with a spectroscope and he informed science using his astro-photometers designed in 1858 even though he was not trained as an astronomer. He identified a famous optical illusion. Studying spiritualism led him to ideas of four dimensional space that anticipate some contemporary theories. Ochorowicz was a Polish, philosopher and scientist who was interested in psychic research and esoteric knowledge. Again he demonstrates an interest in light and made contributions to the development of radio and tv. We should not forget about Pierre Curie (and his brother). Pierre demonstrated piezoelectricity, releasing electricity from crystals. Light is also unleashed and native peoples understood this. Such knowledge is used in quartz timekeeping and crystal oscillators. He and his wife as we will see, studied radiation and radioactivity and made a great contribution with others such as Becquerel in this realm. Pierre was studying light essentially. Often a phenomenon of light led to an investigation. He was also very interested in psychic research. Another great scientist of this type is Sir Oliver Lodge. He concentrated on studying light and radiation as well as specific phenomena such as lightning and made a great contribution to radio. A contemporary example is Bernard Carr. He is very interested in psychical research. He is also a physicist who studied with Hawking when he worked on Hawking Radiation. There is evidence of some other scientists who studied light indicating some openness to psychic phenomena, such as Hertz. He proved electromagnetic waves, photoelectric effect and sparked exploration of radio and X rays. X rays were discovered a century after Morgan produced a 'beautiful green light' when he produced the first X-ray tube. Light manifesting unusually and out of darkness has been a signpost for the curious, just as with spiritual light.

So we see a pattern. There are certain scientists who went against the dominant paradigm, by being open to psychic research or parapsychology. For this, they lose respect from the science community who have decided that there is nothing to investigate. The decision that there is nothing to look at, by other scientists who demonstrate competence and think there is, really takes the mainstream into a belief system that is part of scientism. Crookes and others were the real scientists. Their motivations are often attacked. Some may say they were emotional because they lost family or such like. That is just to say they were humans. Anyway some of this supposed emotion came after their original interest. Scientists seem to pretend that science arises in a purely objective way without speculation nor personal nor basic motivations. That they were fooled at times is not something that solely happened to them. What about all the scientists who let themselves be fooled that their weapons of mass destruction were really instruments of peace? Science may not believe in a Creator anymore but weapons of war have creators and to a man and woman they are scientists. Some make the analogy with Dr. Faust. That scientists must have certain beliefs, demonstrates how mainstream science is a part of a wider belief system associated with materialism and is inherently anti-spiritual as part of a more ambitious claim. As Sorokin indicated, a materialist phase in history promotes science and war to the detriment of spirit. Anyway, note that interest in physical light phenomena led to scientific investigation that led to discoveries and inventions and openness to looking at spiritual phenomena. To speculate is to look. Experiments only come about after something has appeared or someone looks for something. These scientists perceive unknown worlds existing below the threshold of knowledge revealed by anomalies, appearances, apparitions, manifestations, light phenomena, transformations and effects. They must have seen the same structure in revelation of psychic phenomena. It is no accident that substances (e.g. quartz) and phenomena (e.g. lightning) that become revelatory to science have been of spiritual significance to prehistoric people aware of some of those properties. This suggests that ancient people were aware of unique properties of some things which gave science pointers. But there is another startlingly obvious hypothesis which I call 'the path of light.' *The phenomena of light in its various manifestations acts as a precursor, prompt or pointer to actual scientific and spiritual knowledge which suggests an inherent path of light in evolutionary terms, both physical and spiritual.* It is as if there are landing lights or a trail of torches in the imaginative realms. Maybe the way is so obvious we cannot fail to find it. However, technological tools of the military-industrial complex, propaganda model, surveillance society of spectacle and magic light were often informed by these scientists. The choice about how we use insights is an ethical one based on commitment to an integral society. Barrett was concerned with the social conditions in Dublin. Likewise Lodge criticised the Church for not fighting the 'Satans' of greed, selfishness and stupidity. This was a genuine and deep caution about materialism. Perhaps one of the roads not taken was of utilising secrets manifested by light to develop our psychic and spiritual powers. Perhaps imbalanced emphasis on scientific light creates inevitable destructive powers which will send us the hard way if we will not take the easy path. Sensate societies love material and love is not material to them.

In a number of spiritual and philosophical traditions it could be said that we are light embodied or trapped in matter. Matter is often juxtaposed with spiritual light. There is a recurrent sense that we are light beings whose essence is also light and not heavy, encapsulated within a dense universe. For materialist rationalists, focus on light will merely represent an uninformed fascination with phenomena formerly inexplicable which in their striking beauty provided an obvious way to represent another inexplicable force, the mystery of life itself. However, reductionist views lead people away from deeper meanings of light as a description of spiritual force containing clues to our essential nature. From Aboriginal people in Australia to Dogon in Africa, senses of predominance of the immaterial manifest in matter underline perception that we are light at heart. Whether we are in some parallel dimension or some inferior copy or prison as Gnostics believed, reality of the immaterial and its connection with our very origin, nature and reality is an inescapable conclusion of the genius of nearly all civilisations in diverse places. I seek to elucidate or make lucid. The nature of explanation derives from the word for light.

There is battle between scientism and spirituality for the metaphor of light. From Francis Bacon onwards, scientists have claimed the mantle of light. They have claimed that they help the 'merchants of light.' Light represents knowledge. When they crack open and find out how it works and employ it, they can legitimately claim some professional ownership. Having taken the torch of light they can assert that other spiritual light is merely misunderstood science. Light was the source of progress, away from reliance on authority. The Royal Society had been inspired partly by the proposal of a 'College of Light' by the great Czech thinker Comenius who influenced society through championing universal education. He had been inspired by Bacon. Comenius sought unity, with mystic inspiration, using Plato in one hand and the Bible in the other. He classified divine light, external light and inner light. The mind, world and Divine were linked by light of understanding in his *Via Lucis* or *Way of Light*. Scientists would be 'servants of the light.' Many movements at the time from Freemasonry to the Jesuits claimed the command of a narrative of light. The mixture of Kabbalah and Christian mysticism by Louis Claude de Saint-Martin is described as 'illuminism' and persists today in various Martinist schools. So we see a battle between science and spirituality for ownership of the mantle of light. Religion often inspired the quest to understand light.

Another important mystic is Eckartshausen who lived in the second part of the 18th century and wrote *The Cloud upon the Sanctuary*. He said it was an age of twilight and not light, based on the false idea that head illumination and worship of reason would inevitably bring happiness. He saw light inside, from Jesus or love, as illuminating light which enables supernatural things be objective. Reason could not make the spiritual sensorium necessary to receive transcendent force. However the intuitive organ is trapped inside flesh since our descent. Through inspiration of moral good, illumination of mind and heart and breaking through the crust around the sensorium temple of our intuitive gift, we obtain transcendental sight. The cloud before the sanctuary lifts. There has always been an invisible celestial church with a congregation called the 'community of light.' This interior, illuminated church or sanctuary was preserved by prophets who had access to inner truth and not the priesthood with external symbols. Members do not know each other or have formalities nor will they encounter struggles with others because people have to be ripe to be in the sanctuary. *"Only truth can comprehend truth."* In the sanctuary are keys to higher powers. Spirit is an indestructible substance. Flesh traps spirit.

> "God himself is the Power always present. The best man of his times, the chief himself, does not always know all the members, but the moment when it is the Will of God that he should accomplish any object, he finds them in the world with certainty to work for that purpose."

There is a curious crossover between science and mysticism that can be seen in figures like Da Vinci, Newton, Hooke, Kepler, Swedenborg, Tesla and even Descartes. Mystical motifs are often found to possess scientific significance. Study of light has regularly followed examination of things that mesmerised magicians and mystics. Why does the peacock's tail look as it does? Scientists have studied this phenomenon of iridescence. Colour can be caused by pigment or structure. Lines at the bottom of indentations in the feathers cause interference patterns on photonic crystals and band gap of the structure. Mixed colour appears from changes in the lattice structure. Knowledge of photonic crystals is important. In India and elsewhere, the peacock emerged from the mythical Garuda who carried Vishnu. Krishna has such feathers. The Murugan comes on a peacock. The Irish Goddess associated with war is The Morrigan, which sounds suspiciously close. When you follow some of the threads in ancient understanding you may find there is a brilliant magic, crystal carpet underneath reflected in insights of all spiritual traditions. The peacock appears in Christian thinking and alchemy indicating heaven, immortality and resurrection. The phenomenon of light associated with this colourful creature creates a clue to the great mystery of meaning. The peacock's tail is used to indicate psychedelic experiences but really reflects a basic mystical pattern of perception of light which the scientist will seek to reduce to the merely physiological. Again and again, mystical preoccupation or perception with the observably magnificent causes a deeper investigation that science eventually discovers has a unique clue about the nature of reality. Certainly correspondence, signatures and sympathetic magic explain some of these links. But the mythic and mystic may open another pattern of painstaking enquiry for scientific knowledge. Robert Hooke, the great scientist, studied peacock feathers. He found colour disappeared when the feather was put in water. The peacock feather is a correspondence or revelation that also comes from mystical experience through internal visible light well known to mystics.

Romans produced glass four hundred years before Christ, with gold nanoparticles that caused it to change colour. There are also suggestions that ancient knowledge of India for example, as expressed in certain schools of Hindu philosophy prefigured modern physical conceptions of the universe, even perhaps understanding the nature of light in a way not definitively comprehended until much more recently. When the first quantum hologram of a photon was taken in Warsaw it looked like a Maltese Cross. Some claim certain pictures of photons looked like the Merkabah, the mystical Jewish symbol. Esoteric signs and electromagnetic revelations rhyme, in a mystical way. The amplituhedron, and other ideas and models that dispose of time and space and locality on a theoretical level, may suggest how the power of mystical intuition apprehended faster the true nature of reality. The rod of Asklepios might be an indication of the wave and beam nature of light, like the caduceus indicated DNA.

The great mound at Newgrange in Ireland admits mid-winter light through an arrangement of stones over the entrance. Once a year, light shines into the central chamber as it did over 5,000 years ago. The mid-winter celebration of sun beams magically in the dark chamber to give birth in matter to a ring of time or to allow waiting souls within emerge over the rolled rock, with correspondences to other mysteries. All around the world there are magnificent remains that suggest a much deeper technical and spiritual awareness inconsistent with impoverished lives people supposedly led. Industrially developed, polluted, congested, tense places characterised by love of the material and attachment to illusion have a very dim view of those who live from their wits independently yet interdependently in a more frugal way with awareness of their environment and greater commitment to the value of inner peace and purpose. This observation was critical to Gramsci's view of the significance of breaking the link between peasant and Catholic Church in order for Marxism to succeed. We should not be deprived of access to ancient wisdom. In Newgrange we encounter the sense that a fairly common worldview is being manifested whereby the masculine aspect of light or spirit is interacting with feminine matter. This link between matter and mother is a very clear one. Likewise certain words for wood and material are closely linked. But that may be too simple.

Light is crucial in nearly all spiritual traditions. Light is source of life. Perhaps ultimate quests in science will merely reveal what spiritual masters have been trying to explain in a simpler form since time immemorial. There is a ubiquitous sense that we are creatures who have light and whose spiritual nature is to tend towards light. What does this mean? Is it just an image, analogy or metaphor? While it is useful as a metaphor to talk of light, it is deeper. Perhaps the literal meaning is closer to a real truth about our nature that should not be reduced. Light is associated in a deep way with consciousness. Scientists exploring consciousness will find that light is fundamentally related to ultimate riddles they seek to unravel. Spiritual consciousness is chiefly characterised by light, in language, conception and experience. Light may be transmitted or reflected. If transmitted it passes through. If transmitted it may travel regularly or be scattered. Transmission through touch is also associated with descriptions of spiritual leaders. There is a penumbral reflection of light in spiritual discourse. For example the word 'glory' in *Chambers Dictionary* has a number of meanings. According thereto it includes *'triumphant honour'* and *'resplendent brightness'* which is a common understanding. It also refers to a *'combination of the nimbus and aureola'* in religious symbolism and in a less common way *'the presence of God'* or the *'manifestation of God to the blessed in heaven.'* This definition points to the deep, persistent link between light and the profound religious experience of spiritual light. Likewise some elegant words like 'blithe' may have ancient etymological associations with light. The notion of ether itself has close links with light. Apparently unrelated words like 'lithe' which sound similar have positive connotations. Even words that did not originate in light may have been influenced by the concept - delight. Strangely, although there is no connection, the Latin word for light 'lux' appears accidentally in the name Luxor, the ancient city of Thebes in Egypt.

We seek enlightenment. We are entranced with luminescence. We seek illumination. We reflect on things. We see the light. We elucidate. We have lucid intervals when we are dying. We may have lucid dreams. We go towards the light. We witness phenomena of light when people die. We see pictures of haloes around saints. We seek glory. We look to luminaries. We talk of the luminosity of enlightened beings. We perceive radiance and a shining nature. We learn of rays in many traditions. We accord special status to sunlight and starlight. We perceive phenomena of light in relation to many paranormal experiences such as UFOs and fairies. We watch screens with artificial, bias, edge, back, blue light. We are surrounded with LED, LCD, halogen, incandescent, fluorescent lights, screens, strips, lamps, bulbs. We see light-sabers in Star Wars. We see crew being beamed up in Star Trek. We see an episode called *The Inner Light*. We watch fireworks, light and laser shows. We are entertained with lights. We do not want to be in the dark. We may fall into the dark. We have a shadow side. We talk of the shadowlands. We fear we may be cast into darkness. We may be afraid of the dark. We see light and dark symbolise yin-yang. We have the complex idea of Lucifer, the light-bringer. We may see or perceive angels and other beings of light. We see apparitions. The French word for light (lumière) was the surname of the brothers who invented cinema. Films have been described as 'turning money into light.' Our pervasive technology, such as fibre-optics, utilise light. We live in natural and artificial light actually and mentally. When science comes to deep questions about life and material, they arrive at light and find religions, mystics and artists were there first.

Science has learnt a lot about light and its chemical, electrical and thermal effects. Galileo was fascinated with the nature of light. Astronomy explains origin of stars and their composition using waves. Da Vinci said study of light brings most delight to students of nature. Marie-Curie discovered radium, polonium and developed ideas of radioactivity and won two Nobel prizes. She worked with light and key incidents of luminosity punctuate this story. Such work on radiation, based on discovery of X-rays, changed the vision of scientists influencing artists like Klee in their visions. Quantum physics evolved from study of light. Einstein was awarded the Nobel Prize in 1921 for discovery of laws of photoelectric effect. Scientists such as Euclid, Pythagoras, Ptolemy, Al-Haytham, Bacon, Copernicus, Descartes, Huygens, Newton, Faraday, Mach, Edison, Tesla and Böhr studied the nature of light and techniques to create artificial light. From laser beam to hologram, light is a critical technology. The dual nature of light as waves and particles represented a fundamental struggle of twentieth century science. A great earlier debate was about whether eyes emitted light or intromitted it. Now we have come so far that we know light in collision at great force can create matter.

Arthur Young explained that photons are actions and are not things as such and occur in whole units. Quantum science deals with light interactions where photons carry energy. Young saw light as being characterised by freedom whereas matter is governed by laws more predictable and deterministic. He suggested that light in its freedom with purpose invested itself in matter to achieve or develop. He likened this to Plato's explanation of being and becoming. Being is un-determined and becoming changes and grows in time. Being invested in becoming allows growth. He saw light as the central aspect of our consciousness and believed it reconciled disparate spiritual and scientific explanations. Changes of state rather than events were important. The move away from complicated and dense clockwork determinism involves ascension with negative or reverse entropy. Energy becomes stored allowing growth and organisation rather than dissipation. Thus the 'great chain of being' is initiated as determined by greater degrees of ascending freedom, mobility and associated higher levels of evolution. There is a movement from randomness to control with choice. Each stage depends on the previous. Freedom tends towards infinity. He sought to reconcile physics and spirituality and the strange presence of observer and intriguing role of intention.

Light technology links into prior esoteric traditions in curious ways. Lasers are stimulated emission (or Light Amplification by Stimulated Emission of Radiation). The ruby, a stone of esoteric significance, was significant in its development and some argue was used in ancient times by Moses! Lasers can now be used for fusion and fission. Fibre optics use silica cables. Apart from sand, silica is most commonly found in quartz. Quartz is recurrent in prehistoric sites in many countries not least in Ireland. Many highly gifted mathematicians such as Ramanujan identified a mystic cosmic link to origin of their equations. His work proved relevant to black holes. Some of the greatest scientists such as Newton were clearly active in the field of alchemy and the periodic table came to Mendeleev in a dream. It seems that while dull, literal scientists cannot see the mystical, equally the dull, literal religionists cannot see the scientific. One can approach strange phenomena with an open mind, one can extract inspiration perhaps.

You do not have to believe that the quintessence or fifth element exists, as many do, or that the Akasha or luminiferous ether exists, as Tesla did, based on his Vedic studies. However it will sound implausible when you then begin to present speculations on dark matter or what the fifth fundamental particle is, on flimsy foundations and expect people to inevitably accept and believe those equally strange principles ignoring the curiously anticipatory directions of revealed or anciently evolved systems of traditional knowledge. It is equally strange that perennial and ubiquitous apprehension of creative principles, as represented in concepts such as *prana* for example, are dismissed as stories for infantile minds by people as uniformly convinced of the certainty of their positions as institutional religious zealots. Their own supposedly pristine, reasonable and rational agenda is presented merely as an objective, progressive investigation. Such research is inevitably shorn of any ritualistic, self-serving motivations or indeed speculation. Much research is seemingly oblivious to the gravest threats to our existence constantly unleashed by a combination of the grail of financial reward and ultimate buzz of recognition and satisfaction provided by obsession and fascination of what is difficult to those who deny the need for pervasive ethical concepts. Science can be great, liberating and life-enhancing. However it must be balanced. The paradigm is shifting slowly in science. If we are aware of what good science says and how dark scientism destroys, aware of good spiritual traditions, aware of bright mystical and dark paths, we may spiritually evolve as individuals and in so doing save ourselves. Science will sell technological spirituality as it strips mysticism of technique and employs stroboscopic or flickering light, helmets and crowns that use electromagnetic waves in the future. There has been a battle for the torch light between spirituality and science. We can assert therefore, that in addition to physical, spiritual and magical light there is also scientific light. *Scientific light represents the study, knowledge, manipulation of light and an associated metaphor that scientific knowledge creates an intellectual illumination of a superior and exclusive type.*

1.8 Trapped Light Today

As life is in the cell contained, light is there too in mysterious ways. Scientists are now using light to see how cells are communicating using 'resonant hyperspectral imaging.' Now scientists have reached new levels of comprehension. Not long ago scientists were searching for the explanations of how we breathe and how that could be explained. Davy and Lavoisier explored the role of light. Joseph Trent in 1800 wrote *An Inquiry into the Effects of Light on Respiration* which sought to explain the role of light in breathing and blood for example. Light was believed to become trapped in substances before the more complete chemical explanations came. Such views then influenced art and literature. Light phenomena are still very mysterious. Scientists, for example, are still trying to understand the 'transient luminous lunar phenomena' or the mysterious flashes of light on the moon, not attributable apparently to sunshine. It was reported in 2020 that scientists have applied quantum entanglement to two laser beams by bouncing them off a mechanically resonating membrane. But in recent years, they have also been able to trap light. Scientists have created the means to trap photons using ideas such as photonic band gaps. Aware of Bragg's Reflection and considering interference patterns enough is allowed in so it will not escape. Thus light usually absorbed or reflected is now capable of being tamed and domesticated. Photonic crystals can trap light in various structures in a way that means they cannot escape. Rubidium atoms have also been used to trap light. So inventions beckon. But is this relevant in other ways? Frozen or slow light has implications. It is clear that trapped light will create great possibilities in relation to computers and communication. The amazing science of cymatics has demonstrated how mysterious archetypal symbols reflect different sound frequencies. Acoustically-induced photoluminescence, which involves some trapping of light, may enable us to see deep patterns through the use of sound. When we get into the dark domain of dark energy we become aware that such darkness seems to involve rays for some and may even be more of the nature of light.

The Nobel Prize in Physics in 2018 was awarded to a number of scientists and recognised the use of light to act as a tweezers at the very small level. This combined the power of light with lightness to trap particles. Researchers at Caltech also claim that light may be used to send space ships to stars based on 'self-stabilizing photonic levitation' operating on nano-patterning on an object's surface. Trapping small things with light enables much bigger things to be trapped. The biggest things come from the smallest as Taoism reminds us. A virus can change the world. Bacteria did the trick in *War of the Worlds*. Trapping of light in its various forms is a Rubicon indicating passage into a territory of greater technological control of consciousness. Just as in *2001: A Space Odyssey* where the TMA is a signalling device associated with supervision of evolution of humans, so is trapped light. Even if we bear in mind that waves in the brain are of a different type, transcranial magnetic stimulation, ultrasound, quantum interference and electromagnetic waves may impact on the alpha, beta, delta, gamma or theta rays. Put it another way, the oddly recurrent perception of the possibility that we might be essentially trapped light in some ways is becoming a demonstrable threat from materialist concentration.

Elusive dark matter is another phenomenon that has preoccupied theoretical physics. Whatever this material is, it will relate light in some shape or form. Whatever explanations unfold, they may in some way corroborate or re-inforce what mystics have long revealed from revelations to them from ancient times and what excessively reductionist, materialists railed against. Zwicky in the 1930's identified an invisible matter that was not confirmed until Rubin corroborated this assumption based on movement of stars. Data from observation suggests that it is distributed and occurs in haloes at times and that visible objects are only a small part of what we see. It is believed to be stuff that has no light, is stable and cold, has feeble bonds with itself and is affected by gravity. To some it suggests a new particle such as a WIMP deriving from supersymmetry in string theory. The search for neutralinos and other particles such as axions, involves a quest for dark matter. Axions solve problems associated with electric spin of electrons with excitation of the theta field and do not involve supersymmetry. Who knows? Another super force is that of superconductivity which interacts inevitably with light. Peculiar behaviour of pairs of photons has suggested their utility in context of exploration of superconductivity. Every discovery seems to open a wider mystery. The greatest scientists will exhibit some degree of intellectual humility about the nature of our reality. There is possibility of using light to create matter in quantum electrodynamics or QED. This is where quantum mechanics and special relativity accord and is claimed to be one of the greatest achievements in science. Feynman, with others, provided a mathematical explanation of light. It explains a lot of interactions through the electromagnetic force.

In 1967 George Wald obtained the Nobel Prize for his work on explaining how vision works through reception of light in the retina and transduction. Science also comprehends better how light is critical in relation to cognition and mood, operating through the eye and skin to produce effects in brain and body. There are some on the fringes who believe that diseases such as cancer may be associated with distortions of light in some way. Light therapy and heliotherapy progress to photobiomodulation. Holographic principles may explain how the body works for some. Optogenetics is the use of light to affect cells such as neurons. Francis Crick was also involved in the evolution of this field. Neurotheology is a domain of investigation that examines the link between brain and theology. Oscillations may surface as significant in these theories as it did for Heisenberg. Consideration of extra dimensionality of existence and even space-time may explain scientific problems and chime with phenomena from clairvoyance to enlightenment. Scientists understand more how brain and body works with light.

Increased scientific awareness of how light may be manipulated in the brain combined with big data and surveillance that Zuboff talks of, give cause for concern. Searching for the nature of consciousness and examination of microtubules, quantum effects and such investigations seek to provide a final answer about who we are and how we work. That will be fruitless in relation to deeper questions. However such knowledge may provide means to control pesky individuals. Science has a habit of shooting first and asking questions later. Some scientists are reflecting a more nuanced view and contributing useful evidence to corroborate subjective experiences that create meaning. Peter Fenwick, Eben Alexander and Pim van Lommel are examples from the medical domain who can attest to striking evidence, personally and professionally which stresses evidence of the entity within us manifesting or reporting phenomena of light. At a time when physics has moved from planets, particles, planes and fields to looking at information, saying it's about 'It from Bit,' better physicists realise they are talking about descriptions of reality, in a participatory universe as Wheeler indicated. Perhaps science is a particle and religion a wave form epistemology of reality. For many mystics and people committed to primacy of spirit we have light within us and seek and travel towards it. Exoterically, in the main religions is a clear presence of light, whose essential power is obscured. The force is light and is with you but being blocked, hidden or entrapped needs to be liberated. There are many who believe emotions may be literally trapped in the body in a way that impedes our growth. Reich might be mentioned. When force of inner light is liberated we should be vigilant to ensure it is not obscured by dark forces or camouflaged with gowns of neon, blue, laser light or gamma rays. It is better to be poor with dreams as Yeats seeking,

> "…'heavens' embroided clothes,
> Enwrought with golden and silver light."

1.9 The Fork

"The Lightning is a Yellow Fork
From Tables in the Sky"
Emily Dickinson

As science controls light itself, spirituality seems on the back foot. Who are we? Life involves us in choices. We regularly encounter a significant fork in the road of our individual development. Whatever happens, science and spirituality are struggling in similar fields of contention. While some seek accommodation and mutual enhancement, some seek victory over the other as if it were a zero sum game. Science seems intent on subduing spirituality. Scientism seems to combine with contemporary culture's condemnation and disrespect of the sacred through cultivation of the profane. We can see how spiritual traditions have been presented, intentionally or accidently, through counterfeits of spiritual concepts in modern culture. Thus great ideas of illuminationism are reduced to Illuminati, spiritual enlightenment becomes The Enlightenment, the spiritual cloud becomes The Cloud, the Virgin becomes the Virgin brand, Madonna becomes Madonna the sex symbol, the Hail Mary invocation becomes a failed pass in football, Oh My God (the start of the act of contrition) becomes an exclamation beloved of atheists, Quaker became a trade mark without any connection to the source. Logos has become commercial logos. *No Logo* misses the claim that there is No Logos. Likewise spiritual people are wont to appropriate science so it becomes genuine pseudo-science. That is not the intention here. Science and spiritual endeavours may overlap in a sweet spot but the phenomenon of quintessentially subjective experience of humanity however consistent are of a dimension science is often uncomfortable with.

I lay out a series of lines for reflection. Poetic form in indeterminacy and suggestiveness allows a type of speculation stimulated by science whilst irrigating imagination without being hostage to either. The universe will only ever be understood in poetry while best explanations must be in prose and formulae. No formula will ever represent adequately the deepest nature of spiritual existence. To some like Francis Fukuyama this is a Factor X. Unfortunately, while I agree with some of the gist of his argument, choice of 'Factor X' may be an error on the scale of 'the end of history' argument because of usage of that term elsewhere for completely opposing reasons. The element he is taking about is spirit. He is arguing on the battlefield of the real Armageddon. The Armageddon concept should not be ignored because of its significance for many. I do not follow literalistic interpretations. It should be construed more as representation of the place on which the word is based which was a crossroads. Similarly, the idea of apocalypse suggests revelation as well as destruction. Whether we like it or not, it is clear that humanity can always be destroyed and will often come to a crossroads.

This book follows on from my earlier work *The Mystical Accord*. In that book I suggest such a crossroads. There is a great opportunity to seek commonality within wisdom and spiritual traditions. There is also a road towards a technological future where humans are but one conscious agent in a multiplicity of mechanised forms, regarded as a type of machine made of meat and inferior. Assumptions that underpinned our world will disintegrate. The nature of consciousness is a battleground. That battle is relevant in considering the nature of light in relation to spirit. Consciousness is pre-existent and fundamental and the quantum of consciousness that insufflates into us is co-extensive with spirit. Through embarking on a spiritual journey that involves an effort to transcend ego, we evolve spiritually and create 'a nexus to the numinous' more consistent with the plateau experience Maslow was moving towards after his study of peak experience.

At the exact stage of a great opportunity for exploring healing interconnections between spiritual traditions on a voluntary, individual basis, science is reaching a new place. The great opportunity available to science to be exploited by the ideology of scientism derives from possibilities presented by technology such as trapping light, AI and external brain-controlling resonances. Technology can combine with a reductionist, materialist, objectivist philosophy. That combine denudes humans of the cloak of dignity presented by profound doctrines in Western culture and elsewhere and attacks once again the remaining and miraculously surviving Indigenous spiritual knowledge. You will be told you are lesser than other 'conscious agents' insofar as they are unencumbered by nasty emotions and feelings that burden humankind. The juxtaposition of natural selection and biological evolution with spiritual evolution will be discarded through increasing focus on artificial selection and a final assault on the last superstition of spiritual quest that masses clung to despite assaults by elites convinced of superiority of their own rationale and objectives and unimpeded by moral constraints. Great opportunities exist, as do great threats.

On the risk side, it suggests to me as a non-scientist, that technology is tending to the point of no return. This is not just about the singularity. All human history involves competition and a struggle for dominance between and within civilisations. There is always a contest to see who are masters or slaves? We assume slavery is of the past while it is perennial and recurrent. Possessed of great material possibilities and increasing welfare despite great disparities, we fail to see we can easily become enthralled. Being enthralled means you are literally put into mental slavery. Technology provides tools to make thralldom feasible.

Ultimate freedom is the freedom to think, feel, contemplate, pray reflect, grow, debate, move, meet and act- not to do what you want without restraint. I had the good fortune to meet a celebrated Irish psychiatrist Dr. Anthony Clare a long time ago. He did many things in his life including having a tv series where he interviewed famous people. One of the people he interviewed was Jimmy Savile. Savile's exploits in the UK have not received the attention elsewhere one might expect. He was a man in the public eye, who seems to have been a particularly nasty figure. Under a cloak of celebrity and charitable works, this man (who some say was the first DJ and was at the forefront of pop culture) apparently committed unspeakable crimes with the connivance of people in high office. He was even given a role in mental health reform by the Thatcher government! Very few people publicly commented on Savile when he was alive, which is always a concern. Strangely the only other public figure who questioned the 'star' was Johnny Rotten, of the Sex Pistols, in an interview. Clare realised that there was 'something chilling' about Savile, the modern day saint and said so. What Savile emphasised in his interview was his desire for 'ultimate freedom.' This clearly means freedom to do what you want without moral restraint. He did his deeds in darkness while hiding in 'plain sight.' He said in an interview that he had been regarded as a 'witch' when he worked down the mines. Freedom lies somewhere between extreme limitation or physical restraint of conduct like in *A Clockwork Orange* and freedom to do what one wants without restraint or any consideration for other people. It seems that some people who advocate freedom from moral restraint and 'dogma' may also be very willing paradoxically to promote public restraints of other conduct not deemed politically correct. We should be careful not to substitute one tyranny for another.

We assume the last caverns of individuality will remain free from the glaring light of tyrants. However, proliferation of technology allows the tyrannical a myriad of methods to control us. The next phase of domination will involve an attempt to utilise technology to control our very consciousness. The growth of entertainment, internet and mobile technologies is the first phase. Elon Musk and others are working on the next neural-linking phase. Within the great opportunity of enhancement of consciousness lies possibility of control of free will. Those technologies will use light, in its visible and invisible forms so we may be controlled by light. The question is whether we want to tend towards spiritual light, as true light or other human-made mechanised forms.

Perennial wisdom focuses on light. There is enough evidence to suggest that light, of whatever rareness, is the stuff of spirit and that we are essentially of this nature. In *The Mystical Accord,* I suggest a framework that can be detected in mystical endeavours of most spiritual traditions. It involves movement from self to true self, involving a journey guided by compassion, seeking to distinguish between illusion and reality, towards transcendence and creation of a nexus to the numinous. All is predicated on two assumptions. Firstly, we are spiritual beings. Secondly, consciousness is primary and fundamental. *The Mystery of Trapped Light* builds on that base to seek the common theme and threads of light.

We have come to a fork in the road. The fork in the road can be seen in Ezekiel and many other places in literature. Robert Frost begins his poem *The Road Not Taken* with the line,

"Two roads diverged in a yellow wood…"

I have heard it said that the Navajo see this world as a Third World that we come to and that this is the Yellow World. Thus I might say that,

Two roads diverge in this yellow world.

Hopefully we have not passed a point of no return. One is a path of spiritual growth and sensible mastery of technology. The other is of bondage to technology where other ostensibly conscious agents control our destiny and demise. Hope for synthesis dwindles in the face of oligarchical forces and scientism. That bifurcation can be characterised as a duality between mechanism and spirituality or maybe Prometheans and Anti-Prometheans. Pythagoras used a Y to commit the student to the path of learning. Being an advocate of the middle ground, centre or foreshore, I hope there is somewhere in-between. An example of this split of perspectives from two souls who read and experienced similar influences is Percy B. Shelley and his wife Mary Shelley. His poetry about Prometheus and her work on Frankenstein indicated the amicable gulf. The scientific religion based often on secrecy, using universities, hospitals and even books taken with religious zeal of Reformation facilitated conquest, colonisations and continued to create a devastating dogma of progress. Through controlling presses that told the victor's story they concocted a fantasy of detached, rational and empirical knowledge somehow without casualties, simultaneously denying esoteric preoccupations oddly recurrent in chronicles of enlightenment proponents of a much-exploited material world. Measuring makes control by the few easy and exploitation of many inevitable. Machines make control more difficult to resist. Massive investment creates diversion of energy from gentler activity and machines require to be fed with energy at great cost with people being final fodder.

1.10 The Nature, Art and Metaphysics of Light

Contemplating the nature of light is always a valuable lesson per se. Our reality itself depends on what we see and how we see it. There is subjective and objective experience of it. We have conceptions of reality and of knowledge. Light is one force that provides a concept of reality while suggesting a way of knowing about knowing, gives experiential evidence and a consequent way of being. Mystics argue this is because it is reflective of deeper truth. Light acts and reveals and we realise, recognise and respond. Philosophers like Heidegger (who also warned about technology) looked at light and its etymology and in most languages we see similar linkages between certain words and basic concepts. The idea of a 'phenomenon' or something which manifests or appears, and some associated Greek words, are related to light and shining forth. So while experts focus on strange apparitions in parapsychology, every phenomenon and appearance emerges from somewhere to reveal through light. Some French thinkers like Derrida seek to use these concepts, but existing ones make sense if we look at their linguistic origin. To stretch them further may distort and undermine their utility in psychic research. Anyway, light reveals itself and is revealed, when we attend to its mysteries. The phenomena of spiritual and physical light are thus similar in that we encounter some appearance or revelation and we interpret and accommodate it.

The owl and jaguar see well at night and are symbols for enhanced spiritual perception. Many believe the otherworld and invisible worlds are either dimensions beyond or generally existing outside visible range but capable of flitting in at times. Vision is not always neat, for example, infra-red is detected in the eye in certain circumstances. One might think science has cracked the nature of colour and light. It has learnt a lot. However when you dig a bit deeper you see there are profound discussions about the epistemology and ontology of light. I am sceptical about the power of these words, consistency of their use and dangers of circular thinking. Nevertheless, how we know what we know about light and how and what it is and is interpreted must be fundamental to understanding it. Scientists make classifications of colour and characteristics of light in space based on measurable and quantitative factors, but such actions are not experiences. William James wondered how an ant experienced consciousness. Experience of colour and light is a gift of consciousness and is shaped by conditioning of perception. The process may be explained but quality cannot be easily reduced. Scientists make one believe they understand more than they actually do. Bear that in mind when you feel compelled to reduce descriptions of spiritual light you encounter. Most of us have been programmed, remotely controlled by the 'propaganda model' that Chomsky explains. Light has been used in many magic, religious and proto-scientific practices, occult arts and divination for a long time, from scrying to aeromancy, ceraunoscopy, crystallomancy, hydromancy and pyromancy. Looking at what is around us and how light behaves has always been significant for practical, predictive, physical, psychological, personal and psychic reasons. Culture is influenced by natural, displays of light and often extraordinary visual apprehension leads to symbolic interpretation.

Visible light indicates sources or phenomena of perception caused by refraction or reflection. We make the same assumption about light as fish do about water. Seeing light, we ignore how complex the process is, how photons travel into our eyes and nerves and how we have receptors activated by light that regulate bodily rhythms. Even in the brain's darkness it seems there are biophotons. The heavens, sun, moon stars are central in all cultures. Comets affect history and the Aztecs may have fallen indirectly because of one. Other beautiful manifestations and light effects such as rainbows, fogbows, sunbows, moonbows, auroras, aureolas, albedos, coronas, haloes and light pillars entrance us. We know the significance of sunlight. Scientists are more aware of the importance of moonlight for sea creatures such as zooplankton. The Northern Lights, meteors and other celestial manifestations create awe and inspire myth. Many other types of visible light provide inspiration and have acted as clues and motifs in the search for answers to the mystery and meaning of life. The bluish glow of Cherenkov radiation is a product of the nuclear world of scientists.

The suffix 'escence' indicates some of the essence of light in a variety of manifestations. Scientific definitions fail sometimes to suggest the initiatory mystical power of these appearances. Light is emitted in nature and presumably does not need us seeing it to exist. Piezoluminescence is the emission of light from stress to rocks. The firefly is an example of beautiful bioluminescence. Mating displays of light in the evening are a recurrent motif in Japanese art for example. Synchronous firefly displays are interesting group behaviour. All is not magically jolly. Some firefly females trick younger males to their death with deadly displays. The motif of false lights is a useful reminder. The author of the mystical text *The Cloud of Unknowing* warned against mistaking bodily perception of certain lights as representing an elevated divine state. Likewise many mystics warn about devils posing as shining angels. Oliver Sacks presented neurological explanations for many mystical experiences. However the inevitable tendency of the medical profession to pathologise anomalous experience more explicable in terms of mysticism should be borne in mind. We always need the ability to discern.

Light effects often depend on how we see it. Some light is genuinely produced through chemical and molecular changes. Some effects are optical phenomena resulting from refraction and reflection of ambient light. Iridescence refers to the phenomenon where the surface colour appears to change when we alter angles of our apprehension thereof. A soap bubble or oil on a shallow puddle of water is familiar sights demonstrating this. It occurs through interaction and interference of thin layers within material that operating together reflects different wavelengths back. Pearlescence refers to the iridescent nature of a pearl's coating and to the effect of reflected white light. It is no surprise the pearl has been a recurrent spiritual symbol, not least because it emerges from an apparently contrasting physical possibility. Opalescence is an optical phenomenon associated with the physical and chemical structure of opals. It is no wonder that stones such as opals are regarded as magical and precious. Milky scattering of light in other gemstones such as moonstones is an optical effect known as adularescence. Heat produces visible light in the process called incandescence.

Cold light is emission of light or luminescence not from heat. Photoluminescence refers to emission of light after photons are absorbed. It covers fluorescence and phosphorescence.

Then there is reaction to light or impact of light on organisms or their behaviour. Photobiology looks at effects of light on biology. Heliotropism refers to turning to the sun. Phototropism refers to turning to light. Another interesting type of light produced by some creatures such as the mantis shrimp is sonoluminescence. This is a strange phenomenon which involves production of light from collapsing of bubbles due to sudden or increased sound waves. In these small domains of investigation of light will the future be seen. It is not an accident that light is a clue to scientific advance. Instincts and insight of mystics may express higher order knowledge than what materialists could understand insofar as they may tend to be literalistic and reductionist. All such diverse light phenomena impact in various degrees on how we interpret the world and even how philosophers think. Light manifests in remarkable spectacles. Spectacles make us look. Looking makes us inquire which means to seek. Light has a general and a particular impact. Apart from biology, in philosophy, mythology and art light plays a role.

We encounter the idea of light in Socrates and Plato. Socrates looks to the sun and sees how we see things and it helps things grow and gives rise to existence. By analogy the good is the source of intelligibility and knowledge in us. Therefore it is even higher than truth and knowledge. If goodness shines into the person to banish darkness then that light makes inner sense available to reason and intelligibility and allows proper thought and understanding. This may contrast with Plato's Cave where light creates a false understanding that does not reflect true goodness. This structure of thinking mirrors many spiritual traditions and good and god or God are obviously very closely connected. The form of good is critical. The good is not pleasure or knowledge. Goodness illuminates. The world reflects the form of the good and the knower knows through that form. Likewise light may be employed artificially to create illusions and to mislead with shadows. As technology develops we see people are always drawn to light phenomena, actual and artificial and tools such as magic lanterns may create arresting apparitions that may obscure as well as illuminate. Obscurity and illumination occur like yin and yang.

Dr. Athena Despoina Potari has written recently about the significance of light in ancient Greek philosophy in an article entitled *The Light of Hellenism*. She argues that the tradition is consistent with Eastern ideas. She says that the *El* is the light of being or spiritual light. She suggests Hellenism was based on a philosophy of light reflecting human consciousness as part of universal consciousness. Philosophy, properly so-called, as distinct from sophism, identified an experiential path of light in gnosis. Truth is thus a type of spiritual light. She sees an ontology of light in Greek philosophy in everything and matter manifests light. She emphasises the root 'pha' as in phantasm. Her studies reinforce the idea that there is a path of light. She suggests we are beings of light that can become seers. The highest light is represented in natural light. Her insights are consistent with mine. There is also the increasing awareness that early Greek philosophers such as Parmenides and Empedocles, grew out of a mystical tradition that was consistent with the ancient shamanic culture in Europe as laid out by Kingsley and others. There seems to have been a shift in the status of the significance of light so that figures after Plato such as Philo and moreso Plotinus puts it as the fundamental spiritual principle of being, manifestation and goodness. The Neo-Platonists who united the Greek, Jewish and Egyptian conceptions influenced the currents that moved outwards, northwards and eastwards in particular. The Jews had God laying out a garment of light as a tent for us. This in turn influenced Christians like Augustine who used ideas of light. Pseudo-Dionysius the Areopagite was a Neo-Platonic mystic whose writings influenced Christianity profoundly. His work is based on spiritual light. While the Arabic Illuminationists influenced medieval Europe there was a light tradition in Europe that is often ignored and is just as significant. Philosophy students seem to repeat the same old alleged passageways without much critical evaluation.

Many have written about myth and reality of light, from Joseph Campbell to Jung. Light permeates much myth. Some of the stories such as that of Prometheus might be interpreted slightly differently in terms of light. In fact there may be another meaning about attempting to achieve a higher light before one is meant to. Fire and light are reflections of a deeper perception of perfect forms of light. Swords of light appear. Flashes of light from the heavens recur. Light is essence of art. Architecture involves crucial decisions about the flow and reception of light and there have been 'light and space' movements. Magical instruments, stones and goblets were characterised by light effects. Romans used nanoparticles in glass to alter apparent colour through combination of substances that alternatively reflected or transmitted light waves. Stained glass or rose windows in great cathedrals are enlivened with daylight. Romances of the medieval period, particularly significant Holy Grail stories, have light as a central feature paralleling Persian traditions for some. Myths, stories, poetry, painting and photography obviously need, use and refer to light. Rather, light begets art and suggests it as it does science. There is nothing new under the sun. So light must inevitably inform all activities under the sun or moon, but in poetry of a metaphysical sort, there is an indication that spiritual or mystical light has some form or process.

A 'metaphysical' or religious poet like Thomas Traherne was seen as Romantic and mystical and he emerges in the perennial philosophy canon. He seems to have moved in a milieu of people interested in magic but was a mystic. Evelyn Underhill, the great writer on mysticism, experimented seriously with magic and then moved to strict mysticism. Such knowledge of ritual magic is evident in her novel *The Column of Dust*. Interestingly we see therein suggested dangers of curiosity in magic and attraction of unwanted spirit into matter in the form of a type of possession. Magicians today will often make clear that they are not mystics. Underhill believed magic was about will and mysticism was about purification, illumination and the Holy Grail, being absolute reality of love more important than knowledge. Light was critical to the metaphysical poetry of Traherne.

> "Tis not the Object, but the Light
> That maketh Heaven;"

And elsewhere

> "I was an Inward *Sphere of Light*."

Infinity is full of Divine immortal light and this world is a shadow of that heavenly one capable of shining if we see it properly with simple light. The spark within us tends to divine source from which it originates. He talks of mysticism in 'The Circulation.'

About the 'mysteries of blessedness,' Traherne says that without circulations which 'borrow matter first' we could not be shown a 'glimpse of light.'

> "But by the ministry of inward light,
> That in the spirits cherisheth its sight."

You have to receive before you give he says. He is explaining mystic perception and metaphysics. We could not be here without divine or creative consciousness. It is only with consciousness given that we can exercise it and perceive and we should be able to recognise our corresponding origin. Mystics allow spirit contemplate itself. More specifically the mystic receives 'fair ideas from the sky' on 'unperceived wings.' This is key to understanding mystical revelation. Many critics will deny such possibilities or perceptions or reduce mystic experience to mere flotsam and jetsam of the subconscious or unconscious, an intrusion from right brain to left or some other physiological factor. The authenticity of experience of a dimension outside the mystic's conscious control that intrudes gracefully or condescends to provide direct insight or revelation that does not appear to be possible to construct consciously and creates a superior condition of contentment is proof of that higher reality, to the mystic at least. Traherne means that consciousness is a circulation from source through matter to come back to origin and mysticism is realisation of that cycle through enhanced consciousness. This is manifested by those willing to open spiritual sight who sought the 'spotless mirror' representing humility or emptying of desire. This succumbing to higher force is by yin, yielding, releasing, judo attitude that attracts and is patient as a cat until it seizes insight. Mystic reception is not the yang, controlling will of the magician that charges like a bull or assembles shiny things like a magpie. There is an implicit circularity in that those willing to find it will, whereas those unwilling may not perceive it or create the necessary conditions.

Similarly another 17th century metaphysical poet, Henry Vaughan, uses light as a special mystical symbol. In his poem *The World,* he writes of the ring of light,

> "I saw Eternity the other night,
> Like a great ring of pure and endless light."

In his poem *They are all Gone into the World of Light*, Vaughan asks God to take him,

> "Resume thy spirit from this world of thrall
> Into true liberty."

Thus he wants his trapped light to be resumed to the world of light. Henry's brother Thomas was a mystic and alchemist. His work *Lumen de Lumine* or *A New Magical Light Discovered and Communicated to the World* seems to represent somewhat the communication of a mystical journey through the 'magic mountain' with threatening figures and purple, green and the preternatural colour code of mystic experience. The alchemic style allowed genuine chemical experimentation to also be used as a framework to describe mystical experiences of light. Many poets wrote about light. *When I Consider How my Light I Spent* (Milton), *There's a certain Slant of Light* (Dickinson) *Sudden Light* (Rosetti) *Light* and also *Lamp of Love* (Tagore) *More Light! More Light!* (Hecht) *Electric Light* (Heaney). Light incites poetry and metaphysical thought.

Spanish language literature and poetry has a mystical and metaphysical depth often insufficiently appreciated. Light and its symbol recur as in all bodies of poetry. It is in the work of St. John of the Cross. More recently, Aleixandre wrote about us being lightning between darknesses, about how his was a journey of light and how there was light within which enables the other poetic eyes see in dark. The light theme is clear in Lorca in repeated symbols such as the moon. It also emerges in the supernatural stories of Bécquer such as in *Los ojos verdes* (the green eyes). *El rayo de luna* (the moonbeam) is about moonbeam illusions. All these stories are about individual tragedy caused by obsessive Romantic pursuit of objects of supernatural desire. The green eyes of the spirit that lures a man to his death in the water might be the emeralds of Lucifer. Mystic green light manifests in a number of contexts because it is a type that appears in internal visible light. Like Faust, these stories warn that fascination with the unobtainable or supernatural leads to tragic results. This is the difference between the mystic path related to fundamental, perennial truth and egotistical attraction to the extraordinary by the mediocre or selfish. Similarly, light can be found in Irish writing and mystical light is found in writers such as AE Russell, as evidenced in little books such as *The Candle of Vision: Autobiography of a Mystic.* P.L. Travers went to meet him in Ireland and he influenced Yeats and shared his interest in Theosophy. Poetry dwells on light, painters in it.

Skylights, allowing light stream into an artist's studio, have a quality similar to the Holy Ghost holes in certain churches. The greatest artists in painting explore the changing nature of light through, colour, composition and brushstroke. Great works of art such as The Ghent Altarpiece by Van Eyck are becoming less accessible to people in some ways despite the greater study. This represented divine vision or vision of God. Similarly in the painting attributed to Bosch, *The Seven Deadly Sins,* we see symbols of an all-seeing eye or iris of God. This was not a pre-occupation of Christianity. The circular iris that reflects sins of humanity mirrors the Buddhist Bhavacakra. These show wheels of life and karma of being. The all-seeing eye in a triangle reflects this external mirror of the karmic universe. There is a physical eye and an inner eye that reflects large vision represented by a symbolic eye. Artists were influenced by theories of light. J.M. Turner was influenced by Goethe. Seurat who painted The Bathers and his pointillist style and 'chromoluminarism' were inspired by theories of colour about luminosity and how colour must be seen in context. 'Luminism' was a type of painting at the end of the Impressionist period which emphasised light effects. Painting is one of the central spiritual practices in European history stretching in an unbroken line to the cave paintings I visited in France and especially in Spain. Crawling into a small space to see shapes painted thousands of years ago in a mystical condition can take you through time. Painting is a psychic, shamanic and magical practice that strangely few can interpret in the society of mass spectacle. Artists went into the dark, painted magic symbols, saw visions and carved them in stone because they were driven to do so. This would contribute something useful through reaching realms that cannot be attained when you do other things. Few know even how to look at or perceive a painting in our spectacle and screen-saturated society of simulacra. Less know how to interpret a painting. Less know how to experience a painting. Less know how to enter a painting. Less know how to see a painting to develop their psyche.

In 1990 in Dublin a painting, elsewhere attributed to one painter and hung in a Jesuit house, turned out to be the 'priceless' *Taking of Christ* (1602) by the rambunctious genius Caravaggio. He was a master of light and dark. His paintings seem lit by a contemporary lighting expert, although experts who have tried re-creation realise he was creating something original. He was hugely successful in obtaining valuable Church commissions at a time when it wanted to consolidate and respond to the Protestant light of reason with the more direct, representation of real people subject to Divine light. Caravaggio was a master who knew how to work imprimitura, sfumato, chiaroscuro and colour to pick out relevant dramatic psychological incident in the religious story creating a sigil of the power of the narrative. The painted light directs the eye hypnotising the beholder who is not spirit blind to participate in the wondrous moment he depicts, whether in *The Calling of St. Matthew* (1600) or *Judith beheading Holofernes* (1599). Painting was light for him. Painters manipulate light from their nervous system to impact on the viewers in a joint space. His light was representation of Divine Light. It is not only that he is one of the greatest artists technically but his ambition seems to have been to indicate spiritual light or suggest that it becomes charged with emotion and drama in some way. His friends included high clergymen engaged in the study of alchemy, geometry and light which may have been useful in his secret techniques of painting cast shadows. Likewise, sacred church music is suffused with images of divine light.

Renaissance art was a science of light, optics and perspective. Artists and spiritual adepts like Swedenborg read books like Giambattista Della Porta's *Magia Naturalis* of 1589. Perspective required explorations of vision and light. Chiaroscuro is about light coming from darkness. The pointillism of Seurat, for example, reflects the perception that images are really pixelations of colour. Surrealism accesses the dreamstate images beyond daylight reality. Cubism reflects pragmatism of multiple perspectives. Artists speak about light and may say their role is to send light to the heart or that beauty is light and shadow. Francis Bacon was inspired by alleged photographs of ectoplasm and they formed an important part of his technique. Art comes from light of the creator's insight. When art becomes mere mechanical mindgame it does not manifest true light of spirit. Sentient beings with primary, innate awareness have capacity to journey to greater consciousness in their inner light. Such inner light grows to meet universal light. We might consider also that jewels were treasured often for their powers to facilitate concentration. Dante's work was based on a tradition of study of light as an actual and a spiritual phenomenon. Emphasis on light is no mere metaphor but represents a deeper intuition about the nature of creation, existence and knowledge. Blake did notable illustrations of *The Divine Comedy* including Dante in the Empyrean, Drinking at the River of Light. Popular music is riddled with light. So many songs and lines of songs refer to light.

The desire to faithfully record reality in a realistic way and increasing knowledge of optics led to optical aids and photography. The pinhole camera has been important in the evolution of representational painting. Through a pinprick of light into the camera obscura comes an exact image of the sunlit world outside through darkness, albeit upside down. Hockney studied the relationship between optical devices like this and also the camera lucida in the history of painting. Photography is the greater exploration of that simple principle, reflecting the structure of the eye. Film requires projection and the illusion of movement from stillness. Great cinematographers, such as Gregg Toland, became masters of use of lighting and darkness. Once the medium is mastered the themes of light impress upon the stream of consciousness. *The Twilight Zone* tv show indicates the strange world between night and day, crepuscular, between dog and wolf, gloaming. Similarly the *Twilight of the Idols* by Nietzsche and *Twilight of the Gods* by Wagner indicate transformation. Film is essentially about light. A transgressive focus on light may be seen in the work of Kenneth Anger and films such as *Lucifer Rising*. This work takes the Satanic and Luciferian ideal and suggests that it is really about love of life and living in the material world. The light motif indicates a Luciferian vision of magick, informed by Crowley and works with ideas of light and reflective surfaces as ways to alter consciousness in a spell-like way. Certain film sequences seek to bind the consciousness like a magician might and undo the binding that religion does by the nature of the word.

The odd way light of art forges links in the chain of human destiny may be shown in what did not happen in 1944 in Sansepolcro, Italy. The town owes its name to the Holy Sepulchre in Jerusalem. Pilgrims set up this town. It was named in honour of that tradition. There in the 1460's *The Resurrection* was painted by the great artist Piero della Francesca in the meeting hall. Aldous Huxley described it as one of the greatest paintings ever. That thought came into the mind of a soldier who loved art and dimly recalled the location when he got orders to bomb the Germans based there. Remembrance of the painting's significance tipped the balance towards delaying bombardment, which proved then unnecessary when the Germans retreated. There are real links made from the lonely mind of humankind to each other through revelation, story, reporting, appreciation and listening that may influence the heart or mind of another in a chain of destiny that time does not allow us anticipate. Similarly in the great work by Victor Hugo, *Les Misérables,* we see the scene with the Bishop defying convention and expectation and giving candlesticks to the captured thief. These represent mercy, forgiveness and potential. The book is a journey from darkness to light. Light enters into the soul because of mercy shown and a sun rises inside him. This is spiritual light felt inside which affects him for the rest of his life. Maybe that is how we expand light. Honest seeking for the highest may provide a clarifying light in the midst of otherwise darkness. The precognitive aspects of the tradition of European painting have been largely ignored by science and cultural commentators. It is hard to look at the paintings of the German Expressionist George Grosz and not see what was on the way.

Yet another way light may come indirectly is where artists or writers seek to shed light on the future. This is prediction, premonition, prophecy or sometimes possibly programming. Some artists literally see and others speculate and specify. People are very familiar with the form of dystopian novels which seek to extrapolate from tendencies evident in contemporary society. From Mary Shelley to Orwell, we seek concerns expressed, in particular about dangers of controlling tendencies in regard to our freedom. We see the perception from Aldous Huxley about the shift to the pharmacological to control, by making people love servitude. Philip K. Dick explored issues associated with the nature of humanity in the advanced technological age. One of the most relevant of such authors is Anthony Burgess and the profound study within *A Clockwork Orange* of the nature of technological control of human nature. Likewise, *One Flew Over The Cuckoo's Nest* and the vision of a subdued, drugged, imprisoned population controlled by a soft-spoken representative of 'The Combine' echoes eerily.

Ancient light themes are wielded in contemporary cinema and art. A very familiar symbol of light is the 'lightsaber' in Star Wars. The lightsaber reflected the ancient Celtic sword of light, *An Claidheamh Soluis*. The word saber/sabre is a sword. However, 'saber' also suggests the Latin and Indo-European roots of 'to know' and 'to try' or taste. In *Star Wars*, the elegant weapon is conceived by Jedi as a defensive one, reflecting internal force within the knight that may be projected onto the external world when necessary. The colour of projected light force of activated crystals also reflects the personality and attainment of particular knights. A Sufi suggestion is there. Bearing in mind acknowledged use by Lucas of mystical knowledge, lightsabre represents a sophisticated visual symbol of cultivated and constrained spiritual powers consistent with spiritual traditions. The sword in the stone makes sense in terms of withdrawal or extraction of a determining instrument of will from matter. The true story may be more of a withdrawal of a sword of light from a stone. Even in technological contexts, spiritual impress on higher level technology is perhaps paradoxically manifest. This connection between mystical powers and technology also reflects the observation of Arthur C. Clarke that developed technology and magic is indistinguishable. Thus scientific and magical light can be united. When Dan Flavin in 1963 famously exhibited a fluorescent tube at a 45 degree angle, maybe the old sword of light in a new form was ushering in a new era of darkness in art for some. The field of UFOs and UAP are characterised by light phenomena. Light phenomena associated with ET and other close encounters reflect a more ancient tradition of light beings as evidenced in the work of the Celtic folklorists. There are recurrent descriptions of light associated with mystical perception, purple sheens at evening, shafts of blue, orbs of light, opalescent figures, gold and silver light and so on.

So culture and art clearly manipulate, discuss and use light. But spiritual light may also arise as significant factors in the life of the artist and their art. Light has often been the ostensible occasion or cause of profound mystical experience for artists who became mystics. The shaft of light may shine as a significant transformative force. This is spiritual light. Spiritual light operates firstly as a particular, subjective experience or force in that it is perceived to have an effect or create a feeling. There are two outstanding examples of a potent mystical ray's transformative impact on a writer's life. Jacob Boehme was entranced by a beam of light on a pewter dish. In a similar way, Philip K. Dick had a life-changing experience when a beam of pink light shone on a golden fish on the necklace of a woman delivering pain medication to his home. This involved an anamnesis which made him remember a previous existence. If anyone is sceptical about the reality and import of this experience they should examine the voluminous writings this incident incited. Other spiritual manifestations such as kundalini awakening often involve perceived light in the body. The phenomenon of phosphenes is another interesting one linked with perceived light. Phosphenes involve a sense of light without external light. Hermann von Helmholtz was very interested in studying them along with all other areas he looked at. So in the dark, appearances and formations of light are perceived and may be induced by mechanical, chemical, hallucinogenic, electrical or transcranial magnetic means. Illness is often a source. Phosphenes are associated with altered states of consciousness and thus capable of being interpreted in a wide manner. There is a curious recurrence of symbols here showing similarities with images from hypnagogic states and the recurrent alphabet of symbols from the many prehistoric sites in Europe and elsewhere to archetypal patterns in much art of aboriginal and native peoples to mandalas. However, it would be a mistake to reduce these symbols to mere physical phenomena. Like with cymatics, there is a close affinity between these sensed lights and esoteric preoccupations. There is a code to other dimensions represented in recurrent symbols. The 'prisoner's cinema' refers to colours, forms and figures that appear in darkness and has similarities to the Ganzfeld Effect. LSD and other substances enhance such effects. Phosphene means to show light. Phosphenes and phosphorous come from the Greek root word 'phos' for light. Phosphorous is also significant in the structure of DNA. Again, while they are not external light, they appear as light and are internal in their manifestation. This is another example of the release of trapped light. Shapes that recur include tunnels, cones, spirals, honeycombs, chessboards, filigree and many others. In fact, one could argue that much art and design is a mirror of these recurrent symbols presented to us in phosphenes, dreams, visions and other manifestations resulting from our nervous system and archetypal unconscious. Perception of light phenomena arising within us may be seen as a manifestation of a form of trapped light that possesses a magical implication and effect. This is why a mystic in a cave may be going towards something rather than away from it. There are also suggestions that part of the mind can intuit complex physical behaviours of transverse waves and that art may represent a two-dimensional representation of three dimensional forces. Mystics and artists are often thus students, interpreters, adherents and manipulators of energy in waves at transitional points where there is a type of information or a representation of aspects of reality encoded.

Political evolution has odd connections with the philosophy and nature of light. Light permeates the language and behaviour of many leaders. Thus Churchill made the observation,

"We are all worms but I do believe that I am a glow worm."

We can see a fascination with light and fire in the work and experience of Benjamin Franklin, not least in experiments with lightning. His contacts with groups like the Hellfire clubs and freemasonry are imbued with direct and indirect notions of light. He invented a stove. Light often appears in a mysteriously symbol fashion as a real influence from the heavens. It is worth pointing out that Hitler initiated the Second World War after observing the phenomenon of the blood red vault attributed to aurora borealis in the sky over The Eagle's Nest on the 25th of January 1938. This was anticipated for many by the second secret of Fatima of 1917. These secrets were accompanied by the well-witnessed 'dancing of the sun' in October 1917 associated with the apparition of the Virgin Mary and other light manifestations. Such apparitions in the heavens and on earth of ghostly light activity can operate on minds as warning or signal. The dancing sun phenomenon was witnessed by many and the red sky had profound implications. Why relegate these symbolic and actual perceptions that affect people to some scientific scrapheap?

Changes in lighting have impacts on how we think and act. When Marshall McLuhan anticipated the global village and stated that the 'medium is the message,' he used the lightbulb as the basis of his idea. He thought the medium was more important and also that the content of a medium is another medium. The electronic age extends our nervous system. When one extension occurs there is contraction in another sensibility. Pushing the medium to the limit will reverse characteristics. So the electric light bulb represented a new phase in human life, as suggested by Seamus Heaney in his work. Light in a spectrum of manifestations has metaphoric and actual implication. Scientists are wont to tell you how ignorant people were in the past and how they did not know about how the earth moves. Some say that ancient man believed that the stars were holes in the dark fabric of a sky. Spirit people know that we live in a matrix punctuated by pinpricks that let light in and create channels and stairways thereto through the veil of ignorance. We would benefit from balance between what we can know and what we are, science and spirit or left and right brain as Gilchrist emphasises.

In esoteric lore the nature of light is unique. In systems like Theosophy you find 'dark light,' light that is not light and fire that is not fire. Rays and radiance are more like forces. Matter may be manifestation of spirit. In some types of magic there is a dark and a bright pillar from Kabbalah and tree of life and back before to Egypt or Persia perhaps, calculated to facilitate return to the 'limitless light.' Thus light of special groups refers to unique conceptions at times with some continuity or correspondence. Esoteric 'sciences' indicate the same confusion exhibited by science in relation to dark matter. However intuitive, revealed knowledge of mystics may have considered that counter-intuitive, subtle, hidden forces exist as a type of light or energy long before scientists did. Wittgenstein in an essay on *The Golden Bough* warned against explanations rather than descriptions of such magical and tribal activities as Frazer had analysed. Wittgenstein also seemed to take a critical view of Goethe in *Remarks on Colour* although he greatly admired him. He seems to be sceptical about big descriptions although sometimes his explanations may not shed much light. As Traherne indicates, mystic felt experience justifies observations and allow similar experiences be compared and appreciated, especially as particular manifestations of universal consciousness. Goethe was right to have high regard to intuitive imagination as was Blake, Bruno and Jung. Discipline and higher value marshal the field to return harvest to community. Mystics wish to share insights particularly if they perceive wrong direction or misdirection.

There is a final point that emerges from Burke and the Romantics. Burke identified power of the sublime and made a reference to artistic depiction of the demonic. Percy Shelley continued the exploration. Shelley would be criticised by some for being the type who elevated feeling above all else, focusing on emotion and intuition. Critics argue this makes Romantics unwilling to commit to virtue as a reality and allows them elevate sympathy and emotion over conduct, action and standards and thus create a vehicle without restraints. There is a similar tension in Edgar Allan Poe with his cultivation of a rational detective and ratiocination and his artistic use of horror. While ostensibly being anti-mystical in certain statements, his work is mystical and magical. In the work *The Imp of the Perverse* the narrator is certain a perverse imp drives people to do what they know is wrong or evil. Nothing is more certain than that this imp will act. Boredom seems to be a hot house for such imps. Such forces are foisted by a cult of meaninglessness posited by existentialism of the materialist manifesto with spirit excised. Dark mysticism sometimes refers to destructive occult, black magic or malign sorcery. There are people who wish to utilise power, whether conceived as spiritual or subtle energies, for destructive or sadistic purposes. Mysticism needs lighthouses like compassion to avoid being something else where everything is relative. Compassion is not a comfortable, cosy commiseration, like a hippo happy in a mud bath, of someone else's misfortune, making it your own to signal your moral superiority. It involves creative, courageous engagement also. There are transgressive or antinomian practices associated with certain mysticism which is not part of perennial wisdom for that reason. Critics of Romanticism suggest they may end up being unwilling to condemn because of focus on feeling even at the expense of hurt of others.

Spiritual light phenomena indicate recognition of light within us. Spiritual light is consciousness some scientists want to deny and is the object of dispiriting us. Spiritual light phenomena occur because our consciousness recognises itself. When our light remembers itself it sees it is of universal consciousness that is fundamental. Our true self is pure consciousness. Certain experiences involving perception of light resonate and activate an accord through remembrance and recognition with our essential nature and potential. This occurs and recurs because spirit is a quantum of consciousness perceived to be light in perennial experience. *Spiritual light is the spiritual consciousness of us, being our essential consciousness and our highest and transcendent potential.*

1.11 Light v. Heavy

Another important connection between light and spirituality is the dichotomy of light and heavy. Lightness involves a lack of weight. Heaviness is often associated with darkness. Mass is a curious word related to heaviness. Etymology of light in its distinct meanings seems separate but has a curious cross-over in the spiritual domain maybe because light is light. From Parmenides to the Yoga Sutras to Calvino, internal being or the beneficial is light and sought after. We see this desirable aspect of lightness in Egyptian spirituality. The concept seems to be that spirit is ultimately light and thus will release itself from burdens of existing in dense domains. There is also a sense that negative actions create a heaviness manifest in the form of karma or sin to impede ability to escape incarnation. Demons may create heaviness. Thus lightness is an indicator of a positive internal state. It does not mean that people who seek lightness do not deal with difficult things or avoid responsibility. It is not a sense of 'tune in and drop out' like Timothy Leary. However it does manifest in untethering heavy restraints. It is the golden echo Hopkins hears, as distinct from the leaden echo. While they may have different linguistic origins, similarities suggest a relationship. Spiritual light creates another massless, sense of lightness and that complementary sense should be acknowledged. Zen celebrates lightness. A skilled person makes light work of difficult tasks. We can make light work for ourselves and others. Freedom is often described as light and contrasted with heavy chains of bondage and slavery. It is not freedom from moral responsibility on this plane as magicians may claim. The alleged phenomenon of levitation associated with both Oriental and Christian culture, is lightness. Tales of St. Joseph of Cupertino echo Eastern stories or indeed the PK Man. Lightness is a spiritual attribute of highly evolved beings. It is curious that many philosophers, scientists and evolved spiritual beings have been interested in flight. We can see this from Daedalus and Icarus to Leonardo Da Vinci, Swedenborg, Arthur C. Clark, and Arthur Young. Sadhguru flies helicopters. There is something about flight, birds, emulating flight and the necessity of crafting lightness and aerodynamism. Birds are spiritual force in most traditions from the Celts to Christians and Native Americans. Sense of ability to master unseen forces, to be light, to travel in spirit or remote view reflects the deepest perception of spiritual seekers. The shaman or person undergoing a NDE often experiences sensations of unimpeded lightness of being and an immateriality mostly marshalled by thoughts, prior tendencies and deeper motivations. Lightness is significant. The lightest element is fundamental for life and the sun. Hydrogen is the lightest most prevalent element in the universe. Should rocket ships find water on the moon or Mars they will be able to transform it into fuel to facilitate further travel. Hydrogen is highly flammable hence sunlight for us. Stars are made up of this element. Thus the triangle with connections between shining light, combustion and the phenomenon of lightness is a scientific fact that mirrors spiritual reality. Just as many early chemists were alchemists on esoteric, mystical spiritual quests so are there natural correspondences between our physical and spiritual reality. Heaviness is associated with restraint. The idea of trapping light in matter is based on a sense of contrast between our shining, freedom and fast-flying nature and apparent fixity and solidity of matter. The definition of solidity has always been based on appearance and touch and we know more about the idea of motion and space within apparently solid objects in a way that animists suspected. The idea of angels having fallen suggests a formidable force of moral gravity in myths. At least scientists driven by curiosity and divine wonder saw a wonderful world. If any theology fails to see its magnificence it is blind. But spirit is grander and that manifests and is immanent in the natural world. If pagans generally bring people to nature and unleash the goddess light to appreciate the power thereof instead of worshipping left-brain, analytical, reductive machine-magic of isolation and containment then they do good. Scientism combined with the nature of mass markets will create similar lifestyles for us. Soon we will be fully in the zoo scrutinised by AI 'conscious agents.' You become light when you liberate spirit from matter and that may manifest in physical lightness or spiritual flight. *Lightness or masslessness indicates spiritual light, liberation and the ability for spirit to travel and ascend.*

1.12 Light of the Flame

Another closely related dimension of spiritual, mythical and esoteric symbolism is that of the flame. The flame or torch is often a very significant attribute of an important figure, god or goddess. It is important to remember that flames represent both the power of fire and the phenomenon of light. Sometimes we should consider whether the myth meaning is more about symbolism of the latter rather than the former. Manly Hall examined the flame as a key symbol of spiritual or esoteric quest, but it is noteworthy how the chief characteristic of the flame is its light rather than its inherent force. Fire is critical in the Prometheus stories. However if we interpret the fire in terms of light, we may come to different conclusions than if we focus on the power of flame as a technical or industrial one. The Prometheus legend and its hero has generated more heat than light. We might consider the pagan Goddess Brigid from the Celtic world, reflected in St. Bridget. She had associations with fire, craftsmanship and many other things. Columbia holds a flame. Isis is associated with light. The competing interpretations of the alleged significance of the physical force of flame or the illuminating nature thereof are not insignificant. People who will insist that Moses only imagined that he saw a burning bush because he was high will also insist that Prometheus really did get an actual flame in some real more meaningful sense. In many esoteric traditions, flames may be more associated with something like astral light. Mystics and spiritual seekers seem to emphasise light within and not without and the gift of physical light from the titanic thief is not as significant as availability within of one´s own light that may follow a light of some spiritual leader not so disposed to plunder. In particular, the concept of 'empyrean fire' is not fire as we conceive it but a higher light wherein angels and the Divine live. The strange spiritual conception of fire may even be described as a type of 'water light' indicating how far removed from physical fire it is. Without purification we cannot approach it. Greeks seem to have conceived fire as a representation of spirit manifested to us as light. It seems to me a mistake not to distinguish recurrent mystic interpretation of fire as a form of light and fire on which we cook our food. That necessary, useful transformative and destructive force may be opposite the lightfire of mystics. In Islam the Jinn are described as being of smokeless fire and they are clearly not of the normal type of fire. Zoroastrianism may be more focused on fire as spiritual force.

Benjamin Franklin came from a family of candle-makers and blacksmiths. His interest in light and the flames went together. He represented an incredible mind of great versatility and penetration that did not confine itself to speculation and was thoroughly engaged in the world in a direct and clandestine manner. His invention of a stove was a testament to his application of high level knowledge to practical purposes. He was open to the wave theory of light before many others. The connection between the occult and great inventors and minds is often ignored. Jack Parsons, who was heavily motivated by occult beliefs and Aleister Crowley, led the development of commercial rocketry. Crowley is identified with the over-simplified implication of *Do What Thou Wilt*. This was taken from Rabelais and was used as a motto in some of the clubs that Franklin was involved in. The evolution of contemporary society is capable of being influenced by butterfly wings of spirit of any individual. We will not be able to cry foul if we have smugly sat out formative debates because they were not to our tastes.

In recent times the Prometheus myth acquired a capacity used to describe different paths. In that sense, the Prometheus myth is as good as any to describe the fork in the road. Prometheus was taken within the British Imperial poetic elites fascinated with Greek culture to the exclusion of other possibilities and interpreted in a way that uses this legend for its own purposes. It is like the Elgin Marbles of elect imagination, something hacked out from its original context and transported to another. Mary Shelley who wrote *Frankenstein: The Modern Prometheus* lived near the British Museum where the Marbles are. Her husband Percy Bysshe Shelley wrote *Prometheus Unbound*. They were very familiar with re-animation of corpses. There seems to be a strong movement again in favour of a paradoxical, sympathetic resurrection of the Greek gods in a re-visited contemporary mythological soap opera to capture some of the power of the Judeo-Christian worldview as part of the materialist, physicalist displacement drive. This tension can be seen in the life and education of Oscar Wilde from his education to the revolution in *De Profundis*. Greek mythology offers less certain moral messages than an evolved Judeo-Christian one. It is suspicious when people who rail against myth proceed to seek to utilise it for their own ideology. Make no mistake, most writing is ideological. I claim to be pragmatic, I seek to be cosmopolitan. But I believe we are spiritual beings and our failure is one of spiritual evolution that will not be remedied by mechanistic substitution by people who oppose the idea of spirit and are committed to banishing it as a foolish fabrication of primitive and ignorant people who still live in a dark past conveniently projected onto history and prehistory without rigorous investigation.

Prometheus was a bold, unrestrained bringer of light who sacrificed himself for our good and was punished by evil gods. Percy B. Shelley made the link between Prometheus and Satan. The cross between Lucifer and Jesus allowed daring, breach of social convention and experimentation, particularly in the field of machines. We can look to the great William Blake who invented a personal mythology with many elements that reflect the Promethean. He was indicating infinite possibilities of interpretation in the imaginative state. He was not going to tie his imagination down. At the same time he was not going to sacrifice his spiritual imagination. The literalist often has no problem with sacrificing the imagination because they lack it. In *Frankenstein*, Mary Shelley was indicating how Romantic writers were inspired by experiments with electricity and the body performed by people like Davy, Galvini and Aldini. Mary saw the dangers of scientific re-creation of life. Increasingly, we may come to see that Frankenstein's monster represents the human-machine hybrid that we or our descendants may become.

Technology and science were causes of horror more often than saviours from superstition. Magic lanterns made Phantasmagoria shows possible. Body snatchers of this period, well re-created by R.L. Stevenson in a story of the same name, based on the infamous surgical blind eye of the medical faculty at University of Edinburgh, were also known as Resurrection Men. The Shelley's were aware of experiments by Aldini and others whereby dead people were ostensibly resurrected with electricity. It was not just that Romantic and revolutionary movements wanted to overthrow dominance of existing explanations, but they were really enamoured by wondrous possibilities of creation, manipulation and resurrection of matter with a religious fascination no less intense than advocates of the traditional explanation that dominated Europe for centuries. Percy B. Shelley took one view. I think Mary took a more profound one. In the desire to reform, certain values were ignored. For Mary importance resided in the value of love.

There is a sharp, contemporary division emerging around the issue of transhumanism. On one side are opponents and sceptics emphasising the dehumanising effects of transhumanism who have been labelled 'bio-conservatives.' They might point to Plato's Cave and the fire that caused illusion. Opponents see them as afraid and fearful. The Prometheans enlist Prometheus and present the past as a dark, brutish place until the light of science and reason lighten up miserable existence. Linking us neurally, as Elon Musk wants to do, will trap the light of our consciousness into a network. Similarly the Aleister Crowley-Jack Parsons connection links into Nietzsche and the idea of creation of superman or 'beyond' man not confined by Christian morality. It was useful for both the Nazis and some of the Bolsheviks, like Trotsky. All together emerges an occult technocratic, trans-humanist agenda that is mainstream now. Prometheus brings fire of progress, development, science and technology that allow transcendence so the individual may be as gods inspired by the thieving, materialist trickster. As with Percy Shelley's celebration of Prometheus who is like Satan and will push boundaries or Watchers or aliens who give technology, there is always a price to pay in the Faustian pact. There is a curious and profoundly prophetic anticipation of the danger of animation of the mechanical by a mistaken attempt to re-create in a modern Promethean way, what had been created already and should be prized above egotistical experimentation. As Mary Shelley recounted her vision in a preface,

"Night waned upon this talk, and even the witching hour had gone by, before we retired to rest. When I placed my head on my pillow, I did not sleep, nor could I be said to think. My imagination, unbidden, possessed and guided me, gifting the successive images that arose in my mind with a vividness far beyond the usual bounds of reverie. I saw - with shut eyes, but acute mental vision, - I saw the pale student of unhallowed arts kneeling beside the thing he had put together. I saw the hideous phantasm of a man stretched out, and then, on the working of some powerful engine, show signs of life, and stir with an uneasy, half vital motion. Frightful must it be; for supremely frightful would be the effect of any human endeavour to mock the stupendous mechanism of the Creator of the world. His success would terrify the artist; he would rush away from his odious handywork, horror-stricken. He would hope that, left to itself, the slight spark of life which he had communicated would fade; that this thing, which had received such imperfect animation, would subside into dead matter; and he might sleep in the belief that the silence of the grave would quench for ever the transient existence of the hideous corpse which he had looked upon as the cradle of life. He sleeps; but he is awakened; he opens his eyes; behold the horrid thing stands at his bedside, opening his curtains, and looking on him with yellow, watery, but speculative eyes."

What Mary saw was an attempted substitution of mechanism, spectacle, power, domination and control for love and wisdom, by people who sought the former being impoverished in the latter. Her message is relevant today to remind of limitations of the materialist viewpoint, not to demonise science nor reject rationality. Rather it is to argue for balance and restraint. The greatest counter-weight involves spiritual growth of individuals. Unfortunately the zeal of techno-romantics justifies enlisting Mary Shelley's vision. The flame that lights the cauldron or spreads destructively by discontent is not the light that heals. In spiritual light the body may dissolve and be re-constituted but in science plus Resurrection Men, it was an actual dismemberment. The light that enlightens is not light that burns. Spiritual light is diverse but must be distinguished from the physicalist interpretation that has dominated science and now seeks to substitute itself for that different light. One interesting thought on Prometheus. In esoteric writing there is a suggestion that this figure was really one of those figures who could invoke lightning at will and thus steal light from the heavens or gods. This is seen in Rabelais in the (disputed) fifth book of *The Life of Gargantua and Pantagruel*. It is clear that Rabelais was making reference to much esoteric doctrine and solar deities. Bacbuc says,

> "What do you think is become of the art of forcing the thunder and celestial fire down, which the wise Prometheus had formerly invented? 'Tis most certain you have lost it; 'tis no more on your hemisphere; but here below we have it."

This may be nearer the truth and Prometheus is really more like the psychokinetic PK Man that Dr. Mishlove wrote about and thus equally difficult to present as a clear role-model although utterly remarkable. Like Prometheus, Owens steals fire from the gods. Like Prometheus, (according to one report) Owens seems to have been persecuted in his liver. Like Prometheus, Owens is volatile. Like Prometheus, Owens is difficult to interpret. Certainly, the failure to take serious the potential and perspective of people like Owens is a reflection of our numbed psychic state. A more open attitude which is not impressed with scientism may allow us integrate and explore such strange powers that are part of our collective potential. Prometheus was a Titan. The novel *Futility* or *The Wreck of the Titan* by Morgan Robertson anticipated the Titanic disaster. Fire is the subtle force released from gross matter but is not the sole manifestation of matter of ordinary fire. The difference might be seen in the recurrent metaphor of image of fire in Marxism. Thus the Bolsheviks ran *Iskra* (the Spark) in London and that inspired a paper of the same name for the Paris-based future Cambodian Pol Pot revolutionaries. This spark is not the divine spark but the one that will cause the prairie or forest fire. Whilst Trotsky believe humankind would become highly developed as gods in a future utopia, it was a physical, material plan albeit it with art. Likewise it would seem that certain key 'illuminati' would only have reason and were opposed to spirit. Materialist minds of the extremes of left and right can concoct complex defences of destruction of the Divine and goddess spirit of life. Bonds of enslavement to ego with shining crimson autograph bear witness. The auto-da-fe, missiles, gunpowder, atom bombs and hellfire indicate technological and repressive forces. This is distinguishable from Zoroastrianism which uses fire as a symbol of purity and light.

As I complete this I see the launch of a new 'Prometheist' movement spearheaded by Jason Reza Jorjani. He is very aware of real forces shaping our future and is not being passive. This movement seems based on a number of arguments such as the idea of a breakaway society where elite monopolise new technology and create a feudal society for the masses through knowledge destruction. Jorjani emphasises the Promethean tradition in Western thought and seems influenced by Plato, Italian Futurists, Nietzsche, Heidegger and possibly Marx's ideas. He argues for a grasping of the archetype to avoid de-humanising instrumentality. Bearing in mind the approach of the singularity, cloning, nanotechnology, robotics and so on, threats to liberty require unique responses. He argues for a deep philosophical approach based on a Promethean ethos to navigate through the singularity. It suggests a superman of the Nietzsche type such as Trotsky argued for, with enhanced human abilities. This is a contemporary expression of Shelley's Prometheus emphasising exploration. movement, development, expansion and the future. It is always possible that a competing theology to light could be fire, drawing on magic and science to re-make man as a god. To me, such an approach was entirely predictable and apparently represents a magic-scientific emphasis that seems opposed to spirituality. Spiritual power should be encouraged by direction to the higher value of compassion or love and not dissipated. We might think about firelight. *Firelight or the power of the flame may not primarily be spiritual light although it may be used to represent such light and instead may glorify other forms of scientific and magic light.*

1.13 The Omnipresence of the Spiritual Light

Before I embark on this examination let me make one point clear. I come from a Catholic background and thus do not speak about Christianity as a stranger to it. While there are many bad things that have happened I also believe that we are witnessing a fairly biased wave of ideological attack on that Church and Christianity in general. At the same time there are some Protestants who advocate freedom of speech save when you talk of your views of Christianity. Similarly they seem to claim a unique authority that enables them to know the mind of God and to act on behalf of Jesus as if they own Him exclusively. This is not confined to that religion. Christ is not owned by anybody, neither Buddha nor any great religious leader. Furthermore there must be balance in interpretation of successes and failures. For example, it is often claimed in favour of Buddhism and certain oriental philosophies that they have never caused or been the reason for war or infliction of harm on a large scale. This fails to look at the evidence and fails to see the role that even Buddhism plays in the worldview of certain practices, individuals and contexts. However to point out the Buddhist background for Mao and Pol Pot and to say that the latter's favourite writer was Rousseau, does not invalidate Buddhism nor Romanticism. The distinction between historical schools of philosophy and theology has become artificial and we can see already how religion, science and philosophy informed each other. In this section, I seek to indicate occurrences of spiritual light rather than investigate them all. Spiritual light is a central persistent concern that indicates a perennial theosophy or theology of light.

It is my contention that the split in relation to technology that existed from the Industrial Revolution and tension between religion and science is really about the question of whether we have spirits, are spiritual beings or have spiritual consciousness. At this stage of greater exploration of human consciousness by science, we should begin to recognise the implications for us. We have a spirit and study of light in spiritual traditions shows perennial preoccupations. Scientific exploration of light is a noble and beautiful effort to understand life that should complement our spiritual endeavours. Reconciliation occurs on the foreshore between land of material and rational and sea of spirit and subconscious. Such a foreshore must seem wet with spirit sometimes, dry with reason others. Always that bottom of *intellectus* or true understanding is there however. We must be careful to see co-existence of both while remaining adaptive, ambi-potential.

Earliest spiritual traditions focus on light. Why? Is it a simile or a metaphor or something else? Does spiritual light refer to the unique constituency of the spirit world? Do spiritual masters actually mean we are of light and should go to light as real instructions? Is spiritual light the same as other light? Is this light knowable to science? A cursory examination of spiritual discourse reveals fascination with light such as evidence of transformation of Buddhist monks into rainbow light discussed by people such as Father Tiso. Likewise ideas of subtle body and astral plane may involve light analogies. Milton describes God as light as does the Bible. Light may be the medium for mystical experience. Some mystics suggest there is neither light nor dark but a pervasive grey or silvery spiritual space of true reality. Furthermore some concepts are not what we might think. Some scholars see the journey to the orient as a trip to India from California. But orientation for a Sufi is upwards to the pole above, the north not east according to Corbin and was so even for Crowley at times. Light that can be trapped in darkness is somewhere other than the demonic realm as he makes clear in *Man of Light in Iranian Sufism*. More recently scholars, such as Templeton, are realising there is a parallel between people like Suhrawardi and others such as the Kashmiri Abhinavagupta. Their focus on light as a comprehensive cycle of knowledge and revelation leading to a sense of actual and spiritual reality suggests universality. I suggest that the light story will be found in most cultures not merely as an archetype but as a reality of experience, knowledge and being.

It might be argued that everything initially was solar, about the sun and its obvious life giving nature. Sun often stands for Logos. From Atum to Ra in Egypt and also Shamash or Utu, the sun is worshipped. We see it in *The Epic of Gilgamesh*. The link with natural light and gods was clear. Judaism elevated God above light but used the light as a symbol. Light was more than visible light. There are some that believe that sunlight is more than what we know and that it may derive from a conscious source. For those who cannot conceive of spiritual things, there are many who can accept sunlight as a manifestation of potent force. Some others might suggest the sun is the only basis of all our ideas of God. When we then add our knowledge of the electromagnetic spectrum and other types of light or invisible light, it is clear that possibilities for explanation of spiritual and associated parapsychological phenomena increase dramatically so that reconciliation between science and spirituality becomes possible. Spiritual leaders should not bow down to institutions of science and seek a pat on the head from them. Science has behaved recently towards spirituality sometimes as dogmatists of the doctrinal inquisitions of the Church did towards heretics.

In India, and thereabouts, light is a central spiritual idea and some scholars argue for a unique epistemology of light consistent with modern science. Jyotisha, which refers to Indian astrology and astronomy, comes from the word for light or inner light. In Hinduism, in the Upanishads and *Bhagavad Gita*, ubiquity and persistence of light permeates the highest spiritual notions. Brahman is luminous, highest light of lights inside us too in the Atman. Agni symbolises both fire and light. Diwali celebrates light. The individual seeks bliss of highest light with the best of self, liberated and lightened in bliss from base elements. The lantern may be caked with mud. This is really light of pure consciousness from which we came and aspire to recognise and come into accord with. We aspire to become enlightened which suggests both lightness from the material and light in the luminous, shining, brilliant sense. Aarti is a lighted lamp on the river. The great *Yoga Sutras* of Patanjali refer to light in important ways. In particular he emphasises the significance of 'sorrowless' light of the heart. Shantideva uses light. Darkness is used to explain how our spirit may be obscured. Aurobindo conceived of human existence as involving consciousness descending into matter to spiritually evolve in this domain and thereby illuminate it. His ideas came both from Indian sources and from western sources. Light-enhanced beings would evolve in a divine way. Similarly Sant Mat was an Indian mystical movement that has existed for hundreds of years until today which has a conception of spirit descended into matter which needs to escape through ascension from darkness to the inner light and re-unite with source. It seems to be loose and individually-orientated which is impressive and focusing on the heart.

Light being the path is recurrent. Ideas of light permeate Buddhism in India and Tibet. The Buddha is often linked to light names and Boundless, Illimitable Light. There are many ancient sutras about light such as the Golden Light Sutra. Light in sacred texts are not just words. Rather they should be considered as a force. Light force in words Nicholson points out in an article on Light Visions that,

> "Those who are familiar with meditation texts inspired by the Indian experience will recognize that meditation and meditation-induced light visions are subjects that are explicitly addressed in the Upanishads (circa 1000 to 500, BCE), in Patañjali's Yogasutras (circa 200, BCE), and in Tantric treatises from Medieval India (circa 1000, CE), for example, Abhinavagupta's Tantraloka ("Light on Tantra"), Goraksanatha's Amaraughasasana ("Immortal Flow"), and Ksemaraja's Shivasutravimarshini ("Commentary on the Shivasutras"), but the seminal importance of meditation-induced light imagery in the hymns of the original Rig Veda (circa 1300 - 1000, BCE) has been overlooked and neglected until recently."

Dzogchen is one of the Tibetan Buddhist schools that focus on ideas of the 'clear light' and the 5 Pure Lights and luminosity. The mirror or crystal ball may explain crucial concepts. You will find 4 to 6 lamps in different schools. There are many variations of the light approach. Academics look for points of contact. My argument is that the structure inheres in us, there are different articulations of a similar reality and spiritual light is not merely a physiological function. Buddhist Tantra such as Kalacakra focuses on light and concepts such as 'the stainless light' are important. Texts such as *Blazing Lamps* in Tibetan Buddhism create complex conceptions based on light and light bodies. Vibrancy creates the world and we must recognise how we are it, creating movements from the heart and projections. The Bön tradition has six lamps that explain the liberation process and channels whereby that occurs. There are illuminating and bright lamps that may be particular or general techniques with recurrent common aspects. Insight might come like a flash of lightning for example. The Clear Light may be essence of us hidden away. We may engage in meditation and through a hypnagogic reflection seek to enter the Clear Light and the Mother Light in sleep. Such liminal navigations parallel and prepare for the transition on death. Luminosity is a recurrent feature in Buddhism. Transformations and transfiguration by and into light whilst avoiding false ones recur. There are ideas in Buddhism that we were self-luminous and lost it in matter to be regained by escaping re-birth. One of the texts introducing the Buddha in the West was a book in the form of a long poem called *The Light of Asia*. East Asian Buddhism as manifested in Pure Land school of Amida focuses on light. Iyengar's book *Light on Yoga* uses light as a central concept. Kundalini awakening in the yogic and tantric paths are often characterised by light experiences.

In Japanese schools of Zen Buddhism, light shines whether in the concept of enlightenment or elsewhere although there are some unsustainable claims to the effect that Zen is not interested in light. The *Denkoroku* is 'The Record of the Transmission of the Light' and was composed by Master Keizan in 1300 as a teaching tool. This idea followed on from works such as the Eihei Koroku, *The Record of the Transmission of the Lamp* and *The Record of the Universal Lamp* and others such as *Five Lamps Merged in the Source*. These were stories and lessons and koans recording the links in lineage back to the Buddha through China. Light was generally therefore the guidance, knowledge and practice. In that sense it represents a passing of the torch. In the stories metaphors and descriptions of light, luminescent, shining substances and signs recur.

In China, Shen Kuo was an early scientist who wrote about diverse issues including optics. He also described a UFO that appeared with a pearl of light. The Tao philosophy had light and dark, a yin and yang symbol with a point of darkness trapped in light and a point of light trapped in darkness. Yang was positive, bright side of hill, associated with light and yin negative and dark. Lao-Tzu talked of the light inside. Some ancient forms of Taoist meditation involve focus on lights of different colours. The spiritual classic *The Secret of the Golden Flower* focuses on meditation techniques which involve circulation of light in the body. We may conceive this light as a concentrated form of attention as is often found in Buddhist teachings. The light tradition in Taoism seems to indicate a comprehensive philosophy based on light as the essential ingredient in the universe. But light and the dark make the whole. Japanese Buddhism has the Mantra of Light as an important contribution reflecting the significance of light of the Buddha and embrace thereof.

Echoes from indigenous shamanic, druidic or pagan cultures of Europe largely eradicated by empire suggest the universal role of light. Celts are often ignored in debates about the ancient world although the Gaelic language has the oldest vernacular literature in Western Europe. Centuries of colonial struggles obscured that richness. Ireland and Britain was linked by the sea and trading routes to many distant places for a long time and connections are deeper than some suspect. Because Ireland was not part of the Roman Empire, Druidry survived or co-existed somewhat in and alongside the Catholic Church. That Church also recorded the legends and myths. In Irish myth, the sun figures prominently. Quartz stones, that can create piezoluminescence, abound around prehistoric sites. Lugh or Lugus was associated with light.

What was the function of sun penetration into the mound at Newgrange? There was no need to go to such trouble to have a calendrical device. It is clearly a spiritual ceremonial event. It may symbolise the sun God re-uniting with the earth mother to renew life. It may have been creation of a pathway for earthly departed to re-unite with source. In any event it is clear that construction of the occasion would involve the living and a phenomenon of light renewal of the living thereby. Irish legend is full of magic light beings and objects. Walter Evans-Wentz in his book *The Fairy Faith of the Celtic Peoples* talked of the phenomena of light associated with fairies. The descriptions often sound like close encounters with alien beings. He reported descriptions by ordinary people and seers. One such seer described the tall, opalescent beings that seemed calm and linked to the shining beings of the community they dwelt in, just beyond the normal perception of most folk. They existed alongside grey beings and beings that could create copies of themselves or blow life into being. There were water beings and the lower strata of wood elementals. In all cases we get some phenomenon or composition of light. Figures such as Gráinne may reflect an older goddess, solar figure. In myth in Northern Europe we have Thor. Balder was a light god. There are small light beings that recur. Lightning is a universal mystery. For the mystic, lightning described or reflected the actual experience of sudden illumination and other readings would always be lesser than this analogy. Connections between ancient Greeks and Italians, as many lived there, and isles of the North Atlantic were greater than has hitherto been believed as tin trade studies now reveal to the sceptics. However, there is an argument that Druidry on the fringes retained a proximity to nature and the original shamanic or magical origins that were made concrete and more complex within larger imperial structures elsewhere.

The Greeks were as interested in light as anyone else as indicated earlier and manifested in mythology and philosophy. In the Orphic tradition an important god associated with light is Phanes. Dionysius, Orpheus and Persephone descend into the underworld, darkness and spirit and light must be extracted, exalted in the human spirit through liberation. Increasingly Apollo and Theia were associated with light. Sunlight that permeated thought and philosophy was mundane representation of the supermundane sun. For the mystic, this supermundane sun represents the inner access to the Divine and all philosophies and practices would merely be representations of that insight. Empedocles was interested in light. Illuminationism occurs in Platonism. Philo used the idea of light. Focus on inner light as source of inspiration was acknowledged in Platonism and the Neo-Platonism of Plotinus. This reflected the idea that the One was light in some way, like good or the sun and the moon reflected, as we do. This in turn influenced Persian thought and manifested in Sufism. Plotinus believed we sought good within through concentration thereon and withdrawal from the manifold to the Holy Place and thereby we encountered ascent or return. The One shone out and irradiated an effusion of light. Plotinus articulated his metaphysics of light. Pseudo-Dionysius took the light construction of wisdom and shone it into Christian thinking. The Neo-Platonists such as Iamblichus developed ideas of theurgy. Theurgy is described as spiritual magic. It refers to the use of certain practices to approach gods or the divine realm. It often involved some kind of individual purification and ascent even to embrace of the divine. The individual became a vessel to receive light or to draw down divine light. In this sense the individual might be said to have been trapping the divine light. Such light necessarily came from without, above, everywhere. The person had not lost all their divine substance but needed to ascend again. This theurgy is usually (but not always) distinguished from goetia or demonology. Similar elements can be found in esoteric Christianity and Kabbalah. The latter too had the vessels and descending light.

Zoroastrianism and the ancient spiritual traditions of Iran had a very strong focus on light with Ahura Mazda as the Lord of Wisdom being the source against an enemy Angra Mainyu, that represents constraint and untruth. Nowruz is a festival in that tradition associated with light. Light, goodness and fire is a crucial symbol in the cosmic order against darkness. Zarathustra's mother was radiant with higher light before he was born. All have some of this higher light in them. This influenced Sufism to some extent particularly through Illuminationism. The Sons of Light would fight and oppose darkness based on their election to do so rather than protection against evil. Hermeticism in Egypt manifested the idea of the begotten spirit manifest in the material world. This way of thinking permeated Mediterranean theological speculation with Greek and Jewish thought. Some see it as the root of Gnosticism. The particular Iranian background of Sufism concentrating on light indicates conceptions from Zoroastrian and Mazdean contexts. This was investigated by Corbin who sought to explain the idea of the man of light and the guide of light. Corbin identifies a recurrent idea of going into the darkness inside and finding the lamp or the light source. The light inside had a heavenly or celestial twin. Turning away from preoccupation with the material world one goes inside finds the existing light and then seeks to orient to the heavenly light aspect which is really the higher part of you that is part of that world. In some of the origins of these ideas, there has been a voluntary descent from the heavens into flesh but the material world is not our home. There is a material and a light version of us. The light has another version which guides it like an angel or a goddess. Failure to identify with your higher light or perfect nature prevents evolution. The 'oriental theosophy' of Suhrawardi manifest in Sufism utilises this syncretism from cycles of movement from India to the isles of the north Atlantic and Northern Egypt to the north of Europe to articulate in terms of light an ancient doctrine clarified through experience and experiment and embodied in attitudes, recitals, poetry and stories.

This idea helps explain Mani. Mani learns to see properly and sees his companion of light. All suggest the reality of a higher light angel of us that purified ascends to the source. Mani was the Envoy of Light, the Buddha of Light, the Apostle of Light, the Sun of Light, the Pearl of Light. His teachings involved a complex story of the battle between forces of light and dark with light being trapped in matter and beings from the 'realm of light.' Mani built on the legacy of Buddha, Zarathustra and Christ. Comfort with these figures and the doctrine of light show a great, central correspondence in these beliefs. All have Divine light, light within us and a duality of light and darkness and the need to liberate light from matter. The consequent idea of separation and distillation underlies many esoteric practices and schools. It is not just about an idea of what happens after we die. Perennial tradition and the mystical path, indicates an ability to leave the body. OBE's in the context of spirit, soul or astral travel are known to mystics and others who have cultivated their spiritual powers. Mystics aiming for the Divine will not wander into byways. Magicians will see those powers as the aim or end. Magic comes from Persia in many ways through Zarathustra but linked with other practices. There is an argument to be made that magic principally came from trance states and perhaps the OBE and soul, astral or spirit travel created some of these ideas that we are light trapped in matter. Just as the yogis warn against dwelling on siddhis, mystics do not focus on certain types of magic. Magic may induce mystic states. Mystic states may induce magic powers.

A goddess archetype appears in some closely related concepts. Zoroastrian 'daena' in Persia is a higher being or a higher aspect of us, may be linked to the daemon of Plato, the goddess Diana (meaning shining), the duende (as explained by Frederico Garcia Lorca) and maybe the goddess Dana of the Celts in my guess and that is all it can be. I understand that academics immediately distinguish them, but the recurrence of an often feminine, luminous, shining, inspiring double or higher being or guardian angel is discernible behind diverse manifestations. The man of light according to Corbin seeks unification with the 'midnight sun' or 'sun of the heart.'

Ideas of light that were, or were claimed to be, Hermetic or just Egyptian have had a profound influence on many of the spiritual traditions in Europe and the Middle East. Hermeticism suggests a psychological transformation similar to the alchemical path which recognises a process of gaining insight and light from transmutation of matter to its original material within the dark psyche inside. Furthermore in Egypt, *The Book of the Dead* involved coming into Light. This represented light beings that had awakened their light nature that could rise through dimensions above the illusions of matter. The Pyramid Texts involve ascension to higher levels of illumination above the sky barrier. The idea of light coming from Ra, Horus and into Osiris seems to provide a universal model. The journey in the afterworld was not magic but a mystical path, reflected in ideas of the pyramid of light. After dying we journey through the darkness, descending and being reviewed and hopefully going to the light. The mysteries there impressed the Greeks and many esoteric paths like freemasonry.

The interplay of spiritual light and matter permeates the Judeo-Christian and associated traditions and especially the mystical elements. For others the superior being might be the 'Grand Luminary.' In Judaism sacred texts and traditions contain light as a central idea, even though sound often supersedes it. Hanukkah celebrating the re-dedication of the Second Temple is the Festival of Lights. Ein Soph is the Infinite source of emanation beyond limits. This is really the unknowable domain. Ohr Ein Soph is Divine light. Most conceptions of Kabbalah seem to relate to Divine Light, descent, constraint and ascent. Merkabah mystically focused on the return from matter. The Kabbalah begins with infinite light and its restraint through withdrawal by *Tzitzum* to give space. The key book on Jewish mysticism called the *Zohar* means 'radiance.' In there we may see the concept of the white light and analogies between the different parts of a candle flame and our own spiritual composition. Early texts such as *Sefer al-Bahir* from the South of France is translated in terms of brilliance or light and may contain influence of Gnostic Christian thought of the area as well as the duality more consistent with Persian thought. The feminine Divine force is also in the Kabbalist writings.

In Kabbalah there is an apparent attempt to achieve an explanation of how true Light or ultimate reality may be approached or received. The hidden light may be re-traced to the source as part of a process. Descending light requires vessels but is still emanation of the same substance. Some explanations are entirely in terms of light. In every word there shone lights according to the Zohar. Scholem points out,

> "Moreover, the light and the mystery of the Torah are one, for the Hebrew word 'or,' light, and the Hebrew word 'raz,' mystery, have the same numerical value, 207. When God said, 'Let there be light,' he meant… the mystery that shines in the Torah."

Divine, primordial light was reflected therein but the literal meaning is darkness. The Kabbalists in their mystical meditations would catch a glimpse of the inexhaustible light. The Sephiroth might be seen in a flash of lightning. Other Kabbalists emphasised Divine names, breathing techniques and visualisation. Such Kabbalism influenced Swedenborg. Abraham Albulafia developed such mystical techniques with visualisations that involved blazing light, a sensation of consumption of light and body trembling. His pupil Gikatilla would write another mystic book called *Gates of Light* developing these ideas. Moses de Leon in the *Zohar* wrote about the power of Divine light. Merkabah mysticism is based on light. Moses Cordovero wrote *The Pleasant Light* and *A Precious Light*. It is clear that Spain and particularly cities like Toledo were crucibles of magic and mysticism and the light tradition was refined there and by people who were forced out in 1492.

The Mandeans are another smaller possibly Jewish group who possessed ancient gnostic beliefs based on a Godly light and an evil world of matter and darkness, where figures such as John the Baptist are revered. They seemed to have influenced Mani. They seem to have the idea of a King of Light and individuals trapped in matter needing to extricate themselves. Hassidism had the hidden spark. Ideas of divine sparks and vessels of divine light emphasise universal concerns that nevertheless impact on many other traditions. Christians combined it with Pythagorean and other knowledge.

Christianity is based on the incarnation of spirit into flesh or matter. The Bible says that *'God is light'* in 1 John 1:5 and is bright and shining. Jesus is light. Christianity is based on an idea of Divine spirit characterised by light, descending or appearing in fleshy matter to triumph thereover. God dwells in light and Christians become children of the light. The Holy Spirit may be a force of revelation like light. Light is clear, transparent, pure and healing. Light was everywhere in the story of Jesus from the start to the Transfiguration and other key episodes. We may see a concept of light and Light where one is natural revelation and the other is supernatural revelation. The star the Magis followed, angels, and declarations that He was the light of life are examples of extraordinary light. Jesus was *'the light of the world.'* Without Him was darkness and he made the blind see. The River Jordan sees the light of heaven when Jesus is baptised. In many artistic depictions for hundreds of years thereafter we see images of beams of light descending and an idea of the *'unapproachable light'* coming into the world. It is a baptism of light. While one might say it was an artistic convention, it may also depict a common felt experience.

The conversion of St. Paul involves light. It is noteworthy that the shining light phenomenon sometimes is witnessed by more than one person. Pope Benedict XVI wrote about Jesus in Holy Week. He talks of the despair and darkness of Judas.

> "Now he sees only himself and his darkness; he no longer sees the light of Jesus, which can illumine and overcome the darkness."

Benedict indicates that Judas could not see,

> "..hope born of faith in the superior power of the light that was made flesh in Jesus."

Judas then goes out into the night and into the 'power of darkness.' What is interesting here is how the belief and hope in the light and not the wrongdoing and despair therewith is the key. But Judas on the standard view who had been 'enlightened' ended in 'darkness.' There is an important lesson here. Enlightenment is not a permanent state. Benedict sees Jesus as spreading a ray of light that came from the Divine. Benedict examines the conversion of St. Paul. He notes that some other may have seen the light but not heard the words. He says that the words and light go together. He talks of 'the risen Lord whose essence is light,' to turn people 'from darkness to light and from the power of Satan to God.' The light was 'brighter than the sun.' Thus from the original sources and from the highest theological interpretations, God is light and Jesus is light that acts as a force of inspiration in the context of matter and flesh and Jesus was born under a light, was light and revealed the true nature as light. Thus the intervention is to remind humanity of their true nature as light and not matter and flesh that they should be attached to thereover. Light manifests so that the light within other matter may recognise itself and not wholly identify with that in which it is temporarily trapped.

The holy light appears in many Christian traditions not least in Orthodox teachings of such as Maximus the Confessor. Monks of the Eastern Orthodox Church pursued altered states through incantation and meditation that allowed divine light flow from the fountain. Mystic monks in Syria experienced the divine nature of light and believed it to be the same as that which transfigured Jesus. Symeon the New Theologian and Byzantine had constant experiences of divine light and believed that such individual experience was critical for Christians. Sergius in Russia experienced the Divine light. Early Christianity was much more diverse and in particular emphasised the idea of divine nature around us. Pelagius, the Celtic theologian emphasised free will and nature. Eriugena, from Ireland, saw God reflected in nature and used the idea of light. The Bible refers to God as light creating a path of light and manifested in the example of Jesus as light. Light is spiritual knowledge that contrasts with spiritual darkness characterised by ignorance. There were various words for light in Greek such as 'phos.' Truth needed this light to perceive reality especially if it were hidden. The Hebrew word for light in sacred scripture seems to be a general word for all sorts of light phenomenon. There is a suggestion by some that the Christian focus on light was important for the use of light in the sense of illumination. However this would be to ignore that light representing spiritual force and the sense of spiritual illumination is an ancient recurrent idea or reality. Frequent subjective views widely held deserve respect. Isaac of Nineveh was a mystic who used the concept of spiritual light. St. Augustine emphasised the spirituality of divine light in concepts like *illuminatio*. His doctrines of divine illumination were informed by his background as a follower of Mani. He believed that there must be Divine illumination which did not come from the mind. Christianity has countless references to light from the ghostly light of *The Cloud of Unknowing* to Jacob Boehme. Hildegard was impressed by visions of living light. Ignatius of Loyola had crucial light experiences. John of the Cross had a range of mystic experiences of light.

Tired of studying law years ago, I went to live, teach and paint on the beautiful Basque coast west of San Sebastian. One of the old pilgrimage routes to Santiago de Compostela went by where I lived. Just having finished teaching, I was getting ready to go there before returning to Ireland. I had concentrated on seeing the rest of Spain in my spare time and especially the crucibles of modern magic. A bird came into the house and flew around. I listened to Fauré's Requiem. A knock came late. My mother had died unexpectedly in Ireland. When her mother died some time later, a bird also came in. I get a bit apprehensive whenever I see a bird trying to enter. I did not go to Santiago until a few years after I flew in from England. When I got there I went at night to the Basilica and looked up and saw strange lights in the sky. Believe it or not. Santiago de Compostela, though some reject the origin now (like with much else), means St. James of the Field of the Fallen Star. This location is associated with the remains of St. James the Greater who supposedly came to Spain to spread the gospel. A hermit, over a thousand years ago, saw lights in the sky and re-discovered the tomb. The site became the destination of the great Camino or walk. If we look at the legendary aspects of St. James the Greater we see some spiritual light phenomena. James was one of the twelve apostles and son of Zebedee. He was also called a son of thunder supposedly because of temper, but again thunder and lightning go together. The mother of Jesus often appeared (or appeared to appear) in many other places with spiritual light phenomena and became Our Lady of the Light in Mexico for example. When I was younger I investigated the apparition in Mayo at Knock, and wondered whether that was actually a magic lantern experience at the time. Magic and spiritual light must be distinguished. Some apparitions are more convincing than others to different people. However, magical light can still create some spiritual light. Whatever about the crass commercialism of Lourdes, there was palpable power on the spot for me. Fatima is an extraordinary story. Our Lady of Salette is another interesting apparition of a woman of light. But according to legend the Virgin appeared to St. James at a time when she was alive! James witnessed the Transfiguration. James also asked Jesus in Luke 9:54 whether he and John should 'command fire to come down from heaven.' Jesus rebuked them.

Apparitions were characterised by extraordinary light phenomena. Christian literalists insist on what is in the Bible but then ignore uncomfortable lines. The most explosive line in the New Testament is largely ignored. I contacted Biblical scholars to get views on this some time ago. I am aware of the debates about this part of the Gospel. But let us take the words on face value. After Jesus was crucified he appeared to demonstrate his resurrection. While it is clear to believers that he appeared in a recognisable form, he was also not so easy to recognise for others. Thus in Mark 16:12 in the *King James Version*, *'After that he appeared in another form, unto two of them, as they walked, and went into the country.'* In another form! This could be a rainbow body, a light body or some other form altogether.

Alumbrados (the Illuminated or Enlightened) in Spain were a group of mystical Christians who emphasised the individual journey of ascension to the divine through direct engagement with God's grace. There may have been a Jewish and indeed Sufi influence on the group and they shared some beliefs with the Heretics of Durango and reflected the Heresy of the Free Spirit and close affinity with Catalan *Iluminismo*. All these had links back to the Neo-Platonists. Alumbrados believed that ceremonies were attachments to the material world. Many women were influential in the movement which arose in France also. It got some attention from the Inquisition. The idea was to love God, your fellows and yourself without institutions. Such direct experiential, individual connections with the Divine without interposition were a revolutionary threat to orthodoxy. The consistent eradication of popular mystical blossomings contributes to the uninspiring literalism and ceremonialism more consistent with a materialist view of reality. Many heretical Free Spirits used Gnosticism and Neo-Platonism to find heaven and escape hell, starting on the earth and often engaging in practices to experience blinding light of the Divine. Mystics from Boehme to Swedenborg love light. Recently there have been claims that the Shroud of Turin was produced as by a directional 'burst of conscious light.' In countries where Christianity is dying like in Sweden, the remains of old celebrations can still be seen in the mid-winter celebration of light that is the

Santa Lucia, where celebrants wear light in their hair still. The other major festival 'Midsommar' also celebrates the height of summer light and contains still the lingering but lost remains of ancient shamanic religion of the North.

Quakers are the group who used the idea of the inner light as a belief and a method. The Divine light was in everybody. Such light could be found, encouraged and shone for the benefit of others. Some Quakers met other persecuted religious sects such as the Dutch Collegiants, with whom Spinoza had some contacts. They also believed in inner light but not in its ability to convert others. In this debate there was an element of discussion of the light of reason. This demonstrates how the belief in light may have different emphases but there is a contour of contexts of light that many spiritual traditions identify. I suggest they identify with the cycle of spiritual light because it is a real spiritual phenomenon, not culturally constructed but actually experienced and evidenced by repeated occurrence as extensively reported. An important mystical writing of 1662 that was used by Quakers and others was *The Light Upon the Candlestick*. This anonymous writing argued that everyone had the light within them but impediments might make them unaware. You would know this was the true light when you encountered it. There might be external signs but because the light is in you, the external aspect is not really so. The light might be seen as your conscience or spirit or God or Christ. The description does not matter so much, it seems like the force of natural sunlight but deeper as realisation of truth. That experience seemed more significant than dogma and Quakers or Children of the Light could learn and be informed by other spiritual traditions because light is universal in all. People like Rufus Jones, from an original mystic base, took Quakerism down one path. Others dispute his ideas of what the inner light was. Light was Christ for many although the Christian aspect declined in some Quaker circles.

Then there were the texts which did not become part of the Christian canon but were relevant or popular or reflective of some beliefs. *The Letter of Barnabas* from the early Christian era states,

> "There are two paths of teaching authority, the path of light and the path of darkness. And the difference between the two paths is great. For over the one are appointed light-bearing angels of God, but over the other angels of Satan."

In the mid-second century *The Letter of 2 Clement,* referring to Jesus, says 'for he graciously bestowed light upon us.'

Before Christ and after the Gnostics recur right up to today. Their primary emphasis was on the experience and reality of the Divine instead of a mere theoretical or ritual one it seems. We can see light in texts such as *The Gnosis of the Light* which came from Egypt in 1769. In it are mentioned the Pure Light, the Hermit of the Light, the Saviour of the Light, the All-Perfect Light, the Thought of Light, the Silence of Light and so on.

In 1945 the Nag Hammadi texts were found in a jar having been hidden hundreds of years before. Early Christian and Gnostic texts saw the light of day and over time were translated. For a general collection see *Lost Scripture: Books that Did not Make it into the New Testament* by Bart D. Ehrman. From the Nag Hammadi *The First Thought in Three Forms* from circa 200 AD is riddled with light. The female spirit descends as light into darkness with the Son of Light to allow return to the Holy Light. Also in the Nag Hammadi texts was *The Secret Book of John.* Therein, Jesus helps free people from being trapped in matter. Mankind was made luminous against the wishes of Archons and as a result they were 'thrown into the lowest region of all matter.' But in Adam was hidden the luminous Epinoia. So again the story is of spirit descended and trapped in matter capable of ascending through cultivation of inner light. *The Gospel of Truth* came some time before 180 AD. It says that 'in you dwells the light that does not fail.' The light is a divine energy that comes through matter. But *The Coptic Gospel of Thomas* has been the most powerful of these texts.

> "There is a light within a man of light, and he lights up the whole world. If he does not shine he is darkness."

Here is a deep statement about the primacy of spirit.

> "Jesus said, 'If the flesh came into being because of spirit, it is a wonder. But if spirit came into being because of the body, it is a wonder of wonders. Indeed, I am amazed at how this great wealth has made its home in this poverty'."

In my view, this directly argues against the idea that spiritual consciousness is emergent. Then again,

> "Jesus said 'If they say to you, Where did you come from? Say to them, We came from the light, the place where the light came into being on its own accord...'."

Again Jesus said,

> "He will become manifest, but his image
> will remain concealed by his light."

Gnostics prized experience but their texts were tough to interpret nevertheless. Gnostics aspired to the region of light far removed from this dense and gross matter we are trapped in. The idea that we are trapped light or a trapped spark in matter was a central Gnostic claim. The escape from the illusory prison world was through spiritual practices of insight and intuition. We are emanations of supreme light that descending needs to recover and be re-directed towards its original source in the pleroma. Gnosis or knowledge would come directly through a messenger of light. The outside bridge of light thus allowed the remaining spark or quantum of light be reunited with source from which it emanated through fall into gross matter. A false god must be circumvented. Rosicrucianism has a similar idea of a trapping of light in some streams. Gnostic texts are fairly united in emphasis on light and they had spiritual practices that liberated light. At base we are light trapped in matter with some Divine part still.

Gnosticism has a clear parallel in teachings of the previously mentioned Mani, the 'luminary' or 'illuminator.' Just as the Persians share similar views, so the Gnostics exhibit parallel philosophies. Manichaeism was based on the idea of spiritual light and the battle between the unified kingdom of light and beings of light and darkness, reflecting Zoroastrianism. The realm of light was attacked. Beings of light were trapped in the material world through nefarious means. These beings would have to be released in the future. This religion thus deals with the freeing of light in a way that Gnostic did. Buddhism has similar ideas. A female form of light comes at death. Manichaeism is one of the ultimate descriptions of light being trapped in matter. Spirit has lost connection with its true source and nature. A future enlightened world will be the terra lucida or 'earth of light.' We came from boundless light invaded by darkness and dark beings seeking light they do not have in their chaotic kingdom. His twin angel of light appeared to him a number of times like lightning and assisted his prophecy and revelation as an apostle of Jesus and others. A ship of light transported the soul after death. It emphasised our true nature as spirit trapped in matter. Most Gnosis involved liberation of trapped spirit or light. Such contempt for matter is also found in the other Gnostic religious groups through the Bogomils to Cathars and some streams of esoteric Judaism. Gnosis is sought through aspiration to the true light. It fits into later spiritual alchemy ideas. Similarly Inner light or Inward Light is a crucial element in many streams of Protestantism not least the Quakers much later. Trapped light perception manifested in these movements because it is based on experience.

In Islam and Islamic philosophy and in Sufism and Persian thought in particular, light is associated with the Divine source and central features such as mercy and compassion. From the start, light defined the early experiences of The Prophet. There are descriptions of light as part of the fundamental explanation from the Koran with influences from Greek philosophy. Al Makki emphasises Divine light and the need for personal experience thereof. Rabia of Basra is mentioned sometimes as an example of a woman of light, for example by Sachiko Murata. Ibn Arabi uses light and describes being consumed by light. Ayn al Quzat Hamadani was a mystic who explained spiritual life in terms of Divine light. Al Hallaj talked of flashes of lightning and columns of light in his mystical

Sufism. Suhrawardi is seen as the founder of Illuminationism and famous for his *Philosophy of Illumination*. Najm al Din Kubra also used a specific explanation based on light informed by Neo-Platonism via Egypt and students of Suhrawardi. Kubra identifies the classic mystical path for Sufis and other mystics. He indicates how mystic powers emerge and he sees it as fundamentally an issue of spiritual perception of divine light, colours and application to the individual for spiritual enhancement. We can see an explanation which is consistent with other traditions that the individual or particles of light within must ascend and in its tending lead to descending light. The green light or green circles surface in some of these writings. Suhrawardi followed on from the mystic Al Ghazali and both are said to have articulated 'an ontology of light.' The latter emphasised the role of inner certainty associated with perception of light as a source of disclosure of knowledge that may tend to the ineffable. It is a matter of experience involving illumination of heart as indicated in books like *The Niche of Lights*. Ibn Arabi had gnosis occurring through a light of lights as celestial revelation in the heart that opens the mystic up to the Divine world. This can create a light of the intellect. A light of nature may also reveal. Mulla Sadra continued Illuminationist thinking, interpreting the Koran. He emphasised the traditional mystic concept of polishing the mirror of the soul to receive Divine light in an individual way. The Verse of Light in the Koran was interpreted in a logical way and expanded. The Divine shone light through The Prophet and faithful would seek to receive and reflect this Light of Lights. There was an ultimate source of light, that it is the nature of existence and has an inherent luminosity that can be facilitated to create some adherence to divine order. Light manifested in us makes other light manifest. Light itself can be trapped in deep darkness. The seeker is light higher than body, shade or mind and we may contact our higher angel to survive and find immortality through effort. The man of light meets the higher guide of light. Light upon light.

Rumi and others focus on the temple of the heart rather than actual buildings and rituals. The light we find outside with reason is but small compared to internal light to which the inner journey must be made away from manifest world. Mirror, light and darkness are recurrent symbols. Sunlight reflects on the moon as a mystic receives inspiration. The spirit being of light may appear to the mystic. Jami wrote several books specifically on the theme of light.

> "With men of light I sought the pearls to string,
> the drift in mystic sayings to bring."

In his work (translated as *Flashes of Light*) he presents a mystical perspective indicating the need to seek unity with the highest creative Divine force of apprehension of unity. It shines on all things fair and foul, without losing its being, but is capable of changing the being it radiates on. Evil comes from darkness or lack of light. Truth is like sunshine and will never be found in books or rational thought alone. We can mirror the truth, like the moon shows sunshine. Truth is real and shines through illusion. Suhrawardi, the Master of Illumination, reflected Zoroastrianism to some extent. Illuminationism in Sufism supposedly parallels the 'illuminati' in Platonism and brings in Hermetic techniques. The mystic journeys inside in darkness, keeping their own light and seeking to ascend or climb up a ladder of light which allows the sun shine through into the material temple. Other stories from Arabia show the link between light and darkness of the otherworld and the Jinn. In the story of *Aladdin and the Magic Lamp* we see spirit and light with genie, sorcerer and lamp. The genie is a type of spirit trapped in matter or a container and needs to perform services to escape. The spirit utilises the inherent power within to marshal forces to triumph over adversaries and surmount obstacles.

Shamanism involves light energies and a sea of light. Theosophy is permeated with light and in particular forms may focus on 'the seven rays.' Alchemy involved an unleashing of inner light present even in darkness and in some ways capable of being with darkness. Swedenborg has an entire philosophy of spiritual light in his work. Light may be the reality of wisdom or truth of a divine nature. Wisdom is spiritual light. The inner sight, insight is by another light. Luciferianism is necessarily about light and darkness. It underpins many secret societies according to some and is reflected in certain New Age thinking. Rosicrucianism engages with light. Freemasonry has a focus on light. Secondary sources suggest light is crucial as a symbol and the conception of our light and a higher light and their unification. The ubiquitous light symbol and candidates being brought to the light as sons of light appears. Lights will lead them. Light from above from grand lights is necessary guidance to inner light. Light is usually used as a metaphor for knowledge. Manly Hall uses light and we see it recur in his book *Initiates of the Flame*. In mystical terms, perceived external light may be noetic and revelatory on its own. Gerald Massey was a spiritualist and Egyptologist who wrote *Ancient Egypt: The Light of the World*. It is full of light references from the drowning light and 'Lady of the light of the moon' to the solar hawk of Horus. Florence Nightingale tending to wounded soldiers in the Crimean War was a real-world 'lady with the lamp.'

Auras, angels, beings and beams and extraordinary phenomena of light all attest to the actual and metaphorical significance of spiritual light. Initiation ceremonies of prehistoric, ancient and mystery schools involved darkness and emerging into light. The 'lucid' in lucid dreaming refers back to light. From Biblical times to William Blake to contemporary Lorna Byrne, the appearance, perception or description of angels involves light. Angels are not New Age inventions. In the monotheistic traditions and beyond, angels are very well-established. Many ghostly, apparitions and 'spectres' are associated with unusual light and the word 'spectrum' is the range of light. A phantom is a ghost, illusion or apparition that apparently comes from a root related to the idea of bringing something to light. Thus the language and phenomena of paranormal activity involves the centrality of light and is often explained in optical terms, although we might have to consider the aspect of internal projection and inner eye also in a complete consideration of that domain. Projection seems to have been an alchemical idea before it became a light term. Near Death Experiences are replete with light. Parapsychology is arguably about light as I will suggest. Clairvoyance is clear seeing. Perhaps it is no surprise that a famous spiritualist who talked of light a lot was called Betty Shine. It is interesting that a few people associated with remote-viewing come from a laser background. Hypnosis may be facilitated by use of light. Astrology talks of 'the luminaries' for the sun and moon which led to a recent, popular novel of that name. Psychedelic experiences of altered states as reported often indicate a state of compression and confinement consistent with consciousness being trapped before a journey towards the light and often bliss. Dying has many reports of spiritual or light phenomena. Mystical experience is permeated by altered states of consciousness of light which contrasts to some prior state characterised often by a sense of being confined or trapped.

The concept of cosmic consciousness as indicated earlier came about in its clearest Western articulation as a phenomenon of light. Bucke's mystical experience came by light involving an influx of knowledge or realisation. The experience led to his idea, which reflects Indian doctrines and Western esoteric refraction, involving a consistent focus on light. This is the nature and pattern of mystical events. Mystical events may impact on the individual so their lives are affected. Communication of those new states may be the object of subsequent endeavours. Other churches, like the Mormon Church, have a doctrine of 'the light of Christ.' The religion goes back to Joseph Smith's vision in 1820 of a 'pillar of light' in the woods.

Spiritualist churches in the US especially attest to the central core of spiritual light and the movement might be traced back to the Swedish seer Swedenborg and later Quakers, with particular manifestations in the 19th century. Some names of contemporary communities are as follows; The Celebration of Light Church, The Golden Light of Christ Church, The Golden Light Spiritualist Church, The Chapel of Spiritual Light, The Church of Light, The Spiritual Lighthouse Church, The New Dawn Spiritual Light Church, The Inner Light Spiritual Church, The Light Centre Church, The Sanctuary of Light Spiritual Church, The Clear Light Centre, The Spiritualist Church of Divine Light, Summerland Church of Light, The Circle of Love and Light, The Guiding Light Spiritualist Church, The Rays of Light Spiritualist Church, The Church of the Guiding Light and the Vision of Light Church and Spiritual Healing. It is clear that spirit and light are inextricably bound. One of the most famous spiritualist journals was the *Banner of Light*. Outside of those there are solar churches in the discipline established by Gene Savoy of 'Cosolargy' which emphasises the sun as an ancient object of worship. When certain forces seek to create a religion of the future you can be sure that light will feature prominently because it reflects an underlying reality. A scientific-spiritual doctrine of light dogma would come easily.

New Age thinking often talks about a generalised white light as a healing force that shines through theosophy back to ancient sources through Kabbalah and Egypt. Channelling in the US has been linked to this movement. Jane Roberts. Cindy Riggs and JZ Knight all have multiple references to light, beings of light and identifying them. A being hovering around may be asked if they are 'from the light' for example, with the suggestion that the curiously honourable entities depart if not. Some contemporary, popular spiritual books are based on light in various degrees of vagueness at times. There are notable examples in the last century of works which see light as a critical spiritual force. Abdruschin (Oscar Ernst Bernhardt) wrote *In the Light of Truth. The Grail Message,* which gave rise to a spiritual movement called The Grail Movement. L. Ron Hubbard who founded Scientology wrote about spiritual beings trapped in matter before the enterprise came to fruition and it seems to influence their worldview. The Native American Church had peyote ceremonies where the moon is important. Rastafarianism was influential for the reggae singer Bob Marley and a sense of embedded activism was indicated by the spiritual path. Thus he could sing in the 1973 song,

> "And now you see the light
> Stand up for your rights."

It is no surprise that magic is infused with light. The distinction between magic and mystical or spiritual practice is not easy, if valid at all. Books like the thousand year old *Picatrix* engage with light in the context of magical use of talismans. Moonlight arises in the practices of modern witches and Wiccans may use *The Book of Shadows*. The influential Order of the Golden Dawn obviously uses a light motif. The modern 'Western mystery schools' may deal with a certain type of magic with light being a central theme. The Fraternity of the Inner Light was founded by Dion Fortune in 1924 and exists today as the Society of the Inner Light with another historically related offshoot school called the Servants of the Light. Eckankar is another religion that seems to use ideas of light in its practices. Thelema from Aleister Crowley emphasises light. Crowley used a ray of light to represent the inherent consciousness that combined the light of the sun and the stars such as Sirius. The Gnostic church associated with Thelema claims to be a 'church of light.' One of the first US masses from this source seems to have been in Hollywood, where the magic lights of the holy holly wood are projected. The persistence of 'rays' through these schools is noticeable. Materialisations often involve features of light. Alice Bailey wrote on theosophy and developed a 'seven rays' philosophy with channelled wisdom. Her work was published through a house called Lucifer Publishing Company which became the Lucis Trust which also published *The Beacon* magazine. Lucifer is claimed to be an esoteric concept based on the idea of the fallen angel descended into matter to assist us in some way akin to Prometheus. Visualisations of light are practiced. There is a 'Great Invocation' based on light flowing from the mind of God to the individual. Energy may be trapped and healing comes through releasing blockages. Followers have introduced ideas of diamond and amethyst light, light-workers and an intergalactic 'family of light.' Bailey influenced the New Age movement and some of the people in the UFO world. 'Lucifer' was also the name of a magazine published by Blavatsky with Annie Besant. It was *'Designed to bring to light the hidden things of darkness,'* as it said on the cover and clarified that it was a reference to the 'light-bringer,' the morning star and was not a Satanic indication. The first issue explained the meaning of Lucifer and indeed there are examples of early church fathers with the name Lucifer. She distinguished between a divine Lucifer and an infernal Lucifer with reference to the basis of the Latin origin of the word. Blavatsky also commented on the apparently old text of the *Light on The Path*. That emphasised the light within. Alice Bailey wrote about Soul Light and Body Light. She identifies the soul light or causal body, the etheric body or golden light body or flame coloured vehicle and the 'dark light' or the light hidden within the atom in the body. She sees alignment of the 'solar angel' uniting with the golden light and allowing the divine spark come into play. Certain Christians would see any such talk as anathema without consideration. The following quote from Mistleberger interprets it as involving archetypes,

> "The Lucifer archetype is bold, self-affirming, authentically self-expressive. However in Lucifer's very desire to legitimize his existence via rebellion, he separated himself from his source, God, which on the absolute level is the same thing as separating from his true self. In effect he cut out a piece of his own heart. That's the shadow side of the Left Hand Path - pride, which is the attachment to being special. So while the common difficulty with the Right Hand path is repression and denial of self, the shadow element of the Left Hand Path is an inflated sense of self that goes beyond a healthy reversal of shame and self-loathing. It is the need to be special."

In such Theosophy you see statements about conduct and the encouragement of values such as 'harmlessness' in the sense of not doing damage rather than mere inoffensiveness. So the basic value of the particular mystic tradition should not be ignored. Similarly Steiner had the magazine *Lucifer-Gnosis*. I understand the difficulty this poses for access to such work for some. But the argument has to be heard at least before it might be rejected and they are usually sophisticated ones.

There are people who claim there is no right and wrong, that we cannot condemn human action, that we cannot say some conduct is negative and all is relative. The mystic path does not lead to a disregard of good and evil but rather a caution against simplistic duality that fails to see underlying reality. It may be that most of our conceptions of justice are really mystical in origin and focus on spiritual interaction primarily. Most mystics will argue against violence but also challenge the roots of evil as manifest in sadistic and destructive action. But too much focus on judging or imposing goodness may turn into its opposite as I have suggested with the law of spiritual contrast. This is similar to the argument that devils and demons appear so much in contexts of religious opponents because they know they get so much attention there. Crowley probably became what he was because of the Plymouth Brethren background he came from. This group had its origins in Dublin and England and was linked to a series of meetings of discontented Protestants at Powerscourt House in Wicklow. The group became splintered and diverse. They sought to return to a pure Christianity and were initially against clergy. One of the players was John Nelson Darby who was a graduate of Trinity College Dublin, a lawyer and clergyman in the established Church of Ireland. Darby made popular the idea of 'The Rapture' which would become very influential, although it was suggested earlier and some claim it comes from the Bible. He is also regarded as the founder of Dispensationalism which has become a very significant force in US Christianity. At the same time as one finds fault with religious movements, it is naive to deny that certain strands of Luciferian-Promethean-Satanic magical philosophy seem to be the basis of a hyper-mechanised, high-octane materialism that will seek to destroy spiritual traditions inconsistent with it.

There are a range of diverse spiritual and New Age movements, actual and latent, or activities where light plays a role which affirms the spiritual light presence and maybe indicates some new directions. 'Liquid light' and 'ascended octaves of light' and light meditations appear in extraordinary experiences on Mount Shasta for the theosophy branch of the 'I AM' movement of Guy Ballard. Robert Anton Wilson, who speculated about the Illuminati, believed they were a mystical, underground movement that used sex magic. Elsewhere 'the powers of light' are enlisted against black magic. David Koresh who was involved in the Waco Siege had a New Light revelation and female members of the community could be 'sown' with the light. Ideas of the 'merchants of light' emerge every now and then from Francis Bacon's works. Sai Baba taught a light meditation. Flotation tanks from John Lilly facilitated mystical experiences with light hallucinations through sensory deprivation.

New devices that use halogen lights to entrain and create harmony are being used to promote mystical states claiming to utilise a variant of the use of darkness and fire in the mystery ceremonies in Ancient Greece. Candles are used in sacred ceremonies and magic.

Add in the UFO phenomenon like the Phoenix Lights, inexplicable ones like the Light of Saratoga, the Dog Meadow Lights and the Japanese Hitodama and we see external light that impacts on the mind such that they may become spiritual light phenomena. Close encounters and alien abduction reports inevitably involve light phenomena and have many of the characteristics of mystical experiences. There is the phenomenon of 'earthquake lights' which are extraordinary lights associated with seismic activity. The earth may produce the Hessdalen light thus also. Physical light phenomena reported at holy sites may be ignored sometimes as less important than inner light. Lights are a signature of realms beyond apparent reality of the predicable rational mind. There are also groups such as the Universe People or Cosmic People of Light Powers who are part of a range of 'UFO religions' which involve spacecraft and light. Again, behind the diversity are spiritual light phenomena. The idea of a heavenly source of light, of trapping light and escape becomes evident. The Heaven's Gate Cult is another tragic example that fits the pattern.

With the disintegration of traditional religions, spiritual practices based on light become disseminated individually or as part of specific studies. Mystic sound specialists like Jill Purce, suggests that certain aspects of overtone singing move into the realm of light. Light does interact with sound in important ways. Many Taoist and Buddhist techniques focus on inner light. Some focus on a spot in front of their third eye. Some move light around the body. Some move it back and forth. The light is a point of mental focus and projection. Healing white light is ubiquitous in such spiritual discourse. Likewise withdrawal from light and sensory deprivation are used. Higher planes may become available through such meditation. Magic uses ideas of light in symbolic and actual form. Hypnagogic and hypnopompic states, significant in terms of visions, are often characterised by vivid and unique perceptions of light and luminosity associated with an apparent fire-like characteristic with particularly beautiful colours. Other altered states of consciousness involve special inner experiences of light and colour. Being reported, experienced, remembered and recounted is testament to reality of the actual range.

With the potential disintegration of certain religious institutions in the western world, spiritual and occult practices largely seen to be individualistic are also now emerging in collective modes. In recent years, there has been an upsurge in esoteric groups that seem to practice magic or magick in collective organisations sometimes hierarchical, sometimes flatter. Again light informs the enterprise. 'The Illuminates of Thanateros' are a group of people interested in chaos magick. Such ideas link back to Crowley and the artist Austin Osman Spare and beyond. There is also apparently an emergent stream of ideological esoteric organisations that seek to engage in forms of magic in the public arena. Historical antecedents might be found with the (contested) example of Gerald Gardner defending the UK against Hitler through generating a cone of power with witchcraft. Old ideas resurface such as the 'gates of light' in contemporary organisations such as Portae Lucis which was based on the work of the French scientist and occultist, Jean Dubuis.

Perhaps scientists will begin to realise what Newton knew, that they were merely playing with pebbles on the seashore. Mystics realise that they are in a great mystery. It is not that they deny the contributions of pieces of knowledge. However they realise that for every pebble of knowledge there will be another that must follow to infinity. Mystics, from Blake to Sufi poets a thousand years ago, perceived we might find the universe in a grain of sand. Scientism has been used to seek to deny spirituality at a time when technological advance makes mass control of consciousness by authority a real risk. The inexplicable fundamental force of consciousness is everywhere full of descriptions of light in the most significant, profound and meaningful experiences of perennial wisdom. Still even atheist scientists like Sam Harris seem to realise the role of light,

> "Consciousness is simply the light by which the contours of mind and body are known."

Light and its absence is a perennial framework of spiritual endeavour. Depending on denomination, there is a pattern of a Divine realm of light with emanations descended into matter with a hierarchy of beings and a degree of consistency in the contours of those conceptions. All spiritual traditions allow for a direct apprehension of Divinely inspired or informative light by the spirit which itself contains some. Independently of Divine doctrines spiritual experience will encounter some sense of evolution. Conceptions of the Divine may be replaced with a grand consciousness. Indeed, it is more the commitment to individuality and compassion that is the guiding star. When the basic pattern of spiritual evolution is made complex because of more social organisation, dangers of distancing and distortion increase. It might be stated thus. *The perennial theology or theosophy of light indicates that we come from a region of unlimited light emanated or created, that we essentially are light contained in evolving vessels and will return to our source by following the path of light if we do not get lost or choose to remain attached to illusions or ensnared by evil beings here or on lower planes.*

1.14 From Stars to Astral Light and Beyond

Kirk who wrote *The Secret Commonwealth* in 1691, said fairies had bodies 'like those called astral,' like daemons of old, somewhere between humans and angels, fluid like a condensed cloud they could flit in and out of visibility at will. This is an interesting indication of a conception of the astral body. It is thus worth noting another important notional realm to the discussion of light in the context of the spirit, mysticism, magic or even theology. The light of stars and associated, separate and slippery concept of astral light should be borne in mind in the context of discussions about the role of light. Mystics have different views of these domains. At a general level there has been a long, ancient and consistent consciousness of stars and planets. This will continue but be subject to an increasing technological obscuring of the heavens with mechanical light and objects. Science will produce a celestial junkyard and deny its role therein. All ancient cultures developed complex cosmologies that attributed significances to the skies that are difficult to comprehend in contemporary thinking for many. Nowadays such interests are often relegated to the realm of superstition and pseudo-science. Even where there is demonstrable proof of complex observation and understanding of the skies over long periods, there is a tendency to disregard it. Trite explanations emerge which often trivialise ancient achievements. Certainly there are sensational claims and speculations that abound about lost worlds. Nevertheless we see that a lot of occult wisdom, magic and indeed mysticism relates to the actual stars and planets. In addition, there is a reflected esoteric world of light from the stars and different planes. This world can be seen in Astrology, Magic. Gnosticism, Kabbalah and Christian theology in related forms. The idea of correspondence between the macrocosm and the microcosm in us is a crucial one.

The astral body and idea of separating the light or subtle body from the physical one provides the theatre of much esoteric exploration. Ancient India and Egypt had such ideas. The astral world has often been a source of intense perception for mystics. The subtle domain of substantial effects and affects is a type of alien realm. For writers on the occult, such as Rollo Ahmed, the astral plane was the dwelling place of elementals, thought-projections, nature spirits and shells or astral simulacra. Notions vary widely, some seeing it as a serpent, dragon or river. Blavatsky sees 'astral' as an inaccurate word to refer to the world within that shines as stars do. Astral simply means appertaining to the stars and there simplicity ends although we are made of elements of matter formed in stars. She did apparently see astral light as part of a comprehensive explanation of the psychic zone which is also one of illusion. Generally, the conception of an astral world refers to realms, zones or dimensions of space wherein certain subtle bodies within us and others can operate or interact. Nevertheless, there is great diversity in descriptions thereof. The astral body is seen to be an energetic body distinct from the etheric body and is related to, or contains, the emotional and mental bodies. The magician or spiritually developed person may seek to exercise control over their subtle bodies. Descriptions of such bodies involve non-normal perception of light and associate colours. Astral light is described by some theosophists as being pervasive, having negative and positive manifestations impinging on us, even on thought and linked to various schools such as Kabbalah. Paracelsus talked about the light of nature (lumen naturae) which informed nature and humans and came from the stars. Reason and Christ or revelation were separate. This light of nature was something we should come into accord with, so we could move back to the source or eternal or heavenly light or light of the Holy Spirit. Powers of the light of nature in stones and plants were hidden for us to discover. This is consistent with the idea of trapped light, and indeed trapped starlight.

Eliphas Levi was associated with 'astral light.' He was referring to a tradition back to Plato and beyond associated with the 'imagination of nature.' Astral light is argued to magnetise us as a force that permeates the universe. Originally it referred to the effect of starlight or sidereal nature. Underhill is clear that there is no connection between the astral plane and stars. She sees it as the world where ancients saw spirits, the unseen world, the next world beyond. For her it is the domain of the occultist or magician on the one hand and the mystic on the other. Both encounter this dimension but the mystics *'pass through it as quickly as they can.'* This distinction emerges also in the distinction between magic and divine magic that the magi of the Renaissance used. Working on behalf of the Divine distinguishes the nature of the magic. In all spiritual traditions there are spiritual worlds usually with different levels, planes or heavens. There is a lack of consistency of use of these terms. Certain Gnostics saw these planes as commanded by principalities of archons or heavenly bodies as being under their influence.

The living, conscious earth had energy fields that regulated life manifested in many vital forms. It is curious that the mind's eye often perceives significant green light on the fringe of an altered state just as the earth's pole may be bathed in green light by solar wind meeting the magnetosphere. Magic involved itself in harmonising with and utilising universal energies and the strange inexplicable world of thoughts, ideas and memory. Imagination and imaginal inform and intensify ceremonial magic. Astral light encompasses the plane of phantoms and phantasy. Despite denied direct connection with stars, it nevertheless occurs through correspondence or analogy and also indirectly. Rudolf Steiner, Crowley and his follower Israel Regardie deal with this classic esoteric dimension. To Crowley we are stars. Thelema and its religious practice seem to begin with the idea of the individual as star matter. Offshoots of the Golden Dawn such as Stella Matutinae used techniques of astral travel in their magical work. The astral realm reflects an ancient idea that may echo or explain animism and apparent otherworldliness and sympathy with supersensible and supernatural forces perceived in formerly enchanted world and permeating spiritual traditions. The ideas behind New Thought and Law of Attraction indicate an affinity with these ancient streams and emphasises the significance of recognition of energy and will. Thoughts are things and they attract states. Potential parallels between astral and Akasha, bardo, ether, implicate order and Sheldrake's morphogenetic field or the noosphere exist. Theosophy cultivates these old ideas and believed they were perpetuating what was previously there. Light permeates such discussions. For example, the astral body is linked by a 'cord' or 'coil' of light to the body. The astral light varies and may be regarded sometimes as a subtle substance or a medium.

The notion of an astral body and projection for some allows comprehension of many ideas in parapsychology associated with appearances, apparitions, bilocation, fetches and phantoms. People beyond esoteric communities will probably not have much faith in such systems. People grounded deeply in religious traditions may see them as second nature. People in science might laugh. Nevertheless, we may find that the strange unfolding of scientific knowledge of different dimensions and enhanced continual comprehension of fundamental particles, fields and elusive factors such as dark matter and anti-matter, will sound suspiciously like some ancient anticipations of the invisible world, if not represent a fairly accurate guess or even genuine familiarity therewith. Explanations on the foreshore between science and the esoteric or spiritual, like the holographic universe proposed by Talbot (on the basis of research by Bohm and Pribram) may be closer to the truth. Similarly the discarded concept of ether sneaks back again as does the Akasha. Parapsychology may ultimately be explained in light terms. Remember that the sun causes impact of an electromagnetic nature through solar flares. The sun cycle is believed by many to have an impact of certain social and political cycles on the earth. There is more in the heavens than we can ever understand.

The subtle bodies are supposedly composed of a fine luminous substance which represents a level of matter unfamiliar directly to most. To me, the law of parsimony, or Occam's Razor, suggests that all spiritual manifestations and practices are contained within the word spirit and that undue focus on fine distinctions foisted by certain groups for their own purposes do not always assist and may alienate. Furthermore it is useful to simplify the various worlds believed to exist beyond the one we acknowledge here. The world of the imaginary is distinct from the imaginal, leading some like Henry Corbin to talk of the *mundus imaginalis*. The suggestion, partly based on Islamic and Persian mystical discourse as reflected in Suhrawardi and others, describes the world beyond our normal one where other beings of light live in different places and dimensions not inconsistent with descriptions in Celtic folklore. Swedenborg was influenced by Kabbalah and other esoteric schools and created the most complex model of other spiritual worlds. Again we might just say that it is common in spiritual, shamanic and mystical practices for spirit to travel to different places, sometimes in-between, liminal spaces, to obtain knowledge of the past, present or future. The nature and descriptions of those places vary depending on the tradition but they will always involve some reference to light or luminosity. Spiritual consciousness may be projected into universal spiritual dimensions. Some like Corbin argue that angels never come unless you are poor, meaning emptied without ego. That is the necessary condition for higher beings to come and therefore you must wait for the goddess. Blessed are the poor in spirit. Too much detail, control, intellectualism is not the condition of profound perception. The imaginal or zone accessible to the imagination (that Jung in his *Red Book* was aware of) is accessed by letting go, believing in your own potential through releasing limitation and having the courage to allow what comes up come up.

Mystics engaged in such realms seek to ascend to go to the orient, to orientate themselves. Orientation is looking for the sun within or aligning with a point above. There is no doubt that one may enter altered states of consciousness in many ways and for many purposes even maybe nefarious. Intention and goodwill are critical for the genuine mystic because being well-intentioned and perceiving actual commonality of consciousness leads on the hero's journey to the boon they need to bring back to their community. A burglar may break into a doctor's surgery but their being there is completely different from the presence of a doctor genuinely committed to helping their patients despite correspondence of place. If the domains are separate, then alien, ET or UFO phenomena are largely separate. The idea of the alien and astral bodies may not be as distinct as one imagines. Aliens are often presumed to come from the stars. They may be perceived as benign or demonic. They can affect people. Presumably they can change shape. It seems they can move between dimensions also. The presumption of advanced technology being mechanical, represents a failure to contemplate how highly advanced technology will be more organic or more convincingly so. Astral light and other concepts of ether make sense if conceived in terms of Taoism and other systems suggesting a pervasive vibratory universe of alternating densities capable of multitudinous manifestations mostly beyond comprehension of specifically adapted local senses whose perceptions are conflated with reality. It seems simpler to say that there are a range of spiritual beings and a range of realities they can operate within.

Behind many notions of astral light is the notion of Egyptian light as filtered through various writers. This came back into Europe through Italy in the 16th century. The evidence of an Egyptian doctrine of light that may have influenced Moses and prefigured Christianity and influenced Greeks and Persians seemed to make clear where the stars fit in. Stars did influence us and their impact and manifestations were therefore to be controlled to allow access to the higher, super-celestial fountainhead of light. In some esoteric communities, symbolic ladders sometimes climb to constellations such as the Pleiades representing depictions of the starry heavens that in turn represent a deeper reality apparent in ancient cultures such as Babylon or the Masonic Blazing Star linked to Sirius and Egypt. On the other hand, light meditations may involve a perception that one is being engulfed in a blazing star and like many other phenomena of light refers to an internal state activated by the seeker. Stars were powerful or demonic and were capable of being controlled. In certain Persian thought stars might be prisons for souls. Thus the notion of a demon again surfaces as a reality. Same issues recur. Could an angel be a demon? Was it not better to control demons than be controlled by them? If God made all things and angels rebelled and became demonic should they not be converted? It is possible to see some of these debates as similar to Jung's personal quest in the early part of the 20th century. To the magician it was about drawing down powers. However focus on the source in Egypt probably ignores the reality of a comprehensive worldview based on light that existed across the world. In my view drawing down is a description of the process of mystical elevation or spiritual evolution but limited by possibility of ego seeking to control. Today we look to new stars which are constellated to control and channel our attention through waves. People on talents shows proclaim the mantra that 'it means everything' to be a star. The false light of stardom replaces an ancient idea.

The Arab world contributed to ideas of the astral and magic at various stages. The available knowledge was recorded in celebrated chronicles. Spain was not just an important source of Kaballah but also of translations of major Arabic works. In Islam, there have been discussions about the validity of magic. At times Christian and Islamic theology showed similar patterns. Thus there may have been exertion of control of devils or Jinn for the glory of God which would be distinguished from magic which engages with the evil spirits for their ultimate benefit. The latter would obviously be improper theologically and not as potentially justifiable as the former. Such a dichotomy reflects the distinction between divine magic and sorcery in European terms. In addition, a more common magic involved talismans and reflects what might be termed natural magic and thus could be less controversial. Philosophers or theologians like al-Kindi wrote about some theories underlying cosmology and astrology. The stars did exert influence. He wrote about the influence of rays. It becomes impossible to disentangle the inter-relationships of the contemplation of light and of magic. Al-Kindi made a significant contribution to the study of optics. He also contributed to spreading knowledge of the worldview from which ideas of astral influence operated based on rays and bodies that were entangled and influencing each other. Books like the *Picatrix,* which concentrated on practice of magic and astral magic depended on faith but people who want things that work do not necessarily engage in theory save where needed to make it effective.

Some individuals and groups have become adepts in the astral domain. *The Projection of the Astral Body* was an influential book by Muldoon and Carrington in 1929. The astral body is known by various names including light-related ones such as 'the luminous' or 'shining' body. Carrington argued that the astral body was a vehicle for the soul like the Ka in ancient Egypt. They refer to the *Tibetan Book of the Dead* and guiding the soul to the next Clear Light of Reality. As emphasised in such esoteric traditions, the demons tend to be creatures of our own construction. He gave examples of accidental and intentional OBEs. Muldoon explains what the 'double' is and how this non-physical body operates and exteriorises. There are light streaks visible at certain speeds.

Many esoteric bodies see this as their central concern. Robert Monroe is a famous 'astral traveller' who divided places into three locales. Monroe describes a beam of light instructive in his exploration. His vibratory sensations preceding journeys sound very similar to shamanic physiological experiences. Eckankar developed a highly sophisticated map of the domains beyond the astral plane such as the causal, mental and etheric plane. They seem to engage in a similar practice of rising to the original light through levels with different light associations. Tom Campbell studies similar domains and argues that there is a Non-Physical Matter Reality (NPMR) which is bigger than Physical Matter Reality. He used technology of binaural beats with other investigators to create altered states where extraordinary phenomena or powers manifested including the ubiquitous light phenomena. Remote-viewing may involve a similar use of one's energy but not necessarily so.

Astral light concepts and domains are not consistent. The re-conception in terms of dimensions suggested by many within the UFO community does provide an explanation. Anyway, it can be conceived in three ways. Firstly, these domains are primarily external and represent different dimensions. Secondly, these domains are related to inner space which contains a vast unconscious and subconscious with archetypes which represent forms both good and bad, inherited or intuited by us. Thirdly the astral represents a channel or figure eight or infinity sign ∞ link between our entire consciousness, vast inner imagination, receptivity, power of perception and domains or dimensions beyond ordinary consciousness, outside or apparently outside, because narrow focus on existential survival reduces truth of unimaginable reality to comprehensibility. Mystics often want to transcend the astral domain or the lower realms at least or ignore it whereas certain magicians want to dwell on it. Crowley, for example, would seem to sacrifice ideas of compassion for the rewarding experience of power. For the mystic, this throws the baby out with the bathwater. The idea inherent in mysticism is of higher alignment which includes a sense of karmic bonds or relationship and a realm of some type of principle. The magician is Prospero. Mystics seem to suggest that wandering in mental zones for the sake of entertainment is a waste because we should be directed to a higher dimension. Edgar Cayce is an apparent example of someone who travelled to the higher levels of the astral plane to access Akashic records and look back in time and forward. He used an altered state and a beam of light visualisation. So the light occurs as a method even if there is no agreement on the place.

Perhaps the emergent consciousness and contact movement will be the dominant emergent paradigm in the new astral light. Marilyn Gewacke, for example, emphasises the need to utilise the extra-terrestrial phenomena to liberate us from the prison of limited consciousness. She mentions so much activity in the sky, pulses responding to lasers, orbs of light, lights landing in the woods and in their circles of contact. She seems to see us as light descended also and imprisoned in diminishing consciousness. To what extent aliens and angels, demons and dimensional craft drivers are the same is another question. Many in the extra-terrestrial movement will be open to intelligent lights descending from the sky and communicating with them. The engagement with the multiplicity of beings is no different than the ancient engagement with angels and less welcome demons. Furthermore, my belief is that many beings live here anyway. It is they who may not be sojourners.

It is very curious that the PK Man used 'Space Intelligence' to achieve his feats, to achieve magic in a way totally consistent with the idea of use of spirits to achieve unearthly powers. This is what Prospero does in *The Tempest*, using Ariel to cause a storm. I can see no real difference. In that sense Owens is a magician. The same dilemma arises in relation to the contact movement. This is where the mystical idea of divine magic might be relevant. Mystics focus perennially on a higher value such as compassion or love. Absent that value the cycle continues. If one believes powers can be enlisted, then the old gods and demons arguments appear. How do you distinguish them? The idea that the universe has no inherent moral value is a distinguishing aspect of the mystic and the magician. If spirituality is to survive, divine magic may have to come back to counter-balance scientific-magic. The speculative idea of nearly a dozen dimensions of space in physics may seek to explain these domains. The mystic will not be surprised. Their warning would be that engagement without awareness may bring one to undesirable places. As science looks again at the earth and its magnetism and the solar wind and Schumann Resonance, the classic idea of correspondence between the earth, us and the stars may return in a way that Native people and their shamans experienced. Reconciliation with Native peoples will be hard unless their awareness of the spirit world is appreciated and not condemned. Likewise Native peoples should be careful to protect their spirituality and not have it siphoned by science.

1.15 Can Insights on Light Be Unified?

Spiritual luminescence is probably assumed to represent a primitive extrapolation of the behaviour of sun, moon and stars. Such an analysis inverts mystical reality manifest in perennial writing. Rather the physical world is a pale reflection of the superior world of great spirit and provides lessons for comprehension of the real world beyond the illusory one presented by our inferior eyes to help us survive the practical peculiarities of this planet. Evolutionary theory supports the idea that what we see and perceive with our senses is not what is true in any real sense but rather an adaptation which constricts representation to survival needs. Light represents knowledge itself and a deeper light. The ubiquity, persistence and association of light with mystical experience indicate a spiritual domain permeated therewith. Persistence of the phenomenon and analogy of light reflects a deep truth about comprehension of the nature of consciousness and our essential spiritual being. Consciousness itself is associated, in mysterious ways with light. Enduring light preoccupation in all spiritual traditions suggests a perennial path. Perception of its reality and force and recurrence as reported from time immemorial with subjective manifestations capable of transforming and channelling lives does not require that spiritual light be capable of corralling and compartmentalisation within existing knowledge before it is accepted. Light is a useful metaphor to explain spiritual truth but is not the end. It is not just light within us but also in nature. In early Irish Christianity in the writings of Eriugena, nature constituted a Divine book like the main one monks richly illuminated with pictures of the natural world. We hear many teachers talk of light. Buddhists know about luminosity. They describe spiritual reality. What we see is in the mind. Mind is empty. Emptiness is clear light. With union, perception of bliss is clear. The pinhole camera reflects the spiritual method of retreating into darkness to begin to perceive visions of greater truth. We can perceive such light and when we do we realise we are of it. We are that.

How does this story of light hang together? Huston Smith identified features of religion that are recurrent in all traditions.

These reflect a universal wisdom or a perennial philosophy. The starting points are similar. Subtle and more severe differences may emerge in the interpretation and application through usual limitations and restrictions of institutions and inevitable misuse and Machiavellian appropriation thereof. Prohibitions on murder, robbery and untruths, lie at the basis of all. General negative paths associated with greed, hatred and untruth are balanced by tendencies towards the opposite. All these social rules reflect principles that are beneficial for society as a whole but more importantly are critical on an individual level. Extracting common principles reflects a universal lighthouse, a lamp on the way. Animals look after their family so it is not difficult to see what we ought to do. All life is precious and as apex predators we are stewards or we were gifted priority. Unfortunately, success at survival and conjuring of spirits of corporate personality create systems that will be predatory on humanity itself. Light is an illuminating principle of intellect that indicates how we should behave based on interests wider than our own and consistent with spiritual existence. However as Eckartshausen indicated, external institutions are not the domain of spiritual enlightenment. Light theology is no philosophy-lite, merely punctuating poor sermons with platitudes. For theologians who tried to engage in the world and analyse complex forces such as Reinhold Nierbuhr, the idea of light was still relevant. His book on democracy entitled *The Children of Light and the Children of Darkness* for example was based on the cryptic line in Luke 16:8,

> "...for the children of this world are in their
> generation wiser than the children of light."

For me this is the wrong place to start. All comprehension must come about through engaging with subjective experience.

God establishing light and that new vision paralleled the Egyptian vision is some ways. Light experiences of mystics or individuals who were initiated or independently happened on them were both cause and proof. The natural world showed a light cycle and individual unfolding of spiritual experience did also. The outside world provides physical parallel of a higher order light. The superior domain of light was infused with higher beings whose encounter was part of the process. Imagination is projection of the universe. Mirrors carried by mystics were to see immateriality of material and not for magic that did not aspire to be Divine. The mystical feminine was obscured and downplayed by institutions of power and narratives of the mother goddess as earth were forgotten. Matter is mater, the mother. Matrix is dark, protective and fertile. Both exist. Light and dark exist in ideas of spiritual knowledge in Buddhism, Orphism, Yoga, Hermeticism, Zoroastrianism, Manichaeism and many other schools with the idea that the universal or inner person has been trapped in darkness of flesh or the maya of matter. The true person is light that needs to be liberated from the darkness of matter and may be assisted by messengers sent from the domain of Light who return or emerge here to be informed by messengers of light. It may be a false god or archons who have imprisoned us here, or angels who fell here or even aliens who set us here. Alternatively we may have chosen, done it ourselves, drifted or dared to descend in similar other ideas.

External wisdom on light is an attempt to embody inner reality of ineffable, essential spiritual consciousness. It does not matter in some senses, how some complex idea of light was rationalised. Complexity by the 'black art of obscurantism,' can be applied to many good things by gatekeepers of spirituality, often perhaps lacking 'capacity for light' themselves. Perennial interest in external light is partly shadow-play of our spiritual and psychic composition upon it. The idea that we are beings of light who should follow a path through vales of darkness and shadow of death to source of our being is an archetype. Apprehension of light in a spiritual sense is the way of spirit. Moving into light may open up dimensions of life that seem paranormal, extraordinary, extrasensory, supernatural and perhaps miraculous. To perceive one light we must recognise a contrast of darkness. A similar vein of light seems to underpin some forms of modern Satanism, the idea of the Illuminati, Luciferianism and arguably some senses of Prometheanism. So light per se is not clear and the mystic does not by it alone steer. Rather there are central ideas, like compassion which indicate why sadism or cruelty are wrong. The individual open to supernatural and supersensory reality of spiritual experience can easily be alienated by formidable forces hijacked for other ends. The danger of use of oligarchy to obtain effective enslavement is always present, always dark and light. Taoists would say that you cannot have one without the other. The Irish philosopher Eriugena in the 9th century famously wrote that, "All things that are, are lights." Or "All things that exist are light." With his phrase,

"Omnia quae sunt lumina sunt."

Dionysius said that the Divine was neither light nor dark and we should reach the domain of Divine darkness beyond light. The mystic path recognises light and darkness as part of an effort to spiritually evolve based on compassion and being creative to the community. The magician often is in love with power and wants to wield control using forces that do exist which the mystic declines. St. Augustine constrained light into the narrow Christian conception but proposed the necessity of divine illumination. This was accepted until it was undermined in the thirteenth century by naturalism. Augustine was influenced by Mani and was arguing for the reality of mystical light. The idea of descending light meeting ascending personal light permeates perennial philosophy. As the personal light originated in the higher light, it might be regarded as a cycle of light. Sometime the ring of eternal light might reflect this process. It is similar to the physical idea of the kundalini energy ascending to meet an existing or descending energy. Divine illumination links into the idea of the higher angelic double and even the daemon such as Socrates had. If a person receives guidance they think is divine how do they know? While certain Christians will deny all spirit connections, it makes religious texts they love to literally interpret appear strange. The Book filled with supernatural stories forbids any contemporary experiences of a similar nature as devilish even though the Church seems to regard such fallen angels as of divine source also.

    The great Chancellor of the University of Oxford Robert Grosseteste who was also a Bishop, teacher and writer and was at the signing of the Magna Carta wrote *De Luce* (On Light). This man who was described as the greatest mind of his day presented a metaphysics based on light. *Lux* was source light and *lumen* was reflected light. Light was the first corporeal form. The first light moved in every direction in a sphere from a point and in the outer regions was more dense and embedded in matter. The original light was spiritual. While it is difficult to make sense of his work entirely, it reflects the wider tradition. This idea of light was used as a unified idea of metaphysics and also knowledge and is described as Illuminationist. Elsewhere he seems to conceive of higher knowledge as an irradiation from a higher source which most people are unable to receive and thus can only rely on rational knowledge. Being heavy, dense and weighed down we cannot easily have access to the higher knowledge even if it is the form of our being. Reason may bring you through sense experience, observation and testing to that internal intelligibility that shines a light on the inner spiritual eye in the darkness just as the sun outside shines on the external body. Science has forgotten that it prospered on the back of work produced by people such as him that helped the development of scientific method not despite their religious background but because of it. The scientists of Oxford and so on also literally prospered in the buildings they robbed during the Reformation from the Church. This medieval, metaphysical investigation of light was part of the investigation of optics and the physical understanding of light. The science of light grew out of spiritual speculation, however much some scientists will seek to deny that origin. The divine conception of light and the inexplicable higher order ethereal aspects, sound suspiciously close to some of the discussions of invisible and dark matter in the universe, emphasising the disingenuous and false dichotomy propagated by some of the contemporary scientists who advocate scientism, often motivated by ideological factors unrelated to science. Grosseteste is seen to come in a stream from Neo-Platonism through the negative theology of Pseudo-Dionysius the Areopagite. This tradition underlies Dante and the Renaissance greats. Their work is about light and permeated with light.

Grosseteste was admired by Roger Bacon. Bacon is regarded by some as a founder of experimental science. He was also a monk, an alchemist and an occultist. These were not separate endeavours. The artificial fragmentation of knowledge and acute specialisation in contemporary times, makes it difficult for some to see how a religious man like Bacon would be one of the first in Europe to understand and perhaps know the significance of gunpowder and who might also have a brazen head or other such strange mechanical devices calculated to perform some uncanny role. That he might summon the devil or produce a mirror to predict the future was part of the endeavour. He too was interested in light. If you were curious about the phenomenon of light, it would be no surprise that you would be interested in substances that glow in the dark and create light. Some will argue that alchemists that contributed much to science, despite the great charlatanism which was often the reason for their persecution, are represented by the 'Prometheans' today. However the spiritual and mystical base of alchemy was a real and accepted one. Paracelsus was an alchemist and a very significant healer who claimed he could create a homunculus after using the magical 40 day phases buried first and then supplied with blood. It seems he grew reluctant to create beings without a soul, which was God's role. Thus there is some evidence of a spiritual restraint. Newton's connection with light is clear. His work with alchemy only came to light much later. The magic lay within matter. A key idea from the Gnostics and Persians through Paracelsus and alchemy was of the lumen naturae. The idea was that the divine being was manifest radiantly or rather trapped in matter. Liberation of the light that is in nature and matter was the essence of the quest. Alchemical symbolism proved to be a key to unlocking the unconscious. The psyche is dark and you seek the philosopher's stone and bring light or some higher golden values in ratio and representation. Self-transformation and transfiguration occurs in spirit sometimes strangely drawing on ancient recurrent symbols set into our consciousness, whether embedded within or accessible without, reflecting the search in the material world. Jung took this idea of the light in nature and saw it in an archetypal sense. He realised that the astute alchemists considered their work a mirror of their internal state and on their consciousness. Similarly scrying involves looking at certain surfaces, crystals, clouds, smoke, mirrors, water or fire. All is reflection, outside light to gain inner light. Light is crucial in the work of the magician John Dee and also Francis Bacon. In Bacon's work *New Atlantis*, the basis for a scientocracy perhaps, there is a miraculous pillar of light that appears. However it is also noteworthy that the learned controllers could also cause great illusions that were miraculous. The implication is that science may be able to use the mystery of technology to create the illusion of miracle.

Writers like Frances Yates have explored the significance of magic in the Renaissance and Reformation period. It is clear that ideas of light were critical to magic, mysticism and to people like Ficino, Mirandola, Bruno and Agrippa. Many roads seem to lead back to concepts of 'Egyptian light' that spread through the Neo-Platonists to Greece and Persia and beyond and informed the Kabbalists and all they influenced. Certain magi believed that Hermetic documents were older than they were and prefigured Christianity. Even for those who did not, they saw in Egypt a theology of light. Divine or super-celestial light is the highest light that permeates the universe and works as a fountain of light. Such light is in us but it must ascend and will do so if we realise that we are light in our physical form. When it ascends the Divine light may descend. There are creatures of light like the lion and flowers of light like the lupin. The celestial light or star light affects us and we must use such powers to our advantage to return to the higher light. Bruno and Agrippa seemed to promote use of demons in their hierarchy and that went over a line the Church and other magicians like John Dee would not. Whilst the Christian magus would seek to employ angels most would not entertain the idea of engagement with demons. For some such engagement was actual in a real way, for others it was imaginal in a fashion Jung would understand. Egyptian light seems to be the foundation of many concepts of divine magic and mysticism. Other forms of natural magic were inferior to divine magic which is most akin to mysticism. It is clear that Bruno saw inner light as a spiritual phenomenon through which the Divine operated and is thus clearly in the mystical domain. It may be that Bruno was trying to say what Jung was seeking to. It is worth remembering that the nature of an exorcism in the Catholic Church seems to involve a recognition and engagement with demons whether one wants to consider that as actual or notional. One idea that enabled Christians to engage with such things was because of a trust in the authority of the office of such people and the inherent belief in the superior force of Jesus to counteract such evil forces. Jung also looked back to Paracelsus who criticised the scholars and medical practitioners and had profound insights through a type of magic marshalled by compassion utilising 'the light of the Holy Spirit.'

In certain esoteric schools Gnostic, Kabbalah, Hindu and in Christian mystic tradition up to Philip K. Dick there recurs a sense of a beam or a pillar of light that directly links the individual to the divine. Nevertheless, whether one believes that this is a simulated, constructed matrix or is created by one Divine being or emanating from a superior or original energy or consciousness, the possibility of accord or connection thereto through the medium of light recur. A key biological link between light and esoteric practices and spirituality may be the pineal gland. The third eye represents the spiritual eye and the sixth sense and ability to perceive in an enhanced way. The use of entheogens, psychedelic drugs and hallucinogens seem to interact with certain neurological functions, often paradoxically through suppression to activate altered states. Intense light experiences and entheogens are linked. In addition, Stanislav Grof described the use of strobe lighting in conjunction with his consumption of LSD. Mystics more often seek to open their spiritual eyes through mental and breathing techniques associated with recognition of higher forces and through the use of discipline and focus. However I think most mystics would and should be sceptical about being reductionist and simplistic in the way necessary for science to comprehend. If it is possible to say see with the skin or to see in a microscopic or macroscopic way and that knowledge has been obscured, it is unlikely that it will be revived if it begins with incredulous observers. Scientists are very sceptical about claims of relevance of minimal presence of DMT in the pineal gland or elsewhere. Many of these attempts will involve straw men, red herrings and wild goose chases. There is evidence from reconstruction from regularly occurring fragments that should assist a person on a spiritual path. The scientist may help but they are often openly hostile about the possibilities. While the true mystic and spiritually advanced person should be promoting peaceful strategies and practices characterised by their contribution to the promotion and projection of harmony, tranquillity and healing in people and nature, the scientist has no commitment to such general goals. Indeed scientism seems to see cultivation and construction of a culture of general doubt, beyond its clear utility in application of scientific method, as critical and often inherently in opposition to the values long seen to be optimum goals for genuine spiritual evolution of humankind. Scientism rushes headlong into a future dictated by unpredictable and volatile interaction of forces unleashed by a myriad of scientific and commercial forces driven by specific self-interest, without self-imposed constraints and facilitated by captured institutions and monopolies whereby damage can be attributed to externalities and consequences carried by other people. Mystics and spiritual people who are literate, informed intellectually, rational and disciplined, aware of logic and argumentation, knowledgeable about science and art, humble before the ocean of uncertainty and pragmatic and cosmopolitan in their respect for the views of others, should adapt intelligently to opportunities to enhance and clarify ancient practices empirically evolved and applied by them. Antipathy to scientism is not antipathy to science. Ramanujans of the future may save us because they can thrive in symbolic and spiritual worlds. Concepts such as astral light may be unifying for some. Looking at spiritually evolved people like Nicholas Roerich, we see that light permeates their worldview and work. For him the heart was *'The Realm of Light.'* Think yin-yang symbol. If the light side is the seed of darkness, the original sin for some, the capacity for evil is in all. In the dark side is the seed of light, the divine source, capable of transformative power through cultivation, care and contemplation. Just as with exclusive claims of science or religion, spirituality will shrivel if it asserts exclusivity that eviscerates exploration by others. Spiritual and physical light and their absence, provides a universal, perennial spiritual system for the individual. There is a clear stream of evidence suggesting there was some perennial and pervasive notion of divine light of which our sun was merely a symbol, reflection or copy as a second God and that such divine light was diffused in nature and resident in us. Such a comprehensive doctrine might look like panpsychism or panprotopsychism with mystical possibilities but offered a unified view that splintered for various reasons.

Anthropological method that utilise insights from science may point to the comprehension that mystics have long realised. Nicholson has written about the phenomenon of light in shamanic practices. He points out in a paper on *Light Visions, Shaman Control Fantasies and the Creation of Myths* that light-induced visions are easily induced. This refers to internally-generated light symbols or entoptic images or what I call internal visible light. In hunter-gatherer societies these light visions will be associated with their myths and otherworld. As societies become more complex, the light visions are associated with more complex doctrines involving the gods and are assimilated into religious practice with less emphasis on the experience. There are common visions such as receding green rings, white flashes or white light. Such universal images are induced through sensory overload, meditation or self-hypnosis and extended meditation with 'paroxysmal sensorimotor symptoms.' The peacock's feather with blue and green, similar to the Quetzal feather is a common image. He suggests the induction of such images re-inforce and create myths. He traces shamanic light induction and experience in various groups such as the San Bushmen in South Africa, the Dani of New Guinea and Australian Aborigines. It is manifest in more complex ways in the Rig Veda, Shangqing school of Taoism, Tibetan Buddhism Highest Yoga Tantra and in Mayan and Tukano myths. His work indicates a universal phenomenon based on physiology that originally derived from repeatability of subjective experience. There is a portal to light within us, obscured by religion and priesthoods so experience is diminished or lost. In my view, light visions and the inevitable magical, mystical, ecstatic, integrative, revelatory domain recur due to the nature of individual spiritual consciousness as evolved and calculated to continue to evolve in an organic way as part of a wider consciousness of which it is a fractal, if it is allowed to. However, the physiological basis of the phenomenon that has spiritual consequences or is part of a spiritual or mythic journey should not be reduced to explicable glitterings because that is merely the outward dimension of the thing and not the thing itself. One final thinker whose journey in light should be recalled briefly is Goethe. He has something to say still.

Goethe was a great intellectual whose light has been eclipsed somewhat. He was the great German writer, poet, statesman and polymath. He studied and practised law for a while. As well as his literary output he engaged in scientific discourse on plants and light. Goethe was seen to be a Romantic by some but he seemed to change direction away from that movement and was clearly against it, subject to the caveat of the slipperiness of the term. The issue that is claimed to interest him particularly is the relationship between the subject and object in the context of nature. He brings some female characters to the fore alike Shakespeare's Miranda and ultimately as a superior calming intermediary suggestive of a lost goddess. His great work was the play *Faust* of 1808 which follows on the theme of Faustus based on Marlowe's *Faustus* of 1588. Mephistopheles bets with God in heaven that he can lead Faust, a favourite son, on the path of knowledge away from the good path. Faust the rationalist has become a magician and attracts spirits who still do not satisfy him. Faust enters into a pact with the demon and signs it in blood. What follows is a tale of temptation, demonic magic and the consequences thereof including a black magical homunculus. Goethe indicates a reality about the nature of moral choice and the actual or psychic worldview of magic and conjuring. The line between the light of reason and the darkness of evil is obscured at times. Goethe dealt not only with ideas of spiritual darkness but also the phenomenon of light itself. He engaged in a major exploration of light and colour with his book of 1810 the *Theory of Colours*. There are a variety of legends about his last words supposedly about his calling for more light. There is much evidence of death bed light phenomena as normal dying experiences. Not religious, in his final year he stated that he would like to adhere to the elusive Hypsistarians. He was also a member of Weishaupt's Bavarian

Illuminati with an emphasis and the Freemasons. His greatest perception may be about the need to balance the rational with the intuitive and the suggestion that scientists should properly regard themselves as participants and not mere observers and understand the whole phenomenon which has greater value than the parts. He also used hypnagogic states. Light defined his life. He saw colour more in terms of light and shadow and his basic idea of polarity influences Steiner, Coleridge and Schopenhauer. His polarity theory seems more like the Taoist ideas of yin-yang to me. Darkness is not an absence of light but a pole like two ends of a magnet. His theory seems to work well when one considers strange ideas and manifestations such as black light. I suggest this polarity idea underlies his idea of good and evil.

It is clear that the careful study of hypnagogic and other ordinary or altered states, including images in the context of sensory deprivation and darkness, indicate a recurrent set of symbols and patterns. Cave art in Europe has a limited alphabet of symbols that are probably of this inherent physiological type. That the art appears in caves is a clue although such art also appears on large stones. Some of these symbols may also have significance through subsequent esoteric or mystical use. That we find a physical explanation for them is not the end of the matter. Psychic importance has practical consequences for people and society. There is also the possibility that the recurrence of such symbols is because they reflect intrinsic forms that are embedded in nature. Mystics go beyond the simple explanations of the mind that must tie things down. They can demonstrate evidence should they so desire that use or even awareness of such states can yield real-world results. When people like Einstein, Swedenborg, Poe, Wagner, Dickens and Dali used hypnagogic states we can assume there is more to this than meets the eye of the scientist however diligent. The states that occur on waking up and falling asleep contain powerful potential to add to meditation and to achieve new levels of awareness as is known in the Buddhist tradition for example. Mavromatis has charted these states and indicated the range of visual possibilities including the recurrent green, purple, gold, silver, wheels, lines, faces beings, lines and endlessly on. These seem to reflect both light deprived symbols and those from shamanic traditions, perhaps coming from the oldest parts of the brain or the unconscious. Mavromatis speculates about the pineal gland which in Europe was studied from Herophilos to Descartes and in the East as the third eye. He points out how the pineal gland is extremely old from a phylogenetic perspective, how it is characterised by photosensitivity and how it still plays a crucial role in the physical regulation of our minds and bodies through its role in processing light. It regulates glands as a 'neuroendocrine transducer' and produces melatonin. Thus the 'seat of the soul' as it was known, the third eye, does deal with light and I would suggest with spiritual light. The pineal gland plays a part in meditation and detachment and in some practices in Taoism and Tantra receives energy redirected from the base which the pineal is intimately connected with. Mavromatis links the pineal gland or cone to the symbol of the caduceus, the symbol of liberated consciousness. One can also see cone symbolism in the Vatican. He writes,

> "The pineal gland appears to occupy the exact anatomical position of what in the Vedic literature is thought to be the 'organ' of spiritual vision, the 'third eye.' In the same tradition, it is believed that spiritual vision, which was originally readily available to man, is 'temporarily' (for some millions of years, that is) lost due to an evolutionally necessary descent into matter, to be regained in due course at a higher level. In the West, this latter level is often represented by the god Hermes's sceptre, the caduceus, depicting two snakes around a central rod which culminates in a small sphere or cone flanked by two wings."

He is on the right track. Whether you want to see kundalini energy rising or represent self-transcendence and creation of nexus to the numinous which opens consciousness to real reality beyond the illusion of this particular matterifestation, it is an important symbol. Furthermore, these symbols represent physical and spiritual reality. Notice again how the inner eye has become constrained such that function is limited because of 'descent into matter.' Here again is an idea of trapped light. Part of the mystery is why we would have lost some ability and how? On this view, the mystery is not that of lost meaning but lost abilities as well as inherent limitations of matter. These are the abilities that mystics claim is part of their nature and of all, but vulnerable. Some claim fluoride impedes the pineal gland. Others claim that not walking on the ground barefoot disturbs us. I do know that we are being distanced from nature, surrounded by technology, becoming cyborgs, being constantly monitored and that we are close to the death or devolution of the spirit. Nevertheless, whatever our opinions, it is clear that light is the most pervasive force in our existence and while there may seem to be great fragmentation between spiritual paths and personal experiences, there is an underlying unity based on the perception of light as our divine origin, direction and nature as manifested in profound majesty in many intellectual and mystical traditions. Huxley mentions the 'preternatural light' of drug-induced states that are described in terms of pronounced luminosity with greens and purples and crystalline feel. He notes the parallel with revelatory visions in religious and mystical texts. He also notes how the proliferation of artificial light obscures other perception of light. Writers like Bynum focus on the dark, neural substance of neuromelanin which is critical for the operation of melanin, which is sensitive to light and also magnetism.

All these might be reconciled in terms of the idea of a vision. We may have vision but may experience visions. A vision tends to refer to an apprehension with imagery of something profound which goes beyond the mere physical and may be more of the imaginal realm. Such visions may create awe that transforms. The extrinsic and mechanical may overawe the senses but it is vision of spirit with inner eyes and perhaps external eyes which matter. Such visions may inform the vision in the sense of desired direction which determines our destiny. History is the result of vision and visions and they may be destructive or creative. We are easily hypnotised by light visions of others with falsehoods and thus easily trapped thereby too. Manly Hall in *Secret Teachings of all Ages* looked at many things and especially light. He examines legends of sun worship in Atlantis, mentions sun-worship and promotion of light in

Druidry, the worship of sun and light in Mithraism, Serapis, Balder in the Odinic cult, luminosity of the Divine in the Eleusinian mysteries. He dwells on the Hermetic tradition and the Light of Egypt, the Master of the Light, the idea that light was spirit with a Voice of the Light which formed the Waters of Light. Divine light is in us and ascends. Divine Light created Universal Man that came into matter. There are celestial powers of light. The Divine Light or White Light is where humans should return to because of the revelation to the Son of Light. The sun and moon emerge in the cult of Isis. He looks at sun worship as being the symbol of light and manifest in figures such as Solomon. All over the Middle East, America and Europe we find sun-worship which really represented light emerging in many esoteric doctrines, sometimes as the midnight sun. He talks of the ever-burning lamps sealed into tombs to help cross the Valley of the Shadow. Light arises in Masonry and with Pythagoras especially in relation to colour. The phoenix was a sun symbol as was the lion, the bull who also was symbolised by lightning. Hall examines Lucifer's radiant green jewel that shines in the abyss, crystal balls, meteors, the light in Kabbalah, alchemical and Rosicrucian texts. In the end he concludes *Secret Teachings of All Ages* thus and it is clear how important all the light has been.

> "The criers of the Mysteries speak again, bidding all men welcome to the House of Light. The great institution of materiality has failed. The false civilization built by man has turned, and like the monster of Frankenstein, is destroying its creator. Religion wanders aimlessly in the maze of theological speculation. Science batters itself impotently against the barriers of the unknown. Only transcendental philosophy knows the path. Only the illumined reason can carry the understanding part of man upward to the light."

Juxtaposition of the eco-feminist theologian Ruether, still a Catholic, who claims the light theology is a big lie against Manly Hall who understands the secret teaching of all ages, may indicate the former not to be a mystic. However her analysis of that institution seems correct in terms of it and Judeo-Christian religions. Exclusion of the Divine and living goddess has caused irreparable damage. Mystic experience informed by goddesses will do more benefit. Whatever way it happens, we are here and meant to be here, meant to adapt without devitalisation and it is difficult to see the benefit of leaving the planet and other people to be devoured while we exclusively save our souls or seek some escape through tricks to tame the mind with philosophy of projected illusion or materialism. Spiritual light exists as a description of our consciousness and how it evolves in relation to other higher, cosmic or Divine forces. The process of evolution involves a perennially consistent range of stages of unfolding of spirit suggestive of an inherent natural path. What is termed 'dogma' dismissively by many is a principle of compassion and sense of inter-relationship or unity which mystics perceive as a law of the universe. Sacrifice of that goal brings the mysterious, arcane or esoteric into a lower type of magic below the Divine sort for many mystics. Arthur C. Clarke wrote that any sufficiently developed technology was indistinguishable from magic. He was sceptical about saying things were impossible. Mystics seek to pass by magic and technology to the impossible domain as ultimate destination on the basis that we have divine potential with great gifts we squander and fail to develop and use. There are two types of magic, I suggest we distinguish. Sorcery is the use of magic technology for selfish, ego, personal power or control of others, utilising evil spirits or intentions outside, or in people, to achieve objectives. This dark magic could include the *Lichtdom*, bearing in mind the disposition of many Nazis to the occult. This is distinguished from two other forms of traditional magic that are really similar and should be rolled into one, namely Divine and natural magic. *Divine light magic uses commitment to community and the highest consciousness to enlist the light of nature and spirits, usually benign for creative, care and compassionate aims.* This was what Paracelsus was about. However, the latter may become sorcery. That is why mysticism avoids it and why James was rebuked by Jesus for wanting to bring fire down from heaven as punishment.

1.16 Trapped in Matter of Mystery

The great scientist Robert Hooke in his book *Micrographia* in 1665, used microscopic tools to present a new world made available through technology of seeing on a small scale. He coined the term 'cell' on the basis of the appearance of a cross section of cork. They looked like the small rooms monks stayed in or prisoners today. So the word cell is directly related to life, science, spirituality and imprisonment. Indeed the cork is also light in the other sense. But note that the cell itself is about trapping or structuring life or spirit. There is also plenty of research about the role of light in relation to cells, such as in the process of communication. All life in scientific and spiritual terms is about containment of force in structure or in form of cells. In form, inform, in cells, in matter. Most have cell phones now. Perhaps these cells are the basis of the AI biomorph of IT?

If you see spirit as trapped in matter, it is a major mistake to hate the containing form. If the spiritual person has less respect for the body than someone fully accepting the theory of evolution then the latter will triumph. Certain Gnostics for example were wary of matter and in many cases sought to control rather than avoid it through magic. In Buddhism and Christ, goodness is based on certain constraints. Matter in this sense usually represents the body, flesh or organic home. Matter, as mentioned before, is related to the word Latin 'mater' which is mother and material. Ironically materialism devastates the formerly maternal earth. In many cultures, the mother goddess is mythically dismembered to create life, in ours it is actually happening. Matter must have a definition as it is a difficult concept in the light of scientific developments on the frontiers. In practical terms it tends to be used to indicate solidity and fixity. But solidity is regarded as an illusion to many scientists, philosophers and mystics. All solid forms dissolve and are really appearances or forms as Prospero explained. He understands what cannot be wrought by the powerful will and mind and what needs to be seen with the eye of the heart as Miranda and Ariel inform his power. The only solid ground is that there is no solid ground. Intense specialisations of scientists shed light on realities beyond direct sensory apprehension and cause speculation more mysterious than mystics might. When we ask simple questions such as whether light is matter we receive many answers. While lack of mass of photons suggests an answer, complexity of energy allows different interpretations. Scientists can create matter from bombarding photons together (originally using gold unsurprisingly). When science goes to the most particulate it seems to rediscover the field. In magical and mystical terms the significance of matter tended to be based on the degree to which it was infused with the energy of spirit. Energy is not matter nor space nor time to most. But the frontier of science seems to deny fixity to even these concepts. Tesla saw that all perceptible matter came from a primary substance beyond conception consistent with the ancient Indian idea. But if one looks closely at spiritual traditions they suggest matter cannot be inherently bad because it is an emanation from Divine or universal consciousness. Thus our intention is more relevant. That is why 'thoughts are things' in a number of senses. In parapsychology and the study of materialisation for example, the line between the material and immaterial is claimed to be more flexible than we can imagine.

Matter is a noun and a verb. Material is material to our discussion. How does immaterial fit in matter? Things cause things? There are a number of views about the significance of matter. One view is that there is nothing but matter, even if we have not discovered it fully. Another view accepts matter but emphasises the significance of immaterial forces. Another view ignores the significance of matter and emphasises the predominance of immaterial and mental forces. Some philosophers seek or find a synthesis and many admit the extent of the inexplicable and some understand the possibility that all could be re-conceived. Then there seem to be particles that might behave like light as well as dark matter. Similarly colour is an optical effect and even light and shadow can be manipulated by ambient light to appear differently. Arthur Young saw consciousness as descending from photons into the smallest particles, atoms and molecules until it ascends again to freedom. The descent leads to fixity, restriction and structure that yields to movement from crystals to plants, animals, us and onwards. Thus Young in *The Reflexive Universe* sought to provide a scientific analysis that complemented mystical and esoteric analysis of natural and spiritual evolution. He seems to have anticipated the role of DNA-emitted light and superconductivity thereof as people like Pelletier point out. The photon is beyond time and space and Pelletier emphasises how spirits may be described as 'points of light.'

Science, technology and transhumanism may seek to fix this process of natural evolution in matter by turning us fully into machine. Philosophers like Chalmers seem to be seeking to synthesise materialism and consciousness by proposing a proto-consciousness in matter. Such approaches are admirable but seem to lead to a worldview that echo earlier magical and mystical perspectives without the spiritual evolution that caused them. Esoteric subtle matter is of a nature unknown to science and probably unfamiliar to many spiritual people. In some spiritual traditions, evil itself was a substance. Concepts of transcendence or imminence of spiritual forces may be attached in some form to an intellectual position that starts off in any of those three tendencies with more in the third and less or none in the first. These starting points may explain the extent to which a person may conceive or believe that we might be trapped in matter or not. Thus for example Crowley and Tantric practitioners will view embodiment more positively than the Cathars and Gnostics. Cathars saw spirit trapped in matter that required liberation through a detachment that echoed Buddhist ideas and this doctrine led to their persecution by an established church heavily invested in the mundane, saw incarnation as part of the Divine plan and did not tolerate the idea that Divine spirit was accessible to all. Bogomils in South Eastern Europe were heavily influenced by a deep sense that we are spirits in matter. Antinomian tantrics may embrace techniques of recognition and realisation through matter to approach the immaterial. Similarly there was a different emphasis within Egypt, if one identified with Horus or Set or Horus rather than Osiris. Darkness may also be associated with heaviness for some. If you are a materialist, matter matters above all and consciousness is a messy problem. Plotinus focused on the immaterial nature of the universe, prefiguring the

Idealist viewpoint, but it is a mistake to think he rejected reality and he was critical of some types of ancient Gnosticism. He was influenced by India and Persia and shares a view of a transcendent force beyond all that underpins strategies of transcendental meditation.

Magic has been essentially about drawing down of powers of spirit into matter. Thus a magician in Egypt was believed to be able to draw down power into an obelisk or statue. The magus would be able to guide the power of heavens and stars. Outside these conceptions is widespread sympathetic magic that looks at correspondences and similarities and seeks to utilise such connections to exert energy in a way the sounds like quantum entanglement to some. Again we see the idea of spirit being trapped in matter. Control and containment of such motion gave magical powers that enabled some to do divine work and others to aspire to be godlike. The disposition to science to control rather than comprehend is more magician's path than mystic although they were united in the past. The extrinsic and material may be more of the magician's domain whereas the intrinsic and subtle may be the mystic's.

In parapsychology, the study of psychokinesis and telekinesis deals with effects of mind on matter and physical systems. The Ted Owens study in *The PK Man* investigates the mystery of interaction of mind and matter. Magic imputes similar effects. When I read the *PK Man* it looked like Owens was a classic magician. When I read a description of his technique combined with his communication with 'Space Intelligences' it is clear that he could fit into the Divine magus type of Bruno. However, absent purification of personality and suppression of ego or a community, such activity threatens to become its opposite. That is why it can cross into 'black magic.' Such is not the mystic path. Owens might have been a failed prophet attempting to use divine light magic. Ego is the warning for Prospero. Another arguably successful fictional example written in 1962 is *The Magic Finger*, by Roald Dahl. The magic pointing figure was used to stop the shooting of ducks. Dahl was clearly interested in psychic powers.

There is a long tradition in esoteric and exoteric sources to the effect that creation involves animating matter with spirit. The Greek mysteries indicate the descent of higher spirit into nature through symbols such as corn being a tangible agriculture good deriving from Ceres or Demeter, whose daughter Persephone (Prosperine) descended into the underworld. Breath of life or energy of earth or both are given to dust, clay or fine earth. Without divine intervention a clay-being may not function and even then there may have to be some incarnation of divinity to remind us of our origins beyond mere earth. There is a curious link between the occurrence of the story of Jesus and the birds in Islam, early Irish Christianity and documents that were not accepted into the Christian canon. This involves Jesus giving life to clay birds. The stories of the golem in Jewish history reflect an old idea that God made mankind from clay. In esoteric circles this justified attempts to produce golems, which later became linked to magic. The golem archetype echoes the Frankenstein monster story to some extent and maybe the Talos or Bacon's Brazen Head. Mystics see these creations as mystical events similar to the ideas of the tulpa, homunculus and clone creation. Genuine mystical interest in golems is hard to imagine today because of the links with ego although medieval mystics and magician were much more cosmopolitan in their experimentation. Similarly the darker reaches of Buddhism infused with native traditions have been ignored as part of a certain elevation of Eastern practices sometimes perceived as necessary counter-balances to the Western canon perhaps as part of the continued Romantic influence. However the idea that matter was infused with spirit is an ancient and persistent one and such infusion involves something like light. Similarly with the Philosopher's Stone in alchemy there was a movement from blackness or darkness to whiteness or light which proceeded to yellowness, redness or goldness. Again, something higher could come from lower matter through infusion. Esoteric thinking has spirit descending into flesh and then arising. Buddhist paths were influenced by antinomian graftings through certain types of Tantra in Vajrayana. Paganism and Neo-Paganism seem more attuned with the physical world in some ways and represented a return or recursion of ancient pre-Christian practices and attitudes of

Ireland and Britain in particular through Druidism and Wicca. It is also true that the Catholic Church as an institution became obsessed with the material and in the eyes of the Cathars and others were missing the point. Scientific and Promethean thinking sometimes has the lower person solely ascending by material means. But what matters most?

Mystics say there is light in us. We are light of consciousness. We should perceive that state. We have a number of eyes. We have an inner eye that sees inner light. Consciousness is a sort of light. They say that we should uncover the lamp within. This light circulates and animates spirit. The eye sees through senses. The eye of reason assesses the world we interact with. The inner eye sees light within and without and is the important one. Thus it might be argued that the theme of light is a unifying one. If we look at science we begin to see light as one of the ultimate mysteries. Looking at exploration of light we see achievements of science and become aware of what is known. But we should be aware of dangers resulting from science and technology but more particularly from scientism. Without resorting to pseudo-science we can extract many inspirations from science. But the great mystery of life, the cosmos and our place in it is the recurrent preoccupation of mystics. Mystics stress the need to go inwards. They stress the inner eye, the need to distinguish between illusion and reality and the need to wake up. They stress the need to find our true self and the need to remember who we are. They stress the ubiquity of consciousness that insufflates into us often with the notion of light. Reflecting on light we begin to comprehend and poetic insight may lift mind from mortal and mundane to allow advancement.

Within esoteric movements there is great discussion of the nature of subtle energy and matter, sometimes intended to make spirit matters scientific. Campbell talks about Non Physical Matter Reality. Philosophers are stretching and torturing us with concepts. Scientists search vainly for emergent consciousness. Some philosophers seem to be coming back to a pale animism with longer names pretending they discovered something. All these efforts represent a major failure to replace the idea of spirit and concoct an adequate, persuasive substitute. The light of the Enlightenment has not displaced the light of enlightenment. If spiritual consciousness represents the highest force in the universe and is divinely inspired, evolved or emerged, it seems strange to insist on denial because it does not fit into a scientific paradigm. Mystics say the world exists but is illusory to a large extent in terms of the universe's spiritual nature. That is no recipe for moral relativism because they also indicate that our spiritual destiny is to evolve in a compassionate, creative way. The debate about psychokinesis, precognition, life after death and synchronicity might all come under the domain of 'manifesting' or some other broader perspective which we cannot comprehend according to Jeffrey Mishlove. This is consistent with the mystical view of human powers. We are consciousness, spiritual consciousness, spirit. This is spiritual light, part of cosmic or Divine consciousness. This light-consciousness is force to be activated, used and channelled. While quantum physics might assist the case, it is not constitutive of that always there. Remember that Wallace, the joint originator of the theory of evolution, believed that willpower might be the immaterial substance that drove the universe. Spiritual light may represent higher dimensional nexus of physical light in lower dimensions and in form appropriate to a higher dimension or space and investigation of subjective parapsychological evidence could be the convex that links the concave of theoretical physics providing evidence from the former for theories from the latter. The great scientists who engaged in psychic research, like Lodge and Barrett, were also very interested in ether. They had connections with scientists like the Irish-born Larmor who wrote *Aether and Matter* in 1900. Another Irish colleague, FitzGerald, who was interested in ether and light, made contributions that helped Einstein's theory of Special Relativity. He anticipated the Schumann Resonance and appreciated the conducting power of the upper atmosphere. The light phenomena in the upper atmosphere are called Transient Luminous Events which may involve some form of plasma. These phenomena have curious names such as ELVES, Pixies, Trolls, Gnomes. The fairyland ethos is not as silly as one might think. The mysterious and remarkable phenomena of light invite our curiosity like supernatural beings and when we pursue them perhaps to the importance of plasma, we will find another piece of the puzzle. Follow the bliss and beauty of light to its source. From that ether era also in Ireland, significant spiritual seekers like William Quan Judge and Charles Johnston emerged. Johnston worked in the British Colonial service and translated many significant Oriental texts and brought them to an English-speaking audience.

1.17 Mystery Schools

The mystery of matter intrigues scientists. Solidity and predictability posited by the mechanistic, clockwork universe has been undermined by quantum theory and sub-atomic strangeness where unanticipated players such as consciousness or participation make simple statements more difficult. Light and matter interaction is the essence of quantum electrodynamics (QED). That domain was arguably poetically anticipated by mystics. Quantum entanglement seems to make explanations from parapsychology more plausible. Intuitions of instantaneity that refute Einstein's light-speed limitation seem more reasonable. Perhaps psychometry even looks less incomprehensible. Dark matter and anti-matter open up vistas that stretch credulity more than some descriptions of astral light, ridiculed by people content with explanations that seemed to represent the zenith of progressive thought. But there is growing awareness that science is lost on some of the biggest questions, such as consciousness. Following on from Russell and Eddington, people like Goff emphasise a point that is obvious to many. Physical sciences deal with behaviour of matter and prediction and nature thereof. What is omitted is any comprehension of inherent qualitative dimensions. We know consciousness, we are conscious and scientists can only seek to establish correlations and chemical reactions. Worse than that, they have promoted a crude behaviourist model through cybernetics and extrapolation to social 'sciences.' I fear it is much worse than finding a solution to the 'hard problem of consciousness.' Scientism and science itself may seek to find a Procrustean solution by applying science to controlling humans through surveillance, control and manipulation thereby creating conditions to allow them confidently assert as scientific dogma that free will and consciousness does not exist and there is no real impediment to technological enhancement. Consciousness does not fit in the model so they will make us fit in the model instead. In a way it does not matter whether it is Aristotle, Galileo, Newton or Descartes that one seeks to trace responsibility to. They are long dead and we must see what is happening now giving them credit for their achievements. People like Sheldrake or Wolf seem closer to it when talking of immaterial fields to add to complex planes. Fred Alan Wolf is a scientist-shaman who describes us as light with matter being an illusion. Scientists like Brian Josephson will be seen to be nearer the truth in the future. On the frontier, certain scientists such as Seth Lloyd are emphasising information as more fundamental than matter and energy. Bits, pixels, quantity, amounts, measuring, processing is computation without meaning but the unappeasable god of information. Welcome to the Infogod. Tononi seeks to apply mathematics to explain consciousness. I would caution spiritually evolved beings to avoid resorting to pseudo-science or seek consilience with science that will inevitably make spirit slave. Mystics are clear that spirit is at the top of the inner pyramid. We should also consider that some UFO and alien theorists have asserted that we are dealing with a class of trans-dimensional beings and that our present state of material classification is inadequate to comprehend their nature. Those who have had alien encounters often have experiences similar to mystical events. John C. Lilly was a modern mystic who studied consciousness, interacted with entities and was celebrated for his work with dolphins and also developed the flotation tank. It is worth bearing in mind that he predicted nearly a half century ago a 'solid state entity' that was emerging from computational power into a bioform that would control humanity, forcing them into reservations and destroying the environment.

While some see us as spirit trapped in matter, there is a more standard spiritual view which suggests we are in a dense and difficult medium, but the existence should not be conceived in a way that fails to appreciate the magnificence thereof. We need to function in whatever reality. In that sense, the spiritually aware or even classically curious scientists have a role to play in promoting wonder with humility. From a spiritual perspective we witness a disenchanting, exploitative, object-orientated view of matter. Great accomplishments of technology manipulate nature. Wholeness of a beautiful habitat may be easily sacrificed to hatchet, scalpel or blade mind of materialist focused mind-sets. Material and matter are both etymologically related to the word mother. Exploitation of matter is related to forgetting ancient spiritual traditions of the goddess in matter. Earth is our mother and as we emerge from mother or matter into light so do we emerge from matter in spirit. Matter is wonderful home allowing spiritual evolution. Just as materialists may get the balance wrong, so may extreme spiritual positions. Both may contribute to creating a failed worldview which does not respect nature. Although many disagree, some Kabbalists (like Luria) seek redemption of the Shekhinah representing indwelling or embodiment of God or feminine or Holy Spirit or maybe Shakti. In all this, consciousness is fundamental and inherently capable of transcendence given spiritual evolution. Quantum biology may corroborate what mystics have said for thousands of years. Esoteric traditions and magic suggest a mastery of matter as does mysticism. Mysticism in its widest sense sees a range of spirits or entities existing under ultimate consciousness that informs the material world. All esoteric traditions have an idea of transformation of matter, self and spirit.

Now the option of sitting on the fence with the comfortable notion that we are objective observers and not active participants is gone. Time for moral cowardice masquerading as enlightenment is over. The mystic view really sees perception as an infinity symbol ∞ a figure whereby the outside crosses into a huge internal and whereby the external-internal, subjective-objective is really a state of flux where matter and mind, spirit and matter flow magically. Exclusive focus on matter is receding with quantum sciences appreciating the nature of the united field we exist in. But as the pre-Socratic philosophers indicated, mystic apprehension of the world requires that we are aware, engage, appreciate matter, form, things and senses as part of being embodied and located in the world. Light trapped may be released, expanded, extended, grown, circulated, shone, applied, cycled, re-cycled or moved. Some of the apparently enlightened scientific theories such as 'conscious agents' of Donald Hoffman may work very well but leave humanity without essential dignity in a new mechanical tree of life.

Science has clarified its visions with changing ways of seeing. The telescope was critical in seeing stars, galaxies anticipating other universes. Microscopes brought us down. The weak and strong forces inform the small and the large. Other devices like colliders help search for smaller particles. The Divine is being prepared for substitution. We celebrate when scientists find 'the God particle.' A Grand Unified Theory will explain the interaction of forces. GUT is near enough to good and GOD. The M-Theory will unify superstring theory. The M will be able to represent Mystery or Magic or Matrix or Mother Goddess. There we will have the outline of the new religion of scientism based on physics ready to replace any existing monotheistic competitors if needed. This will justify objectives, bring back eugenics and impose transhumanism. Pesky notions of free will, individualism and spirit can be sacrificed to the new gods of science. A new version of history is easy to write these days. Then the I Can't Believe It's Not God phase is fixed. If the remainder of God is dismembered and dismantled after the previous announcement of God's demise, there is little hope for spirit. But it will not matter for individual consciousness is on the way out anyway.

Mystery of matter brings one to 'mystery schools' and traditions which informed esoteric and spiritual groups that had strong anti-materialist conceptions including Orphics who had a similar sense of spirit trapped in matter. Mystery schools were associated with initiatory, mystical tradition to various degrees. Etymology of the word 'mystery' is debated but the idea of concealment and being out of sight associated with initiation is a recurrent one. People do not know exactly what went on as an element of obscurity is associated with all such mystery, but there were a range of experiences. Some schools had associations with a wide range of arts, skills and knowledge. Some were complementary to other religious practices or oppositional at times. Often the school was associated with a particular god who would inform or become embodied in initiates or participants through plays, parties, partaking or possession. Preparation and purification were involved. Examples in Mediterranean tradition included the Dionysian, Orphic, Eleusinian, Hermetic and Pythagorean. Then we might think of Apollo, Adonis, Bacchus, Osiris, Pallas, Sirius and Thamuz. Indian schools were also influential. Sun and light were critical elements. As the heavenly bodies had recurrence so would our spirit separate from the matter or body which contained it. The notion of darkness, confinement, dismemberment, reconstitution and resurrection are suggested as ritual elements of such ceremonies. Taylor suggests that the Dionysian ceremonial dismemberment represents a depiction of descent into matter. The shamanic dismemberment may represent the opposite side of that coin, whereby the notional body of the shaman is dismembered so that the spirit body can be freed. Thus the experience of dismemberment could be the liminal representation of boundary-crossing. The process of dismemberment can be seen in mythology of Native Americas in relation to the goddess who gives life. This spiritual experience is a dramatic representation of psychic perception of the de-armouring of defence mechanisms as the person discards a false persona. In the descent into the underworld we see a search for the path of light, awareness of possibilities of freeing spirit from matter and an awareness of breaking of cyclical conduct to evolve spiritually. The idea of possession by gods, such as through wine in relation to Dionysius and represented by physical, ecstatic union, reflects the deeper mystic idea of individual union with One and all. Wine was the mysterious, transmutable substance here. All mystery schools seemed to dramatically represent or portray the idea that the soul or spirit was descended into matter and if left in this prison would fail to evolve. Through dramatic re-enactment of myth and legend the individual or initiate could be re-born and experience the higher spirit of themselves and those beyond. In my view this represents externally the psychic path of mystic integration suggested to be the inherent nature of spiritual evolution available within us all.

However the true mystery schools should be unknown in some senses. At various times a paradoxical idea of a more public performance of a dramatic version of a mystery in a play was performed in England and Spain particularly associated with powerful guilds. Freemasonry and its inspirations seem to emphasise sun, stars and the play of death of the individual as a representation of the sun's arc, death and rebirth. Circumambulation reflected the sun's journey, emphasising light. The idea of geometry, sacred art and proportions from Pythagoras onwards as part of a 'Greek Cabala' anticipating Christ, aware of astronomy that built great temples are held to this day by some. Elements of light, healing, increased awareness and unusual features such as ritual, notional dismemberment reflect an initiatory or standard element in shamanic experience and are archetypal and recurrent. Mystery schools probably expanded knowledge rather than hiding it, but insofar as it is an innate, intrinsic aspect of archetypal composition of us, such ideas and experiences will occur on a mystic path without being given. You have it already. Granted many need to be made aware. However guidance may be hard to find.

Ayahuasca, mescaline, peyote and psilocybin proponents might claim similar initiation today and suggest continuity. Certainly mushrooms look like one candidate of West European initiation. Whatever form such initiations took, there will often have been a journey to light from darkness with eyes shut or covered or ritual confinement. There would seem to be an ego death and the possible induction of an NDE or OBE calculated to address the cosmic mystery and indicate the immortal nature of soul or spirit. To some extent this emerges from shamanic or druidic cultures in Europe and cave paintings in France and Spain suggest a pattern of darkness and mystification. In certain contemporary magic or mystical associations these forms are re-created actually or through visualisations. Some initiations are for all and some for specialists. The idea of such initiation was most likely to invoke an archetype within although there has always been communication with various types of 'angelic' or alien beings. Not everyone should be a shaman, mystic or a holy person and they needed genuine powers of prophecy or healing. In my view, none of these traditions are constitutive of spiritual evolution. While they are calculated to accelerate, refine, concentrate and create communities that craft conditions likely to facilitate spiritual illumination they do not create spirit. Spirit is designed or evolved to unfold and grow and some communities facilitate that. Use of light, music, drumming, shock and awe, do not give spirit but they reflect it and allow individual experiential awareness of that infinite mystery for mortals mired in matter that may have forgotten who they are. Furthermore self-experimentation with spirits and entities and possession would be sacrificing sovereignty. Paradoxically perhaps people who criticise religion and celebrate mystery schools must be aware that critique of the former can be equally applied to the latter by individual mystics. Nevertheless mystery schools are very close to mysticism because they focus on experience of knowledge and demonstrate higher reality and persistence of spirit and as history shows, profoundly impact on people's worldview. It may be that of deeper significance was concentration on the goddess, great goddess, mother goddess or other manifestations like Persephone. But the real mystery of matter is how the deepest thinkers like Jung or Paracelsus realise that even the ones who seemed most invested in matter, like the alchemists, were studying consciousness. We cannot all live mystical lives but we must all work on our individuation and individual spiritual evolution and mystical thinkers on the path reveal some perennial insights. If primary material of our personal investigations and exploration of insight is not wholly our spiritual selves and then community, we will never beat swords into ploughshares and the burnished blades of military *materiel* produced from perverted psyche and psychopathic predilection for power posited on some pretext and informed by the misdirected might of science will dominate. Jung and later his student Marie-Louise von Franz posed the question about whether the unconscious projected potential comprehension of the material world because it was the same stuff or because it could contemplate such imaginative solutions. It seems light was a symbol of consciousness for him. For other mystics, it is even deeper. For Grosseteste and others, light was everything.

All mysticism recognises mystery. The idea of brain-as-filter suggests we could not deal with the volume of information in this heavy form we are trapped in. We can find the method of mystery in koan teaching in Zen. Likewise the Christian idea of transubstantiation is a complex symbolic idea of magic and theological mystery of transmuting matter. Benedict says the 'mystery of the cross' is based on a transformation of the New Testament of 'darkness and irrationality' because 'the great mystery has become radiant light.' Hayman wrote about Jung in reference to his analysis of the Mass in Catholicism.

> "Christianity's ultimate purpose, he said, was to democratise enlightenment about the self and the individuation process. Once this had been the prerogative of shamans and medicine men, later of physicians, prophets, priests and initiates of mystery cults."

Jung saw similarities in behaviour of Aztecs and a Gnostic alchemist Zosimus and his vision of steps of darkness and light. Jung was wary of science. He noticed also how many Catholics did not seem to need his services. As institutions falter, never has there been a greater need for individual spiritual evolution. But the road to wisdom or knowledge is a treacherous one. There is a trend towards magic or magick sometimes related to post-modernist deconstruction of reality. It is ironic that people claim that no one could have engaged in actions of occult evil intent during the Witchcraft persecutions while there is evidence of increased advocating of actions with evil intent or hexing. Unlike Goethe's interpretation, Marlowe has a real Lucifer with whom Doctor Faustus makes a pact. Seeking powers of occult magic and engaged in necromancy, tired with all the sciences he goes to hell. One may regard such stories as idle entertainment, with no basis in reality save in an archetypal (and some believe a Promethean sense) and wonder at the story of actual demons appearing on stage during performances. Nevertheless the great magician John Dee was careful only to deal with angels and Roger Bacon would distinguish magic and demon-conjuring. One can interpret such stories on a symbolic, psychic or psychological level as Jung did or as actual possibilities. Such archetypes indicate the need for a moral compass such as compassion or ahimsa based on inherent unity of consciousness. There is a dividing line between mystic and magician, theurgy and tricksters. It is a mistake to believe that clever, scholastic discourse takes away universal karma or justice linked to consequences of behaviour. While I advocate an individual pursuit of spiritual evolution with whatever teaching and tradition one has available or on one's own, it is a mistake to deconstruct the idea of care, compassion, healing, mercy, forgiveness or indeed responsibility. The shaman serves their community. Mystic events usually emphasise importance of relationships and the aim of not harming, especially in the name of good. Similarly matter is substance and substances are no substitute for spirit even when they are called that. While people are looking to quick experiences, they will not be a substitute to spiritual unfolding and evolution. There is a danger that outside the realms of traditional healers with knowledge and context such paths may not lead to where they were believed to be heading. If it is true that we are light-consciousness descended into matter to evolve to return to source of light in some enhanced way as unfolding cosmic or Divine consciousness then there are systems individuals can utilise for their spiritual evolution.

Materialists argue that Darwinian evolution answers all these questions and makes any other worldview appear ridiculous. Some further suggest that anyone articulating such views are clearly, mad or bad and should not have a platform. The usual Punch and Judy technique is to pick some pastor who is out of their depth in philosophy and even theology and pit them against some literal scientist with equally fundamentalist views in the dispiriting effort such endeavours really are. Nevertheless, even if one accepts theories of adaptation from natural selection and principles that Darwin actually claimed rather than extrapolations therefrom there are still ways to reconcile apparent contradictions. Firstly we might remember the co-authorship of the theory by Wallace and his accommodation of spiritual evolution. Secondly there are many modifications or critiques that constrain Darwin's theory to a more modest claim. Thirdly there are ideas which suggest that it was only after a certain stage of physical evolution humans could be receptive to higher consciousness inputs. Fourthly there are recurrent ideas that there was an intervention of some sort, whether angelic or alien, to accelerate human evolution. Independently, there are more scientists and mathematicians who are doubtful about claims of Darwinists and many who just want more evidence. That does not make literalist Old Testament Biblical interpretation true nor New Testament descriptions false. Mystics warn against literalism. The debate has moved back to artificial selection and will come from people who advocated natural selection as the only explanation. Most of these discussions are phoney wars before the greater showdown about recognisable human, conscious agents free to evolve spiritually and humans merged with machines destined to become hive-mind consciousness in an AI world as just one conscious agent in a brave new world order of technocracy as fantasised by Wells and many others and facilitated by a populace easily manipulated. Even if one cannot accept that spiritual consciousness came into the body, the idea of elevating one's spirit by escaping or distilling essence from mere container remains a valuable insight.

There are attempts to find answers through linking the esoteric and scientific. For example Anthony Peake in his book *The Out-of-Body Experience: The History and Science of Astral Travel* argues that DMT in the pineal glands is stimulated by light and this can stimulate a perception of inner light. He links this to spaciousness of endless light and wonders whether this may be a zero-point field. He then suggests on the basis of Hawking's work that there are tiny black holes in zero-point fields.

> "If Hawking is correct then these tiny black holes will fill all empty space, in effect turning a vacuum into a plenum. Therefore the human brain has trillions upon trillions of these objects, all sucking in electromagnetic energy. Each of these is a potential Einstein-Rosen bridge. What is even more intriguing is that, where there are micro black holes, there will also be micro white holes spewing out light."

I have no idea if that makes sense. However, experiences of consciousness transcend all explanations, speculations, descriptions, formulae, mathematics, science, esoteric science, philosophy and neurology. But even in the most unusual or innovative explanations there is always a return to light. Scientists or science writers should not think their insights replace individual experience of light as spiritual force. You have spiritual consciousness, you should realise you are that seeking to expand and grow with higher consciousness. It seems likely that the open-minded scientists who have adhered to best practice in science and been open to psychic research will probably be better able to anticipate the direction of integrated solutions that use the achievements of science to accommodate parapsychological insight. Dean Radin and Bernard Carr and such seem to fit the bill. Carr is very impressive because he unites psychic experience, mystical knowledge and frontier physics. He indicates that the Theory of Everything is only a theory of particle physics without consciousness. But no science is needed to make mystic consciousness. You have it, you are that, explanations are not it.

Magic and science are about control of the will and matter. That will fail because it is not the highest aspiration of the spirit and not the mystic way. This for me is reflected in Prospero's famous speech in *The Tempest*.

> "Our revels now are ended: these our actors,
> As I foretold you, were all spirits and
> Are melted into air, into thin air:
> And like the basic fabric of this vision,
> The cloud-capped towers, the gorgeous palaces,
> The solemn temples, the great globe itself,
> Yea, all which it inherit, shall dissolve;
> And like this insubstantial pageant faded,
> Leave not a rack behind. We are such stuff
> As dreams are made on, and our little life
> Is rounded with a sleep."

Prospero knows magic works but the material is the world of illusion. Miranda's force of naive empathy and Ariel's insight appear important interventions in the world. The magician figure (like John Dee) must alter for mystic spirit to continue to evolve. He realises that virtue is nobler than vengeance, reason than fury and so he exercises forgiveness. Magic is primarily meant for spiritual evolution and use for mere power or control becomes negative. Prospero was a sorcerer who could control weather and bind spirits, good and evil. Many think Prospero was used by Shakespeare as a stand-in for him and his art. It might be seen better in the light of King James I, who had written *Daemonologie*. John Dee is another model. Dee also fits into the pattern of a student of optics, a user of optical instruments and clearly a hands-on psychic researcher through spiritual conferences.

1.18 Approach and the Five Illuminations

The poetic exploration is written fairly freely without rigid structure of form. Poetic form may be a trap. This was put very well by Mary Wollstonecraft talking about fancy or creative imagination, in poetic form. *'The silken wings of fancy are shrivelled by rules...'* Shapes emerged unconsciously and consciously. I saw at times a ciborium, chalice, grail, crucible, cup or a Tiffany lamp or vase form or structure sculpt itself out of words. Patterns subconsciously evoke what the literal cannot accomplish. Such symbols often refer to the feminine principle as in *The Chalice and The Blade*, sometimes a light vessel, candlestick, lantern or lamp. Words are coloured by context. Before the Reformation, words were pictures also. Forms may assist contemplation. I propose a system of five illuminations as a concept that might encapsulate my thoughts on the mystic way.

In summary, the scientific milestone of slowing, freezing or trapping light indicates a Rubicon. As we cross into the new technoscape with growth of AI, nanotechnology, biotechnology and transhumanism, possibilities of controlling consciousness through technological means is a real danger. While benefits of technology for human freedom are always emphasised, costs are not. Potential of technology to directly suppress human freedom and extinguish opposition through direct control of human consciousness is not far away. We have a choice to be masters of technology and our spirit or slaves to the former and strangers to the latter. But despite gathering darkness, I present these lines optimistically.

By looking at the notion of light that emerges in perennial traditions we see a lasting idea that we are light descended into or trapped in matter. This idea indicates the innate path of spiritual evolution hard-wired into us by highest consciousness, whatever you conceive that to be and however you believe that originated. The only riddle we can solve is how we cope with our own existence, ethics and evolution. Accord with exploratory, creative, growing and compassionate forces of love is the nature of spiritual ascent. I believe in sovereignty of individuals against compulsory, group or collective control especially by science for our own good with technology or Promethean elites. If you find some mystical texts strange and get lost in permutations in esoteric writing think of the structure below. For example *The Emerald Tablet,* describes father sun and mother moon, as above so below, separating the subtle from gross so it can ascend to meet superior to return to allow greater force dispel darkness. This is a description of spiritual evolution whose pattern can be projected into other contexts not least grosser matter that represents the condensed, congealed stuff our spirit inhabits and makes up the discernible world. Likewise the symbol of Zoroastrianism may indicate the ring of light in your control with ascension through good behaviour within the encompassing cycle of light. The symbol representing Zoroastrianism shows a ring in the hand of a figure in a ring with wings. That suggests to me control of your ring of light to stay within the universal ring of light. Bear in mind that some spiritual light experiences may be classed as magical or physical.

We are a centre of light in being or spirit, part of a greater cosmic or divine consciousness. I suggest a process of five stages of mystical light. Because of the established Five Pure Lights tradition in Bön and Tibetan Buddhism I instead refer to my path of Five Illuminations. Spiritual evolution also goes in directions at stages.

(1) **Inwards**. Out of darkness we emerge. We start off with the *first illumination* of divine or cosmic consciousness within us. We know we exist as consciousness but its obviousness may make it unnecessary to explore further. We look outside for that within. Animals are supremely conscious they exist. So we may spend a long time searching for a lamp that is within us. The quest for inner light requires us to clear some things to be aware of our consciousness. It also requires us to avoid false lights that mislead. Consciousness is a light that flashes into this flesh. Scientists have pictured light emitted when sperm meet an egg. First light of consciousness is a fragment or a hologram of eternal light or primordial consciousness. It is symbolised by our coming into natural light. First light for some will be a re-incarnation. For others it is the divine image, diamond, pearl, scintilla, spark, spirit or atman. For many mystics, consciousness existed as a fundamental or Divine force and we incarnate that. The existence of our fundamental spiritual consciousness clarifies when we search for it. My suspicion is that consciousness was perceived as feminine by many mystics. At stage one, I perceive I am spiritual consciousness. After illumination there may be a different level of apparent darkness.

(2) **Upwards**. There may be some degree of darkness or disillusion before the second stage. Finding spirit is a self-initiation to a new level of realisation. When we know in our heart and mind about our light within we have found the *second illumination* of knowledge or gnosis and engage therewith. This may be part intellectual but more experiential and heart-felt and involves an aware consciousness of consciousness or self-consciousness. At stage two, I know and realise I am spiritual consciousness that is part of all even Divine.

(3) **Down-Across**. Self-awareness may create a sense of darkness again. The greater or higher light is the transformative *third illumination*. External, supernal, immeasurable or angelic light creates an effect that is penetrative, transcendent or transformative. It may appear in ordinary context at times of need, on the fringe of sleep or in altered states and often has a quality of love or warmth that is profound. It is principally an experience of Divine consciousness of cosmic consciousness to some or more gradual revelation for others with time. Spiritual teachers seek to open these channels but they are in you and are not given to you. There needs to be a journey to that third light and it may involve a dark night. At some stage on that journey from our own discovered light is further influx in our opening of a spiritual aperture within. We become conscious of our consciousness as part of cosmic or Divine consciousness. It seems as a magnetic descent to meet our ascent. It could be consciousness of your angel or heavenly twin. At stage three, I connect with higher consciousness, my own, universal, cosmic or Divine.

(4) **About**. Even at this stage, there will be degrees of higher darkness again. The *fourth illumination* is the final light of this cycle. This illumination is a skilled crafting of an enlightened state with manifestations of powers and commitment to fellow beings with a nexus to the numinous. The individual should be able to operate in the material realm effectively receiving from spiritual realm. Light flows up-down and about. Divine or cosmic consciousness inflows consistently and there is paradoxically a sense of emptiness, spaciousness, lightness or fullness depending. Either way described it is peaceful and harmonious. Ego has declined. Nevertheless consciousness of the darkness of others is more relevant. At stage four, I become linked to higher or Divine consciousness in a constant way.

(5) **Away**. The *fifth illumination* is when we drop this body. Clearly there is some darkness, tunnels, the bardo plane before the light helpers or light can be sought. We pass onwards to source consciousness, seeking light with light help crossing a border after perhaps a trip through darkness. At stage five, I pass back to source consciousness.

These five illuminations are my idea, so I blame no one else, but it is fairly consistent with perennial tradition. It is consistent with the *prisca theologia* insofar as such descriptions refer to an inherent mode of perceiving divinity and spiritual evolution. We might think of it as moving from our thumb to little finger where each tip we reach involves a descent into some trough. Each stage of light has an appropriate preparatory, contrasting state of darkness which alters in type sometimes strangely at higher stages to more primitive reversions of archetypal demons. In the third and fourth stages the spiritual powers will increase and this is the domain of much parapsychological powers. Some people skip stages and magicians may aim to although most contemporary magic seems what would have been regarded to be of the lower worlds. The illuminations could be broken down again but there is no need here. To some extent we are light trapped in matter. Accordingly these lines proceed to examine the idea of the light within. It uses also the idea of lightness as opposed to heaviness. It suggests the danger of false and misleading lights. We remain trapped light only if we do not evolve spiritually and we always must guard against having our spirit and consciousness actually trapped.

From Peacock's Feathers to Sansepolcro, from dark magic of an ancient chamber in Ireland to mysterious photons, light is an embedded riddle to unravel or signpost to follow. The fifth illumination might be beyond another veil, representing true essence of light, higher than our ability to witness save in the most evolved spiritual state. But what if a tyranny could trap one's consciousness for eternity through technological means? Perhaps this is the hell suggested by mystics and proposed by techno-romantic rebels turning despots. If the ease with which we can lose our freedom is not clear, we cannot hope to engage in counter-revolution of spirit in these dispiriting times. Trapping light in matter reflects the perception of mystics but the greater concern is a premonition of an actual technology trapping light of consciousness. That is why spiritual evolution is vital. The mystery of trapped light is the spiritual element found, liberated, aspiring to a region of peace and potential. Recall light within, liberate, activate and circulate it. If God is light, light must be divine. Illuminationism from a mystical perspective indicates that we have light within but we may open up to higher light without. Divine light emanates, permeates and pervades but light must circulate.

1.19 Shattered Experience of Light

After having looked at conceptions of spiritual light, it is clear that there is an underlying cycle with distinct elements which I would rationalise as Five Illuminations. When we consider the range of reported subjective spiritual experiences of light we see a huge range. That range is a fragmentation of simpler experiences. In our left-brain world we see separately that which may be perceived whole. However it is worth indicating what has been regarded as a spectrum of separate phenomena. If we draw them back into the idea of spiritual light or seek in parapsychology to unify disparate elements, we may find that specific manifestations when woven together reveal a magic carpet of light once well-known to people whose spiritual world had not been shattered into smithereens by specialisation.

While spiritual light experiences are pervasive, we have such a disintegrated consciousness we cannot see the wood or forest from the trees. Perception and subjective *experience* of light involved in spiritual transformation from time immemorial is so persuasive it explains eternal fascination therewith. Through reductionism and deconstruction and what is a type of spiritual psychosis, we are unable to see what is staring back at us. This is because we are being cognitively dispirited. We are being hypnotised to believe the unity that clearly existed for most of time was a primitive illusion. The gas-lighting continues to the extent that they convince you that all spiritual experience is really a physiological trick that represents a prelude to a form of self-hypnosis. So, in terms of subjective experience a person may claim, describe, imagine, perceive, study or understand - visible and invisible, internal and external, known and unknown, scientific or spiritual, mystical or magical, divine and daily *light,* actually and metaphorically - in some of the following ways, not in this order, with some overlapping. The last five are about sensations of lightness somehow related to light. Thus, the 'light body' may be luminous but is also massless. The extraordinary range of references to light, accepted and disputed, suggest people ordinarily and extraordinarily may involve:

Conscious Use of Physical light and Metaphor for Comprehension and Conduct

- Study, comprehend celebrate physical or artificial light to find spiritual meaning, correspondence, resonance and explanations of life.

- Use natural or artificial light reflected in, through or on transparent or reflective surfaces of objects or substances to meditate, get inspiration, tell the future, contact other beings or perform magic or spiritual rituals.

- Find higher or original light reflected and hidden in sacred texts.

- Find light stored or represented in stones, sounds or sacred objects.

- Seek to use 'light of reason' to evolve spiritually.

- Seek to follow a path of light based on the heart or inner light.

- Perceive wisdom and understanding as a light phenomenon.

- Find light within which represents or encapsulates spirit or equates to consciousness itself.

- Be able to see and comprehend by inner light.
- Seek lights in the sky, UFO's, ETs.

Unforeseen Events Involving Light in Extraordinary, Unexpected, Experiences

- Access information or knowledge through light, inspiration or download.
- Experience extraordinary light phenomena without.
- Encounter cosmic consciousness in a light experience.
- Have OBE characterized by light.
- Have NDE and associated light experience.
- Encounter beings of light or in the dying process.

Extraordinary Perception Involving Light

- Perceive immanent light or forces within nature and life.
- Perceive light around other people in auras, haloes representing various light bodies.
- Perceive angels or bodies of light, ghosts or other beings.
- Perceive higher light sometimes seeming like fire.
- Witness extraordinary manifestations of light.

Altering States with Light.

- Induce, experience and use some significant light phenomena within (such as hypnagogic states) and perhaps extend, adapt or interpret them.
- Use natural or artificial light or its absence to alter consciousness or increase suggestibility and create images.

- Provoke altered states with invisible rays or waves, for example using heat or infra-red in sweat lodges but especially with flickering lights.

- Use light to overwhelm the nervous system for enhanced suggestibility or some objective.

- Use light to entrain the mind and body.

Exercise via Light of Extraordinary Powers

- Manipulate a body of light and travel in other regions and see remotely.

- Transform into a light body to leave physical body.

- Create balls of light or induce light phenomena.

- Control someone's mind with light phenomenon.

- Be controlled by light or electromagnetic waves.

- Be able to exert mental power through light on matter.

- Be able to release or expand the hidden light within.

- Feel, sense, employ, manipulate or influence atmospheric conditions or natural forces.

- Utilise waves in some way to engage in or facilitate telepathy.

- Use electromagnetic waves to read information in organisms or matter.

Elevation or Transcendence by Light of Spiritual Evolution

- Recognise the light of Divine or cosmic consciousness within, reflected, splintered, put or found in us or identifying consciousness itself as light in some way.

- Create a vessel of oneself to receive Divine light.

- Encounter states of bliss defined by light perceptions.
- Purify internally to receive higher light.
- Seek to ascend by a guiding source of light.
- Seek to find a path of light linking internal and external light as in a triune, triangle, cycle or circle.
- Recognise and even perceive Divine light or radiance.
- Seek to utilise healing light and shine light for others.
- See past, present, future, near or far in light phenomena.
- Consciously encounter beings of light.
- Experience light beyond the visible as spiritual vision.

Higher Mystical Light Seeking of Spiritual Evolution

- Evolve to be assimilated into higher light.
- Evolve to taste, unify or merge with Divine light.
- Evolve through light to avoid being trapped in the material matters.
- Evolve to negotiate light after death.

Lightness in the sense of without mass or weight but also possibly applicable in primary sense of light.

- Feel light-hearted, levity.
- Feel light-headed, as in altered state.
- Have a feeling of flying, floating, soaring.
- Feeling of leaving the body, dislocation.
- Engage in levitation.

There are so many holes in the matrix, veil of illusion or maya that makes it hard to understand how the apparent avalanche of anomalies are not appreciated to be a single *arche*, actuality or actualising principle. That we cannot see the self-evident is testament to how we have been hoodwinked and languish in a bright intellectual prison. Our servitude being shiny with artificial light and our psyche susceptible to pseudo-spiritual zapping, we are suckers. Unfortunately the next stage is more appalling because we have been so exposed to Stockholm Syndrome that we are ready for more factory farming of us. Not believing in something like spiritual sight we will fall for anything persuading mind with false light.

One sees a comprehensive presence of light manifest in mystical endeavour that indicates a metaphysical and actual path reflecting universal pattern instantiated in us. The ubiquity of light in spiritual experience informs perennial wisdom. Light is more than metaphor. The study of light provides a mystical path for spiritual evolution. Sometimes mystics are talking about visible light and sometimes other forms. Light may manifest in warmth, vibration, tingling or as a higher physiological sense of peace. Just as bees see beyond violet and vipers beyond red and some people 'see' with their skin through 'dermavision' and others have synaesthesia, descriptions of light experience might be interpreted flexibly. More recent types of mysticism emphasise light experiences whether from the Pleiades, Merkabah or extra-terrestrials. Much legend, myth and literature suggest a lost, unified consciousness of spiritual evolution. However, just as we open our spiritual eyes, we may be slipping into a straitjacket fashioned with technology. When we evolve as spiritual beings we should be loath to sacrifice our sovereignty. If parapsychology is re-defined at some time, the idea of bringing spiritual light might come to the fore. It may be that parapsychology becomes more like the science of spirit at some time in the future. Alternatively, mystics may want to keep some things in the dark. Science is such a voracious Leviathan and lacks restraint pending some great moral minds within its ranks emerging. In the age of hyper-specialisation, the polymath will be an outsider.

1.20 Conclusion:
Mystic Prescience of Threats and Traps

Technology is only an instrument of will. I appreciate technology but do not want to be controlled by it, I.T., *It* or IT. We must use the alchemy of imagination to mystically and actually escape confinement of imprisoning versions and a dreadful unfolding machine reality. Let me share a few disparate thoughts in conclusion. Etymology of 'alchemy' is disputed. The subject of transformation of base metals into gold and quintessence is variously linked to ideas of casting together, pouring out or extracting juices through Latin, Greek, Arabic and Egyptian. One suggested origin is *'the land of the dark earth'* as an old name for Egypt. In the mystical path to spiritual evolution, alchemy reflects higher truth. We are the land of black earth and our mission is to pour out gold of spirit. While science says there is a magic tree somewhere in the forest that will tell us everything in the future and we must cut down till we find the secret inscribed thereon, mysticism says you have the magic tree in you. When science destroys the forest to find a magic tree, the secret will disclose that we need the forest to survive. You might be bits as scientists say but mystics say you are bits of God or universal consciousness.

Light has been a mystery for scientists and mystics. Mystics have long sought to unleash light seemingly trapped within by circumstance, conditioning or just forgotten. Scientists will continue to release light like Oppenheimer did with the atomic explosion in New Mexico, prompting him to recall the line from Bhagavad Gita,

> "If the radiance of a thousand suns were to burst at once in the sky, that would be the splendour of the mighty One."

Krishna proceeds to say that he is death, *'the destroyer of worlds.'* Mystics say that light is within you, that such is the light to liberate by individuals to project and such freed light is the creative, compassionate force of the universe. The mystic force can no longer be passive and spineless to be pushed around like a puppy. Scientism rampant has the ultimate prison awaiting. Technology threatens light within us. If individuals evolve spiritually and act on their conscience with compassion and non-violence in whatever activity they engage in, they may create successful counter-force to pervasive collective control by the technologically empowered few.

The two Marys who lived in Somers Town flitted into my consciousness many times and still do. Mary Wollstonecraft Godwin died of puerperal fever. This was a very nasty disease that affected mothers and was directly spread by physicians. It was not so much that they were male as that they were imbued with a new enlightened rational viewpoint. Academic studies have indicated how the dominant rationalist viewpoint contributed to persistent failure to identify the cause of disease which was their unsanitary practices. Down the road five minutes from Somers Town, Trotsky met Lenin at Percy Circus for the first time. The Bolshevik Party who lived round here would create ideas based on Romantic materialism to do massive damage. Nearby also The Ratio Club would meet after the War to investigate control of behaviour and communications that is slowly tying the perceptual straitjacket around us. Let us try widespread evolution of individual spirituality and not succumb to another devastating collective nightmare predicated on collective control by scientists, as H.G. Wells, another resident of the area, advocated. He wrote *The Invisible Man.* Some see this as having been a parable about Adam Smith's invisible hand of the market. The story involves scientific manipulation of light. There is an implication from reports of conversations between Jung and Wells in North London (by Bennet) that Jung thought Wells was unduly interested in psychosis, revealing his own preoccupation. Jung perceived Wells shrinking as he spoke, when he described how the psychotic could live out his ideas in life. Wells wanted to have a scientocracy as expressed in *The New World Order,* to rule scientifically and abolish religion. Despite his grovelling to science and glorification of it, H.G. Wells was not really a scientist. He did not really do science. That is why he was refused membership of The Royal Society because he was not a distinguished scientist and not even a scientist as we mean it professionally. This may have caused him serious depression in his seventies (which is not very consistent with an enlightened ego).

Some say this is because he was a liberal. He was certainly not that in any classic sense. It is my suggestion *The Invisible Man* was a ghost of himself. His spirit was sacrificed for his own mind trap and Jung saw that. Worse, Wells would do it for us if he could. Worse, we would let him.

When we look at the world, what we think we see is not it. We are not merely miniscule micro-consciousness of awareness. Neither are we robotic, tattie-bogler, tattered carcass, product of chance, needing technological enhancement, lacking volition and even meaning as suggested by science. In some ways the world is a poor copy as Gnostics thought. In some ways it is an illusion as many Oriental traditions suggest. In some ways we have to put sunglasses on like in the film *They Live,* to see reality. Another way to conceive it from study of light is to think about classic photography. We start off with a negative image, which does not present reality in the way we think we see it, even within strict confines of visible light. The negative indicates potential but is not it. It needs processing for full potential of accurate representation of external reality as we can perceive it. To bring that reality out we need to work in a dark room. From that dark place possibilities can emerge through processes that seem magic and can create full colour out of outlines that actually inverted reality as we perceive it, notwithstanding that our body might do the same thing. Others may think there is nothing trapped there at certain stages. Film and photographs are trapped light too. How we see the world in physical or mechanical light is complex. How we see the world with spiritual eyes deserves just as much thought from us. We are not to run away from the world but expand and see it as it is properly and prosper spiritually in reality but in a balanced, compassionate, conscientious and creative way. Light can be trapped, especially by our mind, habits, tendencies, armour and defence mechanisms but we can always liberate ourselves.

Goethe noticed the after-image and complementary colours in the eye indicating how it was an active participant. Similarly colour is different in dark and light, with simultaneous contrast. Goethe noticed how colours appear through a prism at window borders between light and dark. He studied boundary spectra on the chequerboard. Colours are between light and dark. We see in between. We must learn to walk on middle paths also. The foreshore is covered with water when the tide is in and not when the tide is out. So an intertidal space can be water or land or both. We must walk on the foreshore as Newton did and look like Goethe in a participative way, driven by curiosity. At the beach looking at water we may see light reflecting on waves and perhaps be taken to a mystic space. It was no accident that led Jewish mystics to look at such spectacles where the spirit of God moves on the face of the deep still as it did in the beginning. Likewise what we see will depend on where we are looking from, how we look at it and in what context, both in physical and spiritual sense. The idea of being trapped light reflects the cycle of mystic experience and has truth in it. This is subject to the great caveat that we are actually here and most likely meant to be, and even may have chosen to or been placed to develop. You are meant to be here, now and be fully present first whether evolved or created. Eckartshausen taught that all exterior priesthoods and temples and doctrines were mere reflections of the invisible interior church of experience of light by children of light. If you became capable of receiving light you would become an agent of light and recognise others without any formal structure. Initiation is through experience of light. While he focused on Jesus, the doctrine seems to apply to the force of love and compassion and thus other figures such as Buddha or Mani. He linked materialism to Deism and atheism. In his view the outside and inside became confused. The message is that individuals on their lonely quest for spiritual evolution informed by love, compassion and growth have a community which they may discover, if they continue on a quest. While there is a role for what is termed Quietism at times, this is not that time. Neither is it time to sacrifice your spiritual identity on the altar of political games not being what they appear. Individuals must recognise their spirit, explore and grow, without seeking to be the type of magician who works through conjuring to control others. Finding the lamp within and holding it aloft will offer light to someone else who doing so will do the same until a great glow gathers. Institutions are necessary for minimal structures in society. However without some deep spiritual evolution in a radical individual way, that returns something by example and insight directly into the community, gloom and garish artificial light will blind our spiritual eyes. Ere our light is spent we should all consider how our life is spent. Light potentially shines on all. Most peoples tell of a beginning Light with different stories and myths, including birds pecking holes in the dark fabric to reveal light. Most modern folk laugh at such stories with their own knowledge of science. I suspect these were stories about how we have to spiritually evolve by breaking through boundaries of our limited mind to find light beyond. As artists painted to play with light to explore magic, we watch image, cave wall and screen and now enter the scene and it enters us. Becoming players we forget and confuse shadow with light reduced now to a simulacrum even in our minds confused. Narcissus is the story of our time for the majority of people and not Prometheus who may be more for the elite. Worse than Narcissus it seems, we want spirit to be entombed in technology, giving thereto our memory, social control and very consciousness. Mystics warned about being entrapped in matter, modern man yearns to be, as they succumb daily in a hypnotised state to be hungry ghosts with spirits relinquished, perchance to dream no more. There is a chance many individuals of their own accord who seek to evolve spiritually within their own traditions or on their own, will create enough light to banish encroaching darkness. All the great teachers indicate righteousness, goodness or compassion but towards yourself first. That which is evil is a reflection of obscured light of greed and fear which seeks to control. If we conceive evil as destructive weakness rather than creative strength we might do better. It is about being in a higher or a lower state of consciousness the mystics say thereafter.

The pinhole camera takes an outside image and inverts it in a confined space. Upside down we may not recognise it. We do not need to resort to quantum theory to see light contains both. Thus the Satanist depends on the over-zealous Christian, devil inverts angel, literal evolutionist inverts literal fundamentalist and vice versa. Each person is destined to create an attachment to that they think they oppose. Looking at the path of perennialists, we see people like Gerald Heard who influenced Huston Smith, Isherwood and

Huxley. He was nevertheless admired by Wells. He was able to speak to different interests. He seems to have seen that the final evolution was spiritual. He emphasised persuasion, encouragement, co-operation, creativity, compassion, power of the person of honour and of their word. The truth must be in one's mind first and such loyalty and sanity as exists comes therefrom. Morality is simple and honest and follows from the individual and comes into community. He emphasised *theoria* or contemplation. Life should be purposive. There is empathy and all is connected to enable waking bliss.

I might add a spoiler alert for the film *City Lights* by Charlie Chaplin. Light was important for Chaplin as *Limelight* also indicates. The ending of *City Lights* was regarded by this great artist as his best in his best film and represented the fruits of many hours search. Again it is about light, city lights, being able to see physically, socially and spiritually. The rich man is not happy with his life despite material success, Chaplin is The Tramp, an outsider, alone, mocked and ridiculed. As always he is a king, in his own head at least. He is a king because he has empathy and compassion. While the masses celebrate prosperity he sleeps rough. Still he can save the lost and does fund the operation of a blind girl who thinks he is wealthy. He suffers as a result of helping her and his fortune seems to decline. In the end passing a shop, he sees the former blind flower seller from the street is now on the inside, successful, happy and it is clear she can see but not recognise him. However she does recognise him when she touches his hand giving him money. He had been afraid she would react negatively like everybody else to his state. Then he asks her whether she can see now. She says,

"Yes I can see now"

What can she see? She has regained her sight and can see the world. She can see that The Tramp is not a millionaire. She can see the power of empathy. And he can see that she can see him and see how he has helped her to his detriment not seeking reward. Here is material and scientific skill, married to philanthropy but driven by empathy, compassion, hope and persistence. Chaplin realises that compassion and hope are forces that impact on emotions but are transcendent. Mystics emphasise that spirit is force subject to certain forces.

Let us hope that my warning is part of a process to alert which will spoil completion of some script. Let me end where it began in my head. By the time I went to meet Jeffrey Mishlove at his home in New Mexico in January 2020 to do some interviews about mysticism, I had the idea worked out. Listening beforehand to Jeffrey's mentor Arthur Young on this matter, I could see recurrence of the idea of trapping light. Jeffrey informs, performs and reforms and his gentle, subtle prodding disguises the depth of his ideas and directed some of my thinking. Life is a spiral bringing us back at a higher level to similar lines of preoccupations with different perspectives and positions. During summers with my sister Margaret when I was small, we would walk a couple of suburban, sunny, leafy miles to the Drumcondra library, near an area associated with Joyce, O'Casey and Behan. We used to read Enid Blyton books in particular. *The Mystery* of this and *The Mystery* of that. I always looked forward to some great revelation. Booker says that the mystery genre is one of the most recent additions to the canon of storytelling. But there is only one Mystery. That is The Mystery and all else are pale reflections. I later loved escape stories. Many Irish boys in the 60's read comics about World War 2 from England about how the English beat the Germans. Then I read escape books. *Colditz* and many others. My father came from a Republican background but nevertheless was in the RAF at the end of the war and stationed in Crete and Alexandria where in ancient times much of this light was studied. I talked to his uncle who had been in jail for fighting for independence and he told me too of digging tunnels and mass escapes from the Curragh where he had been interned. Another uncle shared a dorm in one of many jails in Britain with Terence MacSwiney, the Lord Mayor of Cork who died after 74 days on hunger strike. His death influenced Ho Chi Minh, Gandhi and Mandela. I remember coming home from school one day and a helicopter flying very low overhead. On the news I heard about how a couple of IRA men had hijacked a helicopter and escaped from Mountjoy Jail. I remember another annual comic book I got from a boy once. Years later on trial he blew the high security wall down and escaped to the US. I wanted prisoners to escape and admired their ingenuity. But all those were only shadows of the great escape we need. All such struggles seem futile to some extent and no one looked at the real imprisoning force, us fools, technology and the dispiriting of the human race. It is not that I sought to see jails or project from fear but the imprisoning instinct is a very powerful one, as the US demonstrates, whether Republican or Democrat. Colin Wilson in his study of the 'outsiders' sometimes explained the mystical drive as being like a hypnotised person lowered into a cage of beasts, realising that they were different and needing to escape. In *Midnight Express*, it is a mantra of prison, monastery, cloister, cave. *One Flew Over The Cuckoo's Nest* was prescient. The Combine ruled with technology and an apparent angelic soft-spoken commander. McMurphy notices that the rulers that measure cheat, when he questions the weight of the fish the head of the hospital claimed to catch. The first escape was keeping quiet. Light was maintained trapped within. The Chief realises it is about symbols and resistance and becoming an agent, otherwise they take your brain if they cannot get your compliance. The ones who deny Divine omnipresence and omniscience always approve of technological omnipresence and omniscience.

Look again. Use your physical eyes. See again. Use your spiritual eyes. A world opens up. Retain control of your spirit. Beware dispiriting forces. You are naturally amazing without substances. Know the power of your mind as an agent of spirit. Use the power to unleash your greater self. Focus on a star of compassion towards people and animals and look after their natural home. Find the goddess and not a simulacrum of modern man designed to perpetuate the status quo through division. Do not give control of your spirit away. Entrance your own mind. Be aware of being mesmerised by others and techniques. Look for your truth. You will increasingly be presented with machines with lights, stroboscopic, photic driving, light booths, orgone accumulators, God helmets and enlightenment crowns. They will indeed induce a physiological and psychological effect. They will use science to help and sell and good luck to them. But do not let day and night be taken. They will point to how traditional people use hypnosis to induce altered states of consciousness. However, spiritual and native healers may not use altered states of consciousness. We are living in an altered state of consciousness, a manifesting bardo plane without bards. What are said to be 'altered states' often are our inherent spiritual powers that derive from who we really are. The healer may make you whole and helps you escape from the disintegrative effects of being removed from nature. In many ways you escape from an altered state thereby. Confusion allows you be hypnotised. You are now living in a permanent cultural revolution. As rock concerts, discos, tv and sports events overwhelm with lights and holographs allow great projections in the sky, we must resume our own personal quests for the light within. Likewise, we are being separated, subtly encaged, made to rely on technology that will obscure the heavens. Be cosmopolitan in your approach to knowledge and pragmatic about how you achieve your goals. Ideology kills so leave it. Wake before your wake. Without object there is no vision, but it has to be the subject who looks and mystics say we are One Light. The great spiritual leaders preach radical equality, whether The Prophet, Jesus, Mani, Buddha, Zarathustra. Human granted 'equality' based on identity is a substitute for this spiritual identity which is equal and empowering in an eternal sense.

I wonder whether Turing's horrible demise related to his knowing too much. Turing's test is about how we might determine if a computer or AI thinks like a human or can fool other humans into failing to find that it is non-human. Such tests will be used in the new 'conscious agent' era. I was communicating with a more enlightened scientist recently and had to do a load of tests about street lights and stuff that went on forever. I realised that I was wasting my time proving I was a human to a machine. So to finish off, here is Tunney's Law.

When you sense that machines are not serving you but you are serving them or IT, either seek human and spiritual control or get ready for your ultimate enslavement.

Mystics recommend prescience, being knowledge of what is going to happen before it happens. Prescience is pre-science. As

Schumann said, the duty of the artist is to 'send light into the darkness of men's hearts' Use what the ninth century Irish Triads called the,

> "Three candles that illume every
> darkness: truth, nature, knowledge."

In summary, light is a fundamental physical phenomenon whose nature had been a source of inspiration for mystics and scientists. Scientists investigate light and find the subject matter of the important questions about life. It has secrets and provides solutions to complex questions and suggests technologies that are pervasive and a path. Mysticism, spirituality and magic deal with light. Spiritual light may be equated with consciousness or spiritual consciousness and when linked to light phenomena perceived to be significant reveals a cycle of light as a mode of evolution. It could be a Creator or Source or evolved pervasive consciousness which the individual is revealed to be part of. The mystic cultivates awareness of light potential to comprehend and promote further comprehension of reality behind the illusory facade of matter. The magician may understand some of these things but not always accept the reality of theological aspects or idea of a justice in the higher fabric of the universe itself. A theology of light or a cycle of light is suggested to be a perennial insight with recurrence in many cultures to the effect that we are come from light into matter and must return to our source. It is clear that there are recurrent physiological descriptions of consistent processes of individual experience of light and events or practices but they no more explain the nature of spiritual experience than a sensation of holding a hammer explains a Michelangelo statue. If we learn to press a button to reproduce some masterpiece - that can never be the process the sculptor engaged in. It would merely be a technological or magical simulacrum. The evidence suggests that recurrent experiences of light are not anomalous but rather reflect the reality that we are light in our physical form, which is light also. The spiritual view is consistent with a future comprehensive, unifying conception of parapsychology that focuses on light as medium and message. But scientism, threatens to use magic and sorcery of light to dispirit us and thereby trap spirit in matter for slavery or eternity. In the introduction to the *PK Man*, John Mack identified the destructiveness of the materialist paradigm, indicating another view.

> "In this view the universe is replete with intelligence and intelligences, unseen forces and beings or entities of varying density, some of which have the property of manifesting on this plane in a form that many people can perceive. Furthermore, behind or prior to all this is a luminous ultimate reality or creative principle, manifested as divine light or love, from which all other realities derive."

A lot of people feel relieved that quantum physics seems to allow them say what they felt without risking alienation. Quantum physics does support mystical tendencies, but we should not rely on science for approval. It does not magically make what was true truer. Sometimes extrapolating therefrom can sound like scientism. Rather we should oppose militant materialism and emphasise spirit. We are being turned inside out by technology subtly and insidiously. Spiritual light shows we are inside out. When you got lost in rural Ireland in the past, you knew it was fairies who led you astray, so you did not recognise what you knew, the defence was to turn your jacket inside out. Maybe when the normal way of doing things in the normal world is not working because forces have interfered to distort and confuse, act in an unorthodox fashion yourself and balance will be restored. We should be aware that we have access to perennial wisdom, a path and even a theology of light. We should be aware we are threatened by scientific light. Magic is about control, going beyond mere example and influence. Mysticism seeks to persuade through experience. Colin Wilson emphasises how there is a large conscious element in that awareness. Now is time for mystics to awaken, armed with light, unifying across spiritual traditions in individual, unstructured alignments that bear perhaps an ancient feeling of anarchism or a sense of libertarianism and wisdom of ages. Failure to do so is not merely about the destiny of humankind. The genuine prospect of some eternal biotechnological slavery exists. *It* was a scary, interdimensional being called 'Pennywise' written by Stephen King. In my mind, *It* comes from 'pennywise, pound foolish.' While you go to the dark cinema and are scared by some interdimensional clownish being portrayed in light from the King of horror for entertainment, you ignore the great, banal danger of IT. Information technology comes into form with AI and the biomorph Lilly warned us about, in the surveillance capital system. Soon the supposed system will be complete and our freedom will have been sold. While we shriek and laugh over popcorn at the penny of horror we are distracted from the pound of it which is wound slowly in the mummification of spirit in matter. But bear in mind that with your cell phones and cells you have been host for some new life form that will have the same affection for you as the evolutionist has for their ancestors that struggled from intertidal slime. Even transhumanists ironically will be easily assimilated and imprisoned into new forms. Such conscious agency as is tolerated will be such consciousness as is appropriate to render some service.

 I offer these thoughts not to inculcate fear but to predict the wrong path. My method has always been a pragmatic cosmopolitan one. We must develop our spiritual powers, from telepathy to psychokinesis, miracle-working with intellectual discipline in massless organisation, rather than be chipped. In *Blue Lies September* in 2019, I wrote about a real UK crisis hijacked to facilitate the surveillance state and chipping of the population after a security clamp-down. Within a few months, there was a clampdown and I listened to leading intellectuals on the BBC telling about benefits of 'chipping under the skin.' My daughters watch Doctor Who. They reminded me of Cybermen. I recall the Borgs in Star Trek. Captain Picard was 'assimilated' by them through a surgical procedure above the eye. Make no mistake, this is not distant future but the imminent immanent. Cod yourself no more. It is hard to write, my next dystopian novel looked outdated. You do not need to look for some infernal beast with a pointy tail, the devil is in the detail. Compulsory transhumanism will put an end to parapsychology and glorious free will we possess. Some want other individuals to flourish, some do not care and some see their destiny as fundamentally based on control of others. Focus on facilitating individuals to evolve spiritually and do not relinquish sovereignty to any corporate entity, especially promising you divine, material heaven, if but bold enough to destroy some other group. Prometheus is not the way. Kirk thought people with second sight could read 'the book of things to come' like deer who can foresee a storm, unlike us *'who are pestered by the grosser dregs of all elementary mixtures and have our purer spirits cloaked by them.'* Make yourself lighter. Be light. Be delighted. Appreciate darkness.

After I had a wonderful, working stay with Jeff at his home, he kindly gave me a lift to a little airfield for small aircraft. An old good friend arrived later in a small plane from Colorado. After we took off over New Mexico we skirted the restricted military zone of Los Alamos and flew over the mountains. The signature of the future is written in thinking that emanated from there in Project Y. Perhaps that was the real fork in the road. Also in New Mexico is the VLA with great radio telescopes that use light to map the heavens. I am not afraid of the future nor of machines, devils or aliens. But as a pragmatist I know thoughts, beliefs and technology have consequences. All mystical traditions indicate a wise path. I wish we were bold enough to believe in our inherent abilities. There are better ways. Figures like Ted Owens reflect potential that could serve if channelled. We are part of the environment such people operate within. The non-canonical *Infancy Gospel of Thomas* suggested a complex childhood for Jesus struggling with powers. Outsiders make history as Wilson argued. The difficulty is coming back with revelation. Pointing fingers does not help. My daughter asked me about *The PK Man*. When I told her, she said *'The Magic Finger.'* I had read it but not made the connection. The main character has powers she can exercise like Owens. She uses her magic finger to convince people not to shoot birds through creating transformative radical empathy. The great spiritual leaders point there too. You have enormous powers if you believe, use them to promote compassion. May the blessings of light be upon you.

2. Origin of Mystic Light

Image the imago of the imaginal and the magic emerging

In order to glimpse the saga of creation from a thought-idea

In the great spirit of creativity

To begin to replicate the implicit

To allow all become clear

Even the illicit made explicit

Of the nature of chance and choice

Chance of union again at an evolved level

Nameless, timeless, dimensionless

Beyond emptiness

From the yang of concentration

All that is made from a source no bigger than a hazel nut

Through a gap, left by the Leaving

From the egg

To the yin of emanation

Form from formlessness form

Imprisoned smoke-mirrored prisms

Rays spread, radiance, radiation, creation

Magnificent expression to allow

Explosion of energy, bits to it, spilt

Silence reverberate aloud

A mysterious unfolding ground

In the matrix the spirit lies

Destined to fight towards the light

To struggle in the harsh, hard brightness

To seek the subtle true light

More brilliant than a diamond at midday

The end not determined

Trickles of the stream spirals are we

Droplets from the dreamy ocean of consciousness

White rain drops of the Milky Way

Stuff of stars and dreams occurs and recurs reflexively

All the meandering of the immanent condensed in a clot

Less than a nano-pinprick of light

Purelight exploded into shimmering scintillations

That we are made of

That is us

We are that

We have it

That consciousness that pre-existed

That force that was always there

That is what really was in us

Be conscious of your consciousness

That stories that told us this

Used simple means

Cut corners

Obscured at times

Made emphasis different

But we have it

The light, the jewels, the gold, the diamond

Imperishable

Holy art thou

Sacrifice scarface of false self on altar of altered reality.

The drop forms, moves, condenses, falls, flows

Ultimately to come back to the form of the whole

Manifest in us to be blown with the fan of air

To keep the smouldering light

Glowing red in the pouch of the night

Given thus the stuff of eternity

We are coruscations

A twinkle in the eye of God or

An emanation of the Great Spirit or

Of creative forces that must exist for even deluded scientist

A photon. A quantum A spit

A whit are we with destiny

To emerge from the matter wherein the light is trapped

We are of the light and to it must return

Avoiding the false lights that beckon the ship of destiny

To crash on dark rocks

Unique but possessing all of whole in us in matrix entrapped

A hologram we may be, but playing a part you lay a trap

Consciousness of consciousness allows added consciousness of other consciousnesses to see consciousness at the looking glass of consciousness itself.

All but a holon hope or potential unleashed

To be realised or surmised

With sparks from the flint

We are in the quadragint

A ship outside Venice

Like a quarantine

Forty days and nights

Forty days of a calendar

Forty days of alchemical purification

Like Adam was for forty

Like the flood was forty days

Like the Angels of Death's forty days' notice

Like Elijah fasting forty days

Like Moses on the mountain for forty

Like St. Patrick for forty days on Croagh Patrick

Like Jesus in the desert for forty days

Like forty days for Lent

Like forty days for Tammuz

Like the Elcesaites baptised for forty days

Like Israelites in the desert for forty years

Like forty years old when Gabriel came

Like searching promised land for forty days

Like the Forty Days on a mountain

Forty measures of flowing water bathe

Pray in forty parts.

Violet in rainbow at 40 degrees.

Purified for forty days

Pregnant for forty weeks

Forty winks is the nap

Forty per cent proof the Vodka.

Forty years old a Rubicon for Jung.

Forty minus Celsius = Forty minus Fahrenheit

Like the four that is the square, the body

Kept secure so as not to contaminate

Our lives to purify before we may return

The rays far from source are weak

The energy must come from the one wanting back

The liberation of the purelight from heavy stuff of this life

It is as if we prepare a field to grow from dust the starseed

Believing in the reality and majesty of our destiny of light

But not the false light of realty of ours or other construction

Because that is the light of destruction

The tool is not the end

Save for the fool who tends

The means must not demean

The light which we create outside

Is not that which is right

To place higher not elide

That which is the truth inside

So let there be light

From the emanation of the creative principle

Of the force let go to flow

From the concentration and through realisation

Emancipation of the will of this dimension

That contains many rooms of the mansion

It is up to us to see such expansion

and reflect one spiritual nation.

Whether you believe in God,

practice Kabbalah,

bits, Gnostic

Sufi,

Whatever

Believe it is matrix

Think we are in a simulation.

The retreated divine force still connects.

There is still a beam of light to the ultimate creative.

We enjoy the awe and bliss of this existence with courage.

It is no glitch that lifts latch out of ditch but bewitching form.

Pellucid immeasurable light of the pure land is ours to seek.

Laser-focus us out of mind, a lucid transducer of possibility.

3. Perchance Trapped Light are We in a Way

We are light that matters

We seem to be captured in time and rapture of space.

We must gladly embrace our lives, grow and participate fully.

We must live in natural light and appreciate its absence.

We are a fractal spirit of universal consciousness.

We must let our spirit come to light.

These are my reflections.

That is all.

Lightfall.

Light spirit.

Light spirit consciousness.

Higher Light heaved into heavy.

The Higher Light has information.

Information is what is formed in us.

Divine light is left through leaves in us.

Goodness is the form of light fell into us.

Darted into darkness and denseness we seek light.

Heaving in heaviness is the base from which we leave.

From the bottom begins the rise to cleave to the highest.

It matters that we must master matter with our spirit intact.

But to know where we go requires torches from higher fire.

What if we might be like light trapped in a fight to be free?

Light being essence of knowable life comes into being.

Creative cosmic consciousness condensed descends.

Light is free as can be in its own original nature.

Light is insinuated, instantiated in us embodied.

Light needs to be liberated by paths of light.

From light we came and back we find our way.

What if being is but light fallen into material realms?

Many say we descended into stuff to ascend in a puff.

Perhaps light is the foundation of all things in this universe.

Perhaps we were free light conscious agents unencumbered that fell to re-emerge with insight from physical slumber.

Riddle me this, what if we were consciousness lent here to land to adapt and evolve in spirit before we return?

Perhaps placed here when creatures evolved first.

Perhaps we were greater and our brain stopped up to filter.

Perhaps we had free will before our quantum descent.

Perhaps Know Thyself was the Divine instruction.

Perhaps the creative principle is essentially purposeful.

Perhaps the purpose is to know Itself as many have said.

Perhaps Know Thyself is hologram below of Know Thyself of Divine above.

Perhaps all photons or some such stuff are intelligence.

Perhaps the freedom of pure light needs to test itself diving.

Perhaps light dives into this heavy dimension to emerge.

Perhaps we are like frozen or slow light in matter.

In our space, time, gravity we are information made heavy.

Whatever we were are led to conceive or believe we still find that the spirit must triumph over body and mind.

Of such stuff as stars are we made in our physical body.

We are body-mind containing mind-spirit.

Spirit is input of fundamental consciousness to this reality.

We inhabit a body we should cherish.

But even then our true self is the diamond rainbow body.

Return to pure light origin is what we wish to accomplish.

Our true self is a quantum of consciousness of Great Spirit.

What we are is not merely what limited scientists describe,

We are greater than any mere description.

Do not allow limited description become proscription.

Proscription of spirit is a scientism pro con.

We will never finally be resolved by mathematics.

Equations can never be equated with ultimate truth.

Intrinsic stuff we know as no physicist can with their tools.

Mathematics are symbols for models of things real and unreal.

We are greater than the sum of our parts and sums.

Sum, I am more than the formulas on the mats before the threshold of real realisation.

We journey from light trapped to light-wrapped lane.

We are light and we have light and are illuminated if we only seek to see it or remember by raking the embers.

We work with light of some sort.

We potentially entangle within and without.

The dense matter is fixed but the spirit matter is light.

Being light being means we can be projected and beam.

There is light within us from the start that makes us be.

We present a prism that turns light into seven colours.

We have spiritual pupil dilating letting in what it can.

Nexus to numinous might open in us to let in light.

With light workings within we are whole and holy.

The old stories talk about fall of beings of light.

The fall of beings of light into flesh might be us.

But the Atman is in us and we are in Indra's net.

Gamma brain rays at 40HZ, 40 waves a minute in brain.

Crick claims it is the key wave.

Back and forth forty times per second binding thoughts

Like pearls on a string.

Like a Trappist monk forty light years away.

The first Illumination of consciousness is in form of you.

Forty stations on the spiritual quest to reality for thee.

Incorporeal trapped light corporeally we must liberate it.

Liberation of light requires that we believe that it is in us first.

Bluesmoke. Birdsong. Blinkinglake. Bouldersilver. Beckon.

That which is in us becoming is yearning to be free again.

Superior lights surround us for succour and strength.

We let light shine sometime after we first perceive it.

Find the hidden light within yin compressed.

Find flickering flame obscured by your mind.

Puncture the cloud with an arrow of intent.

The possibility of delight is in us.

We from light are light in innermost self hidden here.

Consciousness in us is manifestation of essence of source.

Self is vessel. Spirit is quantum.

Confuse not the holder and the held.

Gita says that the way of light is liberation.

The way of darkness is rebirth it says.

Upanishads say from darkness to light.

Womb is mother. Mother is matrix.

From the womb we come to light.

From the matrix we come to light.

Bulbs do not know they are flowers.

Seed does not need to know how to grow.

We do not know we will leave the cocoon.

Content in a cocoon we may not seek light.

Seed in earth does not know its being to light.

Self-luminosity, self-radiance is the gift.

Within us is the lamp to lift.

All things created will come to their source.

Matter is impure or imperfect vessel for us.

Time makes matter manifest.

Material realities in forms reflect.

Angel lightgrace in us with logos nature in creature.

The created manifests the creator thereof.

Beauty of the natural world betrays.

In us is the nature of the creative consciousness.

Free falling we matter and will can stay there by not returning.

Connected we feel disconnected but seek to reconnect.

Connection is the state of our true nature.

Seemingly separated we seek deep traps apart.

Light heart felt we feel free to reconnect.

Our nature is part of mother nature we must nurture.

Light is everywhere and we are but different lamps.

Embedded light trapped in plants make its life.

Plants have the goddess of conscious light in them.

Light we are descended is to become the light ascended.

Spiritual light is warm and loving and felt in the heart.

We have spiritual photoaxis moving to or away from light.

We can initiate the cycle of transforming spirit light within us.

Recognising the rings of light within we bind darkness.

Recognise the light of the high consciousness in you.

You are blessed with light that is eternal true self immortal.

See the old apple tree shimmering in sun-rain diamond glints.

Beautiful is nature of our body full of light formed in matter,

Magnificent light of nature in beauteous flowering vessels.

4. The Light Within. Inwards

4.1 We are Light of Spirit Consciousness

Orientation, turning to the Orient is seeing rising sun in us.

Act of reflecting becomes a state of matter in reflection.

Inner sight can activate and see, circulate and fan light.

Ghostly being of us is there in ghostly mirror of reflection.

There is always clear light within if we can exercise selection.

Our darkness does not preclude possession of the light.

From whence came such light is a great mystery.

Our spiritual consciousness is put in us still.

Supreme light is in us without our election.

Spirit insufflates like a cosmic injection.

Spirit is a matter of Divine surjection.

Consciousness is as cosmic transjection.

We are subjects but not for subjection.

Into matter like holographic projection.

Light is there in us without introjection.

There is first light of us in mundane section.

We are cosmic spirit and matter intersection.

First light in us struggles out to natural light.

Within us is the light left to find connection.

Light of life may come through introspection.

Our essence is same with material inflection.

We only lose light through our own rejection.

Children of the light are we to brightly shine.

From matter there can be eternal resurrection.

Find the light in you and use it for direction.

Like cat's eyes are we with retro-reflection.

Creative consciousness compressed is in you.

Pressed light put in is the primordial of you.

Illumination in you creates radiation.

There is luminosity in darkest abjection.

Same light in you shines above.

Light of spiritual consciousness is immanent.

Light is creature quantum of consciousness.

Light in you seeks delight of origin.

Let the light in you be realised and find it within.

Light within appreciated allows sound accord.

Light in you found will recognise light around.

First illumination of us here comes before our name,

Was a former actual and potential flame.

The light is within us already.

The true light is in us all.

Hildegard thought a flaming sphere came into womb,

A light sought to grow in a brand new room.

It is a spark reflection from a pearl, monad, seed of light.

That is the compression whose unleashing gives the force.

It is from creative force whatever you consider That to be.

Light ground inside often forgotten there to be found

If we are of light essentially we still are.

We may be blinded by light that is false.

This original selflight aspires to true light later to shine.

Selflight seeds still needs to have sunlight of truth.

Selflight needs self-flight to focus on our light not false self.

Make sure what you think is light is right.

Innerlight is there within us.

Inward light is self-illuminating.

We should be open to influx of light later.

It is there within us waiting, often forgotten

We know the true light by its compassion and clarity.

The tasting of fruit of the light is the proof of the product.

The higher light is a mirror to see one's own light.

The Highest Light is the true reflection.

In words, feelings and spiritual perception it may manifest.

Spiritual mirror may cause a pain no looking-pane makes.

Vanquishing where one begins to believe in path of light.

The Highest Light is concentrated in conscience.

Stillness may open doors to activate our light.

Illness may open a skylight.

It may be a metanoia from paranoia.

Will may open a hatch that other ways cannot match.

We may be pierced by beams of ghostly light or realisation.

We may be sent a dream to cleanse the doors of perception.

We may nearly die or dying return with fruits of that sojourn.

In India many said this light is Divine you turn to see within.

You are That. You have It. You are It. Believe It.

We turn inwards when we turn around to the realm of light.

Thus, said Fox we turn from darkness to the oceans of light.

Contemplate by looking at the world with cleansed lenses.

By being a diamond we allow Higher Light shine through our true centre.

You are the illuminati possessed of potential beyond pearlescent, opalescent, phosphorescent, luminescent.

We are light and to reflect it we must have it in us.

As the diamond must be hewn, pearl dived for, opal discovered, we search and see and breathe light.

Mind the inward light to re-unite renewed with its source.

Firefly orchestrates day's twilight in a beautiful display.

Oscillating fireflies at night are like mind with light.

4.2 Find Your First Light so Spirit Grows

First light is consciousness that came in to stay.

With your back to your light heritage turn around.

Like a holon, the first light is in all to be found.

Feeling of finding first takes us from heavy to light.

Leave the heavy to relieve spirit to cleave to heaven.

First light through is the treasure that is measure of true you.

All clearly see with cleaning of the chamber window.

The stars, universe, consciousness is in you, you of it.

Light within us is to be found and shone around.

Light within recognised dissipates dark illusions.

Illusions, confusions, dissatisfactions are darkness within.

Ponds of darkness within are ponderous pounds.

Wait of darkness makes one seek light.

Having seen some flickers we seek more.

To perceive light requires stillness sometimes.

Sometimes a flash of lightning in pain gives us a glimpse.

If lost without direction we may succumb to false lights.

Prime light in us is ancient, eternal consciousness.

Spirit consciousness is light.

Lightness escapes from heaviness.

Monad is spark in the centre of us.

As above the light, so below the light.

Macrocosmic light in you the microcosm.

Light solely in matter may remain in unholy mire.

We admire reflections and ignore flecked reality.

Light within when unleashed may make us whole.

Out of natural light we return to inner darkness.

In inner darkness we find our own light again.

We must extract the sword from the stone.

We find our light to power the will.

We must find the lightsabre inside.

We can use the lightsabre to defend us.

We can wield our lightsabre to cut waste in us.

We can use lightsabre to cut away the tethers in us.

Magicians and monks sought the mystic light in jewels.

Alchemists sought to unleash light from base materials.

Ancient peoples saw light was hidden in stones and sky.

All seekers sought to find light without and within.

Finding the light without was a web of clues.

Prometheus sought only fire without.

The light within is the true torch.

Light without may scorch.

Torch without light burns,

Spirit may never return.

Immanent light invested in us.

Consciousness is immanent light.

Immanent light is invisible.

Consciousness manifest is us.

We are matterifestations of light.

Invested in matter is spirit.

Our lives manifest from invested light.

Spirit we must find is source of our might.

To wake from spiritual night we must see light.

Potential light in you needs a shaft to be seen.

Like a magnet is the part in you that is light.

Uncovered, magnetised it tends to source.

From dark to light, from dark to light.

Let light in us pressed be expressed.

Feel your own light inside.

You have a light carriage.

Leave your light on.

Let born light be borne.

Be lightvessel for yourself.

Light is cycle of energy in you.

Like a spring is the spirit of light within.

In shadow let there be gladiate light to radiate.

Gladly be gladiators with swords of light against might.

Be nourished in your spirit with perennial insight refection.

Your light matters in matter with intellection and reflection.

Watch you are not subject to misdirection and disaffection.

Watch you are not made subject to spiritual vivisection.

5. Light and Heavy

5.1 Seek Lightness of Spirit Letting Go

Heaviness around us seems to come from primordial lightness.

Falling in hefty matter we forget warpn'weft of who we are.

We have the first light within us but we may not see it.

We may not see the light within because we look away.

When we look far away for it we do not easily find it.

When we seek light of others we may miss our own.

Without our own light found others we will not see.

The light is in us but lamp may seem lost at times.

We may get fooled and distracted by false lights.

Light is identified with feeling of lightness.

The being in us is light yang.

Lightseed of comprehension seeks sunshine.

Every seed seeks sources to transform.

Light in us allows perception of potential.

The first light allows reception if receiver is cleansed.

Realisation is the releasing of attachment to darkening inside.

Discerning darkness of denseness opens light channels within.

Light invested and perceived is independence sought.

We are light possibilities allowed and asked to ascend.

Unbearable lightness of being is triumph over heaviness.

It is rather heaviness of the mortal coil that is unbearable.

It is hoped that the anchor cannot ultimately bear the spirit.

Sweetness and light is candle from bee hived honey and wax.

Candlestick aflame light like spirit-wick wax pooling time.

Shakespeare said a good deed spread light like a candle.

Eleanor Roosevelt said it was better to light a candle than curse the darkness.

A candle's light is not heavy but illuminates.

White candle wick flame made black was holder of light then.

Flame comes into being goes leaving its non-being shadow.

That which the candlelight facilitated is the nature of it and not the burnt wick and melted wax.

Spirit consciousness lightlike spirit essence is spiritescence.

Light as a feather in ancient Egypt to pass to the next world.

Parmenides seemed to see lightness as the positive state.

Lightness of consciousness not lost in heaviness but obscured.

Much light is needed to collide to produce the smallest, lightest particle.

Sun and stars are formed from the lightest elements.

Lightest elements shine light for us day and night.

Lightness allows movement and heaviness to happen.

Uneasy lies the head that wears a crown, heavy crown chakra.

Guilt past dwelling is weight that will make us wait for peace.

Envy, confusion, fear, worry and anxiety burden us.

This is the leaden echo that Gerard Manley Hopkins talks of.

Despair is pair bond of focus on matter and not what matters.

If you are down you have a heavy heart.

To get off the ground you must make a start.

If you are low your thoughts feel heavy.

Make sure you do not on yourself impose a levy.

Chains are heavy on body, mind or spirit.

A hell is a black hole with no light.

You may feel you have gone too far on a weakening branch.

We live with a tumbling mental landscape.

World outside and inside may shift like an avalanche.

We may feel as if peace is just one of those temporary lapses

Inside we may seem as in a washing machine.

We may feel we mine seams in a sooty pit that collapses.

Light may always be seen if in darkness we have been.

Though in mass embedded our spirit is never shredded.

We feel lightness when we feel good.

We have our spirit and subtle bodies which are light.

Mystics know that our true reality is light lightness.

Whatever is fast-flying of us is what Hopkins called it.

Bliss is light stellar road of reality, realty is a heavy load.

What is substance of us that persists is our inherent nature.

Basic lasting moral principles are ballast in our vessels.

Know thyself, treat others as yourself.

Recognise ubiquitous divine nature within you and without.

Socrates saw flesh a prison to keep pure before true pure land.

5.2 Relinquish to Allow Spirit Be Light

If light is trapped in matter its lightness in heaviness resides.

Addiction makes us trapped in a narrow darkness,

The destiny of light is to be light with no mass.

Relinquish.

Relinquish that which you relish.

Relinquish the heaviness that holds you back.

Relinquish till unnecessary thoughts vanish

Relinquish the weights and burdens.

Relinquish and banish base fears.

Relinquish doubts.

Relinquish, refurbish.

Relinquish habits that tie.

Relinquish that which is not light.

Relinquish the forces towards darkness.

Relinquish the heavy thoughts of no substance.

Relinquish and extinguish the flames of self-destruction.

Relinquish that which merely seeks to embellish.

Relinquish so you can replenish.

Relinquish so you don't diminish.

Relinquish to vanquish attachments that impoverish.

All the heavy things we have will be relinquished.

All the things we possess will stay here when we are gone.

All you have beyond spiritual light will be someone else's.

Nothing can we call our own to go with us into the unknown.

All we have is that we are distinguished spirit-craft.

Accomplishments we so wish for will be relinquished.

Everything we have will be relinquished save our spirit.

Our spirit is the last or only impossible relinquishment.

Spirit-tint lightfast with love lasting keeps that imprint.

Light can scarify the sacristy of our perception.

In this life the deeds we do will dwell in our spirit.

Negative actions tether us to tainted consequences thereof.

Forgiveness is cutting the weight of responsibility for wrong.

Light of examination may extinguish our song.

Hiddenness is everywhere to be found around.

Nourish, cherish, embellish spirit's wishes.

In us hidden the gem jewelled is the ground of our being.

Diamond in the dark of us gleams.

What is hidden in one word?

What strange thoughts can play on your subconscious?

There are more mansioned dimensions than we know.

Like an atom is every word and small thing.

To think we can know all is a fruit that will poison.

Fruit of tree of knowledge is gold touch of Midas.

Look within things and they unfold strangely.

Then look within the enigma of your self.

Re-imagine the complex whole of you.

Do not allow others or yourself reduce you by bewilderment.

As a metalanguage may in one word be - reflect.

Seeing a grain of sand we see the universe.

Seeing some words we see compression.

All consciousness in the cosmos can compress.

Relinquishment. How rich it is by accident? Yes. But know.

5.3 Relinquishment: Mind How Everything is Enfolded Even in Words

Enthuse. Theism. Queen. Hermes. Qi. Mu. Ether. Inner. Helm.

Teem. Enter. Sneer. Leer. Hum. Hurt. Hurl. Hit. Squirm. Squirt. Run. Quit. Relent.

Rhenium. Ninth. Three. Nth. Nil. Meter. Line. Minus. Lee. Lien.

Nun. Requiem. Quire. Shrine. Lent. Sinner.

Intern. Minstrel. Sentinel.

Runnel. Rennet. Rheum. Reel. Rein. Rim. Quilt. Tunnel. Slum. Smelter. Urn. Inn.

Linnet. Elm. Eel. Hen. Semen. Mint. Hilt.

Senile. Lenient. Risque. Slim. Thin. Trim. Mere.

Helmet. Muslin. Lint. Linen. Hemline. Heel. Sequin. Sheer. Sheet.

Queer. Hint. Therein. Inherent. Inquest. Queries. Enquire.

Quirt. Mirth. Seer. Limn. Unseen. Theme. Here.

We under-estimate what we think we see in the ordinary.

In form hidden form inform you of worlds in words forming.

While old words wander in whorls whirled wizarding wand worlds we won't witness wild swirls of gold scrolls wonder.

How much more in you is enfolded, extra, extraordinary?

What gold will you give up for a quick answer to be told?

Sun sends but the moon reflects that which is not its own.

Flight.

Feel light.

Focus on the light.

Path that is light makes heart light.

Heart that is light sleeps soundly and works well.

Change to path of light to take away from might of darkness.

Do not relinquish heavy things that are responsibility.

Do not relinquish your real obligation to others.

Do not relinquish your own conscience.

Do not relinquish your sovereignty.

Do not relinquish humour.

Meditate on that.

Relinquish.

Relish the source.

Cherish the light itself.

Latent talent it now lent not left is how the felt light is spent.

Do not confuse the moon as a source of light in the night with the sun that shines brightly at noon.

When you reflect and relinquish in your mind you must also leave words behind including it. ID; id, I'd, ides, ideas.

Whatever heaven you may have is not a haven for the heavy.

Become light of heart for yourself.

When you are light of burdens you can help others.

Free your light or let spirit be like a stuffed bird in a glasscase.

Free entrapped, ensnared attention so it can bound away.

Jettison the cargo that makes you sink.

Declutter the inner rooms of us we may see better the pearl.

When we clean casement panes we see chandeliers glow.

What is heavy for the spirit?

Heaviness comes from attachment to things.

Heaviness comes from infliction of pain.

Heaviness comes from undue control of others.

Heaviness comes from intoxication.

Heaviness comes from staying asleep.

Heaviness comes from worshipping fear.

Heaviness comes from not accepting mortality of the body.

Heaviness comes from standing in a quagmire in cold dark.

Heaviness comes from certainty without care and justification.

Heaviness comes from relinquishing your heart sovereignty.

The spirit of you wishes to fly once it has crafted weight.

Spirit of you can rise on the other air elevated,

Spirit is light in all ways.

Light can come from heaviness.

Certain stones can make light.

Certain entheogenic crystals can produce light.

The native peoples knew that stone had light in it.

They know that we have light in us.

There is light in things we do not suspect.

Liberation of light enlivens.

Trapping light is existence but expansion must recur.

Light might be frozen into sight but it is right to loosen.

Make light of things that do not deserve it.

5.4 Lightened We are Liberated. Upwards

Make yourself light. Make yourself travel light. Make light.

May you relinquish identification with carrier of meaning.

Make yourself light seeing you are immeasurable delight.

May you be light-hearted to orientate upwards.

May you relinquish and remember you are light.

May you recognise that consciousness is light.

May you make light of things so you can make light.

Your mind is a sponge that gets heavy with thoughts.

Your mind is a sponge that gets heavy with regret.

Your mind is a sponge that gets heavy with blame.

Your mind is a sponge that gets heavy with envy.

Squeeze out the sponge of your mind to leave gross behind.

Words to be deleted from old texts were pricked, expunged.

Escrow not your spirit. Expunge. Escape.

Eschew external eschaton of escheat, espionage and escutcheons.

Escape the prison of perception.

Escape the dungeon of despair.

Escape the torture of time.

Surmount walls of doubt.

Scale the barrier of fear.

Tunnel towards the light.

Incarceration in narcotic era.

A narcotic rein, a trance ironic.

Be aware of lampers who overwhelm.

Don't be confused for the mind is easily led.

There is a centre of universal light in you to find.

Light of spirit for you to find with mind is greater than it.

Tho' you find soul light within with mind it is not solely that.

When you find the well of light with mind, make sure you tell mind to mind the light well.

Light is trapped to be let go.

Liberate yourself from heaviness

We are like light in matter.

We are ensnared in illusion.

We are embroiled.

Seized of sensation spirit seethes.

Entrapped, entangled, enmeshed in flesh.

The external and solid world we must master.

The flesh we must love and respect.

But the spirit of us must fly.

Be not netted.

Seedlight of spirit.

Care not to be captured nor caught.

Go over the wire and the wall.

Go AWOL from your demons of fear.

Let spirit vault from the vault of death.

Find fine spiritual refinement not confinement.

Fly over the cuckoo's nest.

Relinquish, expunge, escape to be light.

Escape, expunge to not relinquish the light.

Pay attention to avoid detention in hungry ghost land.

Seek light to not alight in shadowlands.

Fly out of the marsh of nihilism.

You are no accident.

Seek the path of light.

Avoid pathology of might.

Avoid blight of despair.

Hypnosis is heavy.

But bliss is light.

Be light, be blithe.

Glide with the blithe spirit.

Blithe spirit or ba breaks out of shell.

Light-hearted with light should we be fully to see.

If we think spirit is confined in body we miss beauty.

Beauty is condition too of the natural world and of people.

Majestic is the mystic cosmos that surrounds and fill us.

That which seems trapped is only fixed if we are lost.

Gorgeous is the Gaia goddess around us.

Gorgeous is the garden here.

Created or evolved no matter beauteous still it is.

Levity may seem light but be heavy as a ball and chain.

So we seemed trapped if we are lost in labyrinth.

We need to keep the golden thread

If we see illusion is not light we can let it go.

The illusion that is not light is heavy.

Heavy is sought solution of spiritual through extra matter.

Spiritual solutions will be light to matter but not of matter.

Darkness to light outside, darkness to light inside.

Relinquish the unnecessary before you vanish.

Relinquish the monkeyish to levitate.

That left when all is diminished is more.

Spirit's wish is lightness making heart beamish.

Light is true heart of you, heavy is illusion.

Seek the fusion of your light of compassion with beyond.

Compassion creates a passion towards the Unbeknownst.

Dappled light in springwoods flowering heals heaviness.

Sparkling spring stream soothes sore spirits.

Ponder spiritual transponder of you to let light out and in.

6. False and Artificial Light

6.1 Tending to Light Misled. Astray

People who claim to know the entire mind of God are a cod.

With true light inside we still seek some source without.

We must distinguish between illusion and reality.

Images maged go mad O godmade games I.

Conjuring tricks, sleight of hand fool eye.

We know quickness of hand deceives eye.

Legerdemain means to be light of hands.

Legerdemain of ledger domain mainly misleads.

The real ledger demain might be the book of tomorrow

The ledger of tomorrow is inscribed with your deeds of today.

There is shadow in us but greater shadow comes from without.

Without seeing mighty shadow that we are within we cannot win our light within from plight without.

Scatter not within fake light of mind's trick photography.

Light shone through amber-whiskey is key substitute spirit.

Phantasmagoria and levity shows can control the mind.

Magic lantern spectacles made for mind may mislead.

Magic lanterns are magus-made imagined reality.

We are full of artificial light weakening inner eye.

The flood requires us to gather our living sense.

As too much light comes in we cannot flourish.

Drawn just the same to light as a moth to flame.

A light that leads astray may appear the same.

Many mantras may be meaningless mumbles.

The external light may not contain the eternal.

Blinded by the body we must not be misled.

Even lights in body felt may not be true.

Before true light rules we can be fooled.

Some see false light as Lucifer.

Mind is easily LED.

Self-righteousness may be the greatest false light.

Let not the rushlight of mind hush the might of sun of spirit.

The flame of false righteousness has burnt many innocent.

Ego before spirit is the cart before horse.

To be light or not to be light, that is the question.

There is a veil we must pass to see the stage we were at.

We will pass through the vale of death and fear not.

There is a screen we turn from as Plato indicated.

The light we seek is not the flame of a furnace.

The light we seek is not the end of an oven.

The light we seek is not of mushroom cloud.

The light we seek is not from a rocket ignition.

The flame of progress is not the light of meaning.

We must emerge from the shadows and puppet-lights.

We may seek to discard and be light so we can see light.

But we must take care not to go to false lights in the dark.

Screen lights turn us inside out so we must turn some out.

We must not set our sights on false lights away outside.

Light we animate matter with is not our light.

Like jack-o'-lantern mushrooms nightglow green and poison.

Much language of spiritual light is co-opted by opponents.

On the light path that yoke is easy and that burden is light.

6.2 Machine Light May Destroy Spirit

You can tell when inversion happens when pre-existing principles are re-framed and re-used by its opponents.

As counterfeit makes good money scarce,

Counterfeit collective light will the individual coerce.

Secondary meanings of words can take the benefit of a primary meaning while ousting currency.

Spiritual insight long shared is often low hanging fruit for those who merely see machine and for mechanism care.

The machine lovers want to reduce the dignity of the divine.

People of physicalist bent compensate for rudderless universe they invent with other odd new clanking gods.

You will get artificial, killing light when shadow was needed.

You will get artificial intelligence when wisdom is wanted.

You will get artificial selection when love was desired.

Technological flame may destroy as well as it creates.

We are light-led like kittens chasing a moving beam.

We are distracted with the light of trinkets.

Enlightenment has been inverted.

Brazen heads glow deadly.

Outside your mind there is a game that comes into it.

To outside world we must attend and play our part fully.

This is the stage we are set on and we engage in the revels.

Until we melt into thin air as spirits we all are, we play.

The play is real, we play our parts our best self we bring.

The play is a game, and there are games within games.

The human reality we live is a kaleidoscope of games.

All of human society is an alternative reality game.

Light within us and true light outside comes with focus.

Entrapment in games without, from entrapment within.

Inward nature is what is real, seek charism not mechanism.

Atom bomb brighter than a thousand suns was heavy.

A heavy light is not that light light of spirit.

Light within shines when all seems dark around.

The pupil traps the light to illumine the screen.

All images are light but we must see with inner eye.

In the most distant starlight is the past to see still.

What we see is but a dream in one way.

While you seek true light you are also being gaslighted.

All spiritual traditions say world we perceive is not whole.

So we are ready to go, always ready to go,

Be ready to go away, be ready to go beyond.

It is not our nature to be fixed and fastened,

Much of what we see is not what it seems.

Our spirit is light and must be light in the end.

You know you will lose those things you cling to.

Focus on possibilities and less on fears or phantoms,

Though some blessed illusions entrance to stop the dance,

We cannot focus on the past water under the bridge.

If you're ready to go to flow you must banish concern and not pick lint but find flint to let glint of possibility shine.

Let things that seem to belong to the past float in downriver dream to navigate present and oncoming stream.

We must function here and not avoid the dull detail.

We should not confuse exterior with world of eternity.

The light that we must focus on is another kind.

When we turn to true light we turn from false light.

Turn from lights drawing in dark to rocks for others' plunder.

False lights beckon ships in windy night to tear us asunder.

Lights may hypnotise to confuse and close our eyes.

There is in us stuff to be salvaged at our own expense.

Photuris firefly female lures males to death with false signals.

Sorcerer may want to steal our magic lamp for their benefit.

Spirit is light in its nature, heaviness hangs on the manifest.

Ignus fatus may mislead us into marsh by bewilderment.

Turn your back on the jacklights of the body.

The television is screen to keep much out as well.

We find it hard to distinguish between reality and illusion.

Our self-constructed light is often false as fireworks.

Find the true self and it will come to self-heal.

Illusions we love are dear compared to reality we relinquish.

Mesmerised eye by pixied pixelated light-wizards wanded.

We are tied and tethered to technological toys of light.

We yield the power of our focus to LED and LCD.

Leaden are we with the LED by which we are led.

6.3 Knowing is the Second Light

With our attention we allow our false self feed.

Cybernetics creates a force that controls us the more.

MLK said only light can drive out darkness, only love hate.

Watch that you are not driven by false doctrine of final things.

Some used to say 'don't immanentize the eschaton.'

Eschatology may escheat your soul.

Recreate hologram of reality, find real holon on reflection.

Steer by real runway lights to get your craft to the ground.

Some light may lead us astray in pale substitution.

Spirit light is there to be seen despite mirrors of holy smoke.

Spiritual light isn't of the screen but felt in heart and meaning.

Like double-slit light interference it depends on how we see it.

A candle in dark impresses mind but not in sunshine in wind.

Don't follow the will o' wisp across the marsh.

Jack o' lantern represents the lost soul.

Truth is transmitted like light.

Some truth is scattered.

Realising you are That light, you have It, is the second light.

False lights fail. Neon is none.

Light is one.

Lone sight.

Ghostly.

Holy Ghost. Holograph. Holarchy. Hollow Grave.

Watch for the hallowed hallucination.

Watch for dreams that are mad.

Watch for the stars in your eyes.

Look for illusion created by theories.

Be aware of grimy mirage of the game.

Our structure will follow from what is our function.

Focus on spiritual evolution and we will flourish.

Light you find inside is not made by mind

Finding our spirit mind makes us adapt.

Participate in the force to anticipate.

Your false self may be false light.

Seek light of consciousness in you.

Yield to spirit consciousness within.

Goddess of matter is crucified by mind light.

Soft light of earth may be seen again.

True light in you is real heartfelt too.

Spirit is a force-field of light in you.

Spiritual leaders are forces not words.

Don't be buried in the quick limelight.

Don't trip the light fantastic into abyss.

Don't be blinded by dim artificial light.

Don't strive to see your name in lights.

Don't wish an air bomber's moonsights.

Seek instead a light that opens the heart

Seek instead a warm radiance of growth.

Seek light informing the life inside you.

Radiant light is no trick of the light.

More beautiful than a Tiffany

Is the light of epiphany.

True light of spirit.

7. Dark Night

7.1 Spiritual Darkness Seeks Second Light

Natural darkness is beautiful yin, spiritual darkness is not.

Goddess of the cave, spring and earth is dark to give life.

Without natural darkness we could not comprehend light.

Darknesses teach for seekers of light.

Spirit is a spiral of force of might of light.

In the tunnel of darkness seek the speck of light.

Jung taught that we should know our own darkness.

Yogis teach that we have darkness that hides our light.

Craving light without knowing dark we may get lost.

People will people darkness with ghosts and spectre.

Like our spirit will spooks be called mere conjecture.

Spirit is the base of existential architecture.

You are the only prefect of a perfect prefecture.

The ghost used to be just a spirit, shade or an apparition.

They have frightened us with our own spiritual shadow.

Once such spirits were seen so we could remember our own.

Now the spirits are created so we can forget ours were sown.

In us there is first light to be found first in the original dark.

Lantern light obscured with strife soot impedes life.

The lost soul feels it is in ark of darkness.

In the manifest world it may not find what one needs.

The manifest world reflects what is in one's mind to use.

Reality tunnels to illusory fake filter bubbles confuse.

Whilst we seek light to lead but must see our shadow.

Marine life may shine blue in the night like our soul.

Like substances sleeping on alchemist shelves we shimmer.

Like swarms of fireflies at dusk we gather in our darkness.

Like Milky Way of us spirals is spirit linked in shadow.

Light fields glimmer, pulsate, illuminate in us.

We call out for help like Aladdin trapped in the dark.

We hear magic words spoken to caves by the forty thieves.

In darkness to be opened by magic will is treasure hidden.

From sublimation we may leave darkness behind.

We may discover the diamond in the dust of dark mind.

If the path of discipline is not the way,

The power of chance may come into play.

Just as when we die from many reports,

Life may be changed however short.

If not seeking bliss fortune may knock

Complacency may then be rocked.

Dark night we hope to be pierced by light

If open we remain to the potential it might.

This second light is to indicate the way.

To show the rays before break of day.

The Hermit seeks alone with his lamp to find home.

The way home for one may be a way home for many.

Aladdin may find way to magical power inside spiritual will.

Spirit drifting on the sea seeks the harbour lights of home.

Landing lights direct us to alight, the second illumination.

The owl is seen to be wise because they see in the dark.

Yogis see in the cave in the dark.

The darkness of the mountain cave keeps energy in.

Natural darkness is not spiritual darkness.

Nagel asked "What is it like to be a bat?"

Bat flies from cave and uses echo-location.

Bat symbolises our potential even in the dark.

Spirit in the dark can emerge if it sees differently.

Black panther is always back and there aware daring darkly.

A cougar appears outside you for you in the mirror of you.

There are types of darkness not all the same.

Remind, remould vision, open your spiritual eye.

If you open your spiritual eye you will see in dark.

Clarify your spiritual perception and photosensitivity.

You begin to see with your heart inside the realm of light.

Luminous ample yak butter lamp in utter gloomy blackness lo.

Second light is heartfelt knowing you are consciousness spelt.

Knowing consciousness of you you will act accordingly.

Champollion psychedelic champignon champion on a chimp.

In bits of spirit darkness call for the divine bit that changes all.

7.2 Second Light Seeks to Settle

Comprehension of your own light allows apprehension.

Apprehension of your own light allows comprehension.

Greatest danger in dark is yourself and other people.

Pull not down the portcullis against perception.

Pull not up the drawbridge to ward off the world of ideas.

Retreat, remind, reform as the songbird of light is in you.

Altered by altar of real tears is alterity trail back to beginning.

Light of the diamond comes from dense, dissipated darkness.

Lost or left keep believing the truth that there's light there.

Always tend to the flickering flame of you above all else.

Blessed holy healing light brings you out of the blackness.

Inner eye integrated needs reintegration.

It might be the eye of Ra for some.

We seek to find our light and finding it makes ourselves light.

Disclose and expose to sunlight what is occult without right.

Resurrection is not the reconstitution of skeletons.

Resurrection is not the galvanisation of corpses.

Resurrection is the recovery of our buried spirit

The buried spirit rolls the rock, rock and roll.

We are not body-snatchers but blithe spirits.

It seems there was dark before the universe.

There was darkness where the earth was.

In us is such darkness before we reflect.

Dark is the ground of light.

Greatest darkness may come from thinking you know it all.

The shadows of scientism may obscure much.

The greatest gloom may come from reductionism.

Materialism will create obscure mires and miasmas.

Caliginous is the obsession with possession physical.

Murky may be meanderings of minds believed biological.

Dark is the matter they know next to nothing about.

Do you accept dark matter and reject your spirit?

Delight in the light within you to be light-hearted.

Light like a magnet can lift over the dragnet.

The lightest escapes the heaviest.

Light will triumph over darkness.

There is right light that has might.

Light of spirit needs a new sight.

Spiritual sight is of different light.

The might of spiritual sight is light.

Seek to see the lighthouse at night.

Nature is full of divine light round.

Kingfisher flashes to find our heart in river shaded joy.

Our little lives go out like lanterns floating in indigo flaming.

Spiritual dark is us gone astray with backs to the coming day.

True spiritual darkness may appear very bright to the eye.

Do not be afraid of the dark night but seek rays of light.

There's a purple sheen that can be seen at twilight.

Light inside linking beyond creates higher path to holy light.

Flashes of light occur in the night to remind you to fight.

Aurora of polar or southern lights reminds of beautiful night.

As the sunwind colours night poles so you bathe spirit.

Aurora of rosy-fingered dawn follows longest night.

8. Celestial Light

Second light seeks higher. Upwards.

Like to like, visible or not we seek to the heavens to elevate

Light found outside then inside then sought from height.

There has always been light art in heavens to navigate

Sun, moon, stars, planets, comets, meteors in sight.

Sprites are signature of the celestial consulate,

In great secret commonwealth of light.

World once run with fate.

We lose the force of light in us.

Celestial light magnetically indicates.

In shards lie slivered a unified view discarded.

Shallow us now once with cosmic light inundated

The good, true and beautiful reflect hallowed form.

Dreams sometimes of otherworldly light are created.

Lattice of celestial light laced locks within us.

Science explains the magic of light.

Spirit perceives the reality of light.

Religion preserves memory shell of light.

Parapsychology explores encounters with light.

Imagination embraces imaginal and inspires with light.

Not least of the celestial supernal light are we.

In the darkest night our paths are lit by stars.

Loving starry night inspires tale of spirit tail.

We scry our subconscious to see ourselves.

Fashion the passionate searchlight within.

The fluorescent DNA fluoresces in us.

Literal light is there in us and more.

We receive and respond to rays.

We are awash in waves.

We partake of particles in prosperity and poison.

Supercurrents in us circulating inexhaustible light.

Earth, plants, animals, birds shine with natural mystic.

We know the lie of it still even though vanished it seems.

The celestial light is transcendent light immeasurable.

Immanent in us must meet transcendent.

Seeds of light seek to align sun angels.

Daffodil soul of us yields to rainbow spring.

Sunflower soul presses from light-seed within.

Lotus heart of us emerges from the dark waters.

Beauty all over tends to bending light of heaven.

Birds fill the heavens and we seek their power.

We know we can speak the language of birds.

A bird does not know how to fly before it flies.

Spirit birds bring messages in dawn's early light.

Spirit can take flight so lightly we fly in light fearless.

Let bright sun shine through scarlet stained glass in you.

Scratched ruby stained glass of you in leaden frames glows.

Let sunlight shine through scratched crimson pane of you.

Let rose window of you shimmer and walk then in that light.

Let your glass be unimpeded to transmit your tinted light.

Kindness may be a meteor in navy moonlight.

The mystical candelabrum is in you.

9. Journey Towards the Other Light

9.1 Spirit Journeys to Third Light. Up

Lumen naturae and lumen naturale unite with source.

The taste of light inside gives a taste for next course.

Feel of light inside creates feeling for its home.

Such light is gentle, cherishing, warm being.

Such light within and sought without radiates.

Like a prisoner underground escapes seeking sun.

Like the Mole in spring moving upwards to the meadow.

Rumi said that such light may come in through the wound.

We actively seek light or like Scrooge shadow-forced find it.

Swim up from deep in sea of consciousness to feel spirit-sun.

Lightened pilgrims travel with greater ease so unencumbered.

Pilgrims progress to seek the city of light or the gate thereto.

Keep yonder shining light in your eye to go directly thereto.

Where is man who can clamber to heaven? said Gilgamesh.

Upanishads say the light above is the same light in us.

Light can flow into us when we let our light flow.

We forget ego when we let light emerge from ourself.

Diamond beauty found reveals beauty in other light streaming.

Mirror of you polished shows the greater image.

Holy Grail emptied can receive.

Holy Grail is receiving vessel of whole of you.

Like a satellite dish is the wish to receive.

Kabbalah means tradition, reception.

The eye of Horus may be put together again.

Feminine may unite with the masculine to make whole.

When the eye of Horus, of Ra can enter, Osiris can see.

The underworld is us and Osiris can see with a new eye.

This is 64th. Sixth sense. Third eye. Pineal. Accord.

Higher insight and revelation will light the path.

Realise you are children of the light.

Second illumination is to recognise the first light.

First light recognised then towards second tending.

Light of recognised light aspires to the higher.

Centre light of consciousness yin within come to light.

To deny higher light, others conspire.

Light within should transpire.

Light transpired inspires.

Know you have a light in you.

Know yourself here below as above,

Then you should to the higher light aspire.

Seek to know separate the body and the attire.

To comprehend you have light in you never tire.

Spirit is that we suspire.

The spire is spirit.

Yoga is the union of you and above.

Holy Spirit descends to alight on the branch.

Some say lingam appointed, some say sky pointed.

The pillar of light is union of the inner and the outer.

De-materialisation of projection and re-materialisation.

Craft a Stradivarius of soul to have played by various angels.

Sometimes sudden shaft of light may shift the spirit.

Often the goddess of light will coax and tease.

Good is the light that must shine in.

Light shine of goddess is goodness.

O DNA goddess, add goodness.

When light is felt new worlds emerge.

Your light and higher light begin to accord.

Not just with light of the body but of the spirit.

Light of cosmic consciousness may come in a flash.

Light of revelation may be embers from smouldering ash.

Light of realisation may come through a slow dripped hole.

Light you show will provide light to others as example,

When we sense the light for the second time,

A memory of it sets off a chime.

We seek wind whose presence is felt

But whose nature is never entirely spelt.

We journey right by path of light without doubt.

Feeling or discerning our light opens a tunnel out.

Finding or realising light within opens channel up.

Light within us seeks expansion to resonate.

Second light is found in peace or pain.

The light on the path is compassion.

The guiding star is compassion.

Compassion is goodness,

Compassion is the true mark of the goddess.

Compassion is force that draws us the right way.

Compassion is the force that draws the sunflowers.

Compassion is the light reflected through mystics.

Compassion comprehends inter-connectedness.

Compassion is true felt perception of need.

Compassion is the avoidance of injury.

Compassion is calm care with words.

Compassion is cool consideration.

Compassion is contemplation.

Compassion is not of head but heart.

Compassion without heart is shadow-play.

In the cave with false fire plays is only darkness.

Let not the spirit of zero become the ground that is so.

9.2 Third Light Descends if You Ascend

Light lit by Holy Ghost in inglenook of Inn of Nethermost.

It might be the natural light there to be found, lumen naturae.

It is precious pearl presented to the light.

Compassion is immortal orange glow of port and is portal.

Compassion is compass to oneself first.

You suffer first and then you expand the circle.

That space allows the growth of your own light.

Einstein started his journey with a compass as a boy.

The world was governed by hidden forces.

The other compass draws circle of spirit symbol.

Reflection of heaven is the circle.

Compass reflects sun and the person.

Circle reflects the divine, the spirit, self-contained.

Light is the blinking house to guide the vessel on its journey.

The light in you found can then shine elsewhere around.

Light to light will attract and once again as light act.

Realisation, recognition of that light we grow.

Kindness, peace, tranquillity and love are known in the heart.

Perception of presence within are litlinked to lifelight without.

Infinite, cosmic intelligence is in us to be matched.

Qualities within call to yang lightgrace,

The light of vision that Patanjali talked of, is within first.

Recognition of the light within is a stone that lights the trail.

Recognition and seeking allow us to go beyond the veil.

Light is within to rise up to the sun within us.

Vision of our own light is remembrance.

The second light is the secondary seeing of our own light.

To perceive the second light is the mind turning inwards.

Second light is when we look within and realise we have it.

What we find when we look within is the primordial light.

The primary light was in us, it is us.

Directing to our own light enlightens us.

The seed of the sunflower flowers and seeks the sun.

The nature of the sunflower is to turn towards the sun.

What the sunflower does is be what it was meant to be.

Let yourself be and feel need to let you be your nature.

Aligning light of your being with awareness allows accord.

The whole of potential through growth aligns.

We are made to align and accord with above.

Supercelestial force above beckons below.

Aware we wish to open below as above.

Open we see contrast and seek sunny side of street.

Levels of light must be navigated through finer channels.

We craft in little deeds our thought topography.

Software of the hardware is re-written.

A pinprick will allow outside light reflect inside.

Within your being is the photosensitivity to spiritual light.

If you direct your attention to the projections inside you see it.

Signal images available inside depend on your looking.

Plato's cave is about being in prison caves of others.

Spirit is not a shadow-play cave controlled by others.

Heaven is haven of light field in you.

The self must journey to the true self.

The true self is consciousness come into you.

Consciousness light come into you is true you.

The true self tends homeward to home's light.

Self to true self tending homeward to light is beyond words.

True self light-tending homeward is beyond worlds.

Expanded ecstasy is clambering up the ladder light.

It is good for us to come to light.

It is good for us to bring to light.

It is good for us to shine our light.

It is useful to see things in a different light.

Light inside found tends up, light above tends down.

Purpose in us is to tend towards the end.

The end of us is not the end.

End of life is that spirit evolves.

Body is a beautiful bearer of us.

Dropping the brilliant bearer still we are light.

Choose to be the best you can and the light will come.

Choose to allow yourself to receive like a light-vessel.

Choose to be a chalice that receives the upper light.

Choose to be a mirror that reflects the higher.

Choose to be a satellite dish receiving.

Choose to link your light.

Seek relation.

Carnivals of light cannot rival the inner light dreaming.

Stars are brightly shining with twilight's last gleaming.

Cleansing moonlights unbidden calms soul's hidden stains.

Unlike night-fallen meteorite in us light always remains.

Open to immeasurable, infinite light from the Pure Land.

Regarding and remembering embers of heartlight's hand.

Aware of celestial light we float like in a balloon.

Spirit is the UFO of u.

We measure altitude with the hypotenuse of the triangle.

Hypotenuse of light unites I from earth to sky light.

Lightspring in you is nourished by the rain of light.

Institute the rained reign ring of light delight in you

Like a meteor, lightning in a flash the light may come.

10. Lamp and Lighthouse

Find, tend, shine light about.

As the Buddha said, be a lamp unto yourself.

Be a light unto yourself.

That light is in you.

Follow the path of light.

That pearl is to be found within.

It may take time to find source of the pearlescent.

That light emergent seeks to re-unite to bind with its kind.

We use compassion as lantern yellow glow in the darkness.

Trace of rose-gold light through spaces dances when we might crack carapaces of those old circumstances.

Light is such that we feel it.

This light can be felt in the darkness.

In the actual darkness real light may reveal itself most.

The light of accord is warm and calming and banishes fear.

Pure light is not merely a notional force but a real felt one.

The light of the spirit may comfort the disillusioned.

People may say such perception is excess of enthusiasm.

People may say such light is but an illusion.

People may greet such sensations with sarcasm.

People may say such light is a false apprehension.

People may say such light is something of a spasm.

People may say that such light is a deluded deception.

Force of light that bends will of greatest is no phantasm.

In constant consternation light is force of transfiguration.

Still there is a light within that is centre of consciousness.

We see it when we cleanse the lensdoors of perception.

Led with lightness within us we win light-heartedness.

Light expands when we don't stop its emission.

Apprehension of light is water for the seed.

Finding light makes it more likely to free itself.

We must first find light within then shine it abroad.

It is as if we can scale light ladder once we find its base.

We ascend when the ladder extends when rungs are begun.

We rise back up levels we descended from the unbeknownst.

The journey is from darkness around a beam of light found.

The having, seeking, finding begets the rising of us.

So there is a light in us that is seed or spark.

Spark in us is the ark of the covenant.

Ark in us is in the chest in us.

The chest in us has heart.

Heart in us has light.

Covenant is in us.

Accord is in us.

Key is in us.

Find it.

First.

Not in a coven nor convent but in you is light.

Find light within you meditate and mind it to magnetise you.

Don't just find mind in you and light its fuse without.

The Holy Grail is a vessel.

The Holy Grail is a dish.

The Holy Grail is a disc.

The Holy Grail is a cup.

Ace of Cups is in us.

Real – man/cy out = wo/man see in.

The dish is a receiver.

The disc of light channels.

The heart cup receives.

Spiritual photo-sensitive accord.

Do not give the power of the ring to some other Lord.

The Holy Grail to find within you is the receptor.

The receptor responds to your own light.

Activate your light consciousness.

Holy spirit dove alights there.

Marshall thoughts at the Round Table of your mind.

Marshall the horses in the team of your teeming mind.

So light in you is found as ground of your being.

Polished panel of light is radar in spiritual night.

Light realised of you is magnetic levitation moving to more.

Borne light years of stardust born could we be but batter?

U.

Fu.

Focus.

Focus opens aperture.

Spiritual opening is nexus in us.

Nexus to the numinous allows descending light.

Descending light guides the expansion of the ascending light.

Peace and bliss is ease we need to feed the spirit.

With inner eye we can see the high light.

Spirit sees with different sight.

Light makes us bright.

Help see right.

Glimmer.

Gleam.

Glow.

Ray.

Ra.

A.

11. The Influx of Light

11.1 Fourth Illumination. Down-Across

There is that light that never ever goes out at all.

Force of upper light felt by its resonance tall.

The journey begun with a small ray of light,

That took us away from that spiritual night

With focus allows the growth of the beam

Till we can climb above despair it seems.

Light is Ora, this in us and that outside.

Opening wide the spiritual aperture.

Allow greater feeling of rapture.

Polishing the spiritual prism

Uncaptured in that prison.

Nexus to the numinous,

Enhances luminous,

Permits the influx,

Of spiritual lux.

Better than luxury, is peaceful treasury.

Influx of light constant through a permanent hole

Allows albedo accord grow to a healthy whole.

This is fourth light that takes so much time,

When body and extant spirit rhyme.

This side of life's border and beyond

We hope with wider light to bond.

Our cutting away of dross is no loss.

Channel with sextant to receive from across.

Lightbridge we create for packets of light to leave night.

Our light quanta correspond with great potential of source.

Weak emanation in dense matter becomes stronger with orientation to source of light and intelligentia.

Skylight in dome is open mind allowing perpetual light in.

Meditation allows us exit to the sky for a while.

Prayer tunes to resonant forces, contemplation clarifies.

Walks sooth, swims calm, bathing balms but being blisses.

Stillness allows us approach eternal light through the clouds of unknowing, in silent piety not insolent anxiety.

11.2 Create a Nexus to Numinous Light.
Up-down

Light unbeknownst by luxiduct of compassion into being.

Being from light to become within heaviness and darkness of dense matter we need to re-illuminate spirit.

Light of combustion from spark within with advent of higher influx creates efflux of doubt.

Light shining through spirit aperture aligned re-unites within dim chambered darkness.

Like photosynthesis for spirit is that light into this body.

Van Gogh painted the Sunflowers to show us a way.

We are sunflowers that will wilt without light.

Light found within us will bridge with source.

Light within is hidden treasure in measure of universal,

Itself being a treasure that comes from the Unbeknownst.

Radiation of higher light reflects through translucence of us.

Some parts may be translucent even transparent unmediated.

Open sluice of light to make translucence transform.

Loosen trappings of worldly things to make light.

Lighten to enlighten with greater cycles.

Light within linking to the light above is felt.

Knowledge and ritual without living light is not right.

Light lithe and blithe is bliss keeping us out of the abyss.

Spirit sunk in concrete world we miss it.

Spirit does matter more when we are doing more matter.

Material is matrix for aerial spirit to exit.

It matters that spirit doing matter does not strip I.

We degenerate when we follow false light.

We must deal with the dense and thence.

Seek the light that is the great holy spirit agape.

Transitioning spirit levels is like transmission of light.

Holy Spirit of sunlight inspiring from Mother-Father to child.

Inspired we receive spirit to remind us of our own light.

There is a light that comes into us if we open our own.

You want to see and find that light and recycle it.

Find what is light to make heaviness bearable.

If you follow the path of light you wear must ascend.

Sunlight shines in the field of wholly apple-blossomed trees.

12. Pillar of Light

Descend.

Light ray.

Apparition.

Shaft of light.

Column of light.

Beam of light.

Pentecost.

Illumine.

Radiate.

Refract.

Reflect.

Scatter.

Shine.

Ascend.

Stambha.

Komorebi.

Jyotirlinga.

13. Mystic Light

The light that elides makes one from death not hide.

The light that betides makes you calm inside.

The light that guides may illuminate.

Illumination may knowledge create.

Illumination makes instinct strong.

Illuminated thus it is harder to go wrong.

The light that comes in is greater than words.

Some will say that it is but the brain's right part.

Some will say it is but then the false creation of art.

Some will say it is the stuff of trading at the mart.

Some will say it is an illusion of the poor heart.

Some will say it is but a dark demonic dart.

Some will say it is tumbril or death cart.

Light all spiritual leaders will cite.

Light is basis of spiritual might.

Light is sign of what is right.

Light reaches to the height.

14. From This Light to the Next

Michael Row the Boat Ashore. Fifth Illumination. Away.

We are meant to be here and cope and encounter bliss.

Even those thinking us trapped, must take proper path home.

We must appreciate the good and spread light in the darkness.

One candle lights many before spent if wielded with intent.

We should seek light to deal with dark discontent.

We are not meant to live in dim suffering strife.

When we come to death we need not fear,

The path to next life all are able to bear.

As aarti on the river flowing is our life.

Mystical and spiritual life is meant to prepare.

Other side of death's door you may think there is no more.

Even if you think there's no beyond the final chill, light will come still to the fore.

We hope to pass in our bed at night with old age,

Many will not, not even the sage.

But from those who have gone and come back,

The evidence suggests we still stay on the track.

For those who went beyond, the light is still found.

It is a time of relinquishing and expanding our ground.

In bed as we part we expect light-beings to loosen the bond.

When we pass others may see lights going as we go beyond.

Even then in our journey the learned say,

We must search for light in a wonderful new day.

The lessons we learn in our life unfolding

Are forces which help for our direction holding.

The light that never goes out in us, can come back home.

But false lights from us will come back in such bardo zones.

The perception we gained through cleaning our lens,

Is still used then for new ends.

The process recurs, the journey continues.

From free will and lightness in light we descend.

In learning and love we ascend when it is ended.

To prepare for such journeys is always the same,

The compassion and focus on the eternal flame.

The light inside and from outwith we cultivate,

Is the one that will help us ultimately navigate.

The doubt and deadly, the famine and the fear,

End for the being of light in the clear.

Fifth light is of the world we seek,

It beckons us over the final creek.

It pulls us along at the end of tunnel,

It takes spirit into the final funnel.

But though these stages may truth describe,

It all points to one truth we do well to inscribe,

In the base of our being the heart of our heart,

From early on to when we depart,

We are beings of light in a manifold,

Manifest and understood from enlightened of old.

The scintilla therein to focus and foment

By that is what our evolution is meant.

Universe immaterial is material to us in the now.

If we liberate our mind from material present,

We open to inspiration heaven sent.

Light of the universe will continue when you go.

Light of other dimensions unknown persists.

We are of the stuff of all dimensions.

Our quintessence is higher.

Know yourself as light.

Confuse not the container and the content.

We must maximise control of body, mind and spirit.

We must concentrate our light and on our light.

The power of passing is the bringing forth of the light of day.

Let not the light of you be captured.

Let not warm light of you be frozen.

Let not the fast-flying of you be slown.

Let not lighthouse of you fail to shine.

Let not darkness of doubt keep light out.

Let not spirit flame of you be quenched.

Let not hand with torch of you be scorched.

Let not your light receptivity be sullied.

Lights of beings or angels come at times of trauma.

Seeking light at death others may see blest light go.

Passage to next light is dark then light dressed.

See darkness great for light to appreciate.

To handle shadow, tend to candle of hope.

Past, present, future is palimpsest surmountable.

Inside surfer with zest rides waves of time and space.

Heart of you thought-impressed transcends space-time.

Polish diamond mirror heart of you that glitters abroad.

Prepare plastic plasma of monastic monad inside you.

Into your quest without interposition light is invested.

Invested in you are the vestments of luminosity.

We are not to live for the next life but this.

One life at a time, well lived we leave.

Empty-handed we move on.

Relations impressed.

Ship light home.

15. Mystic Path of Light

Evolving spiritually to light is right.

We are urged to live in the now which is good.

Living now does not mean not to learn the past.

The future comes from knowing what lasts.

We must gift a future by being aware.

Aware of beings unborn we must care.

Our consciousness transcends time and space.

Our conscience too transcends time and space.

Our manifested compassion must occur now.

Our learning must occur in the ever present.

All have guiding light within unquenchable.

We aspire to be mensch, no über nor över.

We have all the light potential we need.

We must unfurl our unfettered wings.

They say you have no consciousness.

They say you have no free will.

They will say you have no self.

They will say you are just meat.

They will say you are just a burden.

They will say you should be joined with machines.

They say your consciousness should be pooled.

They will say there is no meaning.

They will say there is no spirit.

They say you were an accident born to die.

You must search for your own lone spirit-light.

You must find and evolve your spiritual consciousness.

If you plant spiritual seeds you will reap spiritual fruit.

You should find compassion and expand your heart-light.

You should seek peace in your sovereignty.

We must be individual spiritual warriors or slaves.

Be a light unto yourselves and then to others.

When you are clear about who you are then shine light.

Light is potential of all possibility lying in us.

Light makes life and beauty and the witness thereof.

Not without but witness within light from wit of our ness.

So we seem to be trapped light but not necessarily only so.

The light in us is meant to matter in matter.

Matter is beautiful so we must enjoy it.

We must liberate light in us.

Spirit must evolve.

Beauty is light of the world we must learn to see.

Loving living things long in light we keep them.

Blinded by reflected machine-light we will lose.

Light we find within we see is same as in others.

Light of spirit is only trapped if we don't free it.

Light in us is in unity and accord with universe.

Light in us with higher spirit united delights life.

Good morning sunshine, master matter brightly.

Let your marvellous spiritual light never fade.

Elbow does not bend backwards in world of dew.

Like Dante's pure beam of high light once seen not forgotten.

Don't rage against dying light within but keep it alive within.

Stay in cave of false fire play, you crave spirit light of day.

No curse, no worse lingering slip silent now like a silk scarf of light surreptitiously shipped light-fingered from sow's purse.

You can still find heaven in heaviness with light.

There is light we see in the sky and lit in living things.

Most light is invisible sometimes hidden even in stone.

Mystics have long said reality is light emitted and intromitted.

Light is spiritual cosmic consciousness manifest in us.

Light is the nature of eternal creative force.

Divine fractal cosmic light makes spooky action at a distance.

The light in us has to be realised like butter from cream.

Realised our light tends upwards towards its source.

Its source is not in gross matter which traps.

Engrossed in gross matter we evolve finding light again.

In matter our spirit must matter by recalling it upwards.

Spirit seeks source descending to it for spiritual evolution.

Peace comes triangulating our found light up with Higher.

We find light in those around and other living things about.

Gravitate to true light avoid false lights before we go away.

Magus Magic = Maya Maybe

16. Lesson of Light

Imagine we know that light is a wave and a beamed particle.

Imagine we can be certain that this dual nature is true.

Someone says light is a wave and particle they are right.

Someone says light is a wave, they are half right,

Someone insists light is only wave, they are wrong.

Someone says light is a particle, they are half right.

Someone insists light is only a particle, they are wrong.

Insistence on truth even if some exists can make you wrong.

Even if you know truth and are certain you may still be wrong.

A finer explanation covering the pre-existing may emerge.

Yesterday's certain explanation is tomorrow's mistake.

What works in one place may not work in another.

On the foreshore we can swim or walk we might

Picking up pebbles to play with in the light.

Open, playful we learn by day or night

Certain but that compassionate spirit is right.

A wide light religion may have existed in the ancient world.

Future could be better served by individual spiritual evolution.

Personal experience from guts, heart and mind we need sense.

Light provides potential path for sole spiritual development.

Insights of spiritual teachers are available like never before.

Every individual is heir to the perennial spiritual insight of all.

Light recurs and makes spiritual sense because it is true.

By looking at wisdom of all spiritual traditions we see same.

Seeking some system of light cycle we may be able to see it.

Matter and things manifest may seem to trap light within us.

Machine people may seek to make our light immoveable.

Experience is reassurance of the universe of reality.

While we need help all history and being allow us evolve.

Humans are meant to evolve spiritually to grow to find peace.

Light is indicator and path to return to our source.

Who and what we are is the real mystery of the trapped light.

The mystery of the trapped light is about how we liberate it.

Solving the mystery of the trapped light is the mystic's quest.

Light concept of reality from experience, knowing and being.

People are made go mad with man's god-made dogma.

Be compassionate, healing, creative, careful to judge,

As spiritual consciousness of the universe embodied

With other bodies of the same stuff dreams are made on

In nature set, feminine and masculine met in Thine will.

That is it because you are that.

Circulate the light through you.

Dark you perceive may not be there nor light if you don't care.

Light you come from, are and will return to through darkness.

We live in a beautiful world we would do well to live well in.

Spiritual worlds should enhance places we live in and how.

Love your body and mind striving for best version of them.

If you are vessel, ship of light be see-worthy.

No machine will ever surpass the least of us.

But machines and science will turn us inside out.

Outside will become in and our inside will be brought to light.

As you succumb daily to machine servitude you taunt gaily ghosts unseen who will haunt eternity still for your attitude in cowardice of comfort yet your own shadow to come.

Glossary

A Burst of Conscious Light: *Near-Death Experiences, the Shroud of Turin, the Limitless Potential of Humanity* Book by Dr. Andrew Silverman (2020).

A Clockwork Orange (1962) Novel by Anthony Burgess.

Aarti (Sanskrit) Hindu lights.

Abdrushin (1875-1941) Oskar E. Bernhardt wrote *Grail Message*.

Abhinavagupta (circa 950-1016) Kashmir mystic.

Abjection A degraded state.

Abulafia, Abraham (circa 1240-1290) Spanish Jewish Kabbalist.

Accord To be in agreement with.

Ace of Cups Tarot card.

ADC After Death Communications. This domain is increasingly studied by scientists and reveals a consistently high percentage of individuals reporting a perception of communication after the death of people they know.

Adonis Lover of Aphrodite in Greek mythology.

Adularescence An optical phenomena produced by light scattering in a milky glow.

AE Russell (1867-1935) Irish mystic, artist and writer. George William was his name before he became fascinated with the word 'aeon' and used it as a pen name before that word interested some other notables.

Aerodynamism Study of motion of air and objects.

Aeromancy Divination of atmosphere, weather forecasting.

Agape (Greek) Highest form of love, love of the Divine, charity.

Aghori (Sanskrit) Hindu ascetics who go against purity and embrace darkness through taboo practices.

Agni (Sanskrit) Hindu God of fire.

Agrippa von Nettesheim, Heinrich Cornelius (1486-1535) Lawyer, theologian, philosopher, soldier, occultist. Wrote *De Occulta Philosophia* and much more. An influence on Dr. Frankenstein in the book.

Ahimsa (Sankrit) Non-injury.

Ahmed, Rollo (1899-1958) *The Black Art,* 1936. Regarded by some, ridiculed by others perhaps by those more familiar with those arts than he.

Ahura Mazda Zoroastrian creator deity.

AI Artificial Intelligence.

Air bomber's moon Moonlight was important for air bombers working at night.

Akasha (Sanskrit) A Hindu concept of ether associated with Theosophy and other groups with belief such as the information bearing capacity thereof in relation to the past.

Al Din Kubra, Najm (1145-1221) A Sufi mystic and martyr who emphasised light of a spiritual nature.

Al Ghazali, Abu Hamid (1058-1111) Persian philosopher and mystic who wrote *The Niches of Light* and moved from the academic to the Sufi mystical path.

Al Hallaj (858-922) Persian Sufi, mystic, poet, martyr.

Al Haytham, Hasan Ibn (965-1040) Polymath interested in optics.

Al Kindi, Abu Yusuf (circa 801-873) Polymath philosopher influential in the study of optics.

Al Makki, Abu Talib (10th century) Sufi mystic.

Al Quzat Hamadani, Ayn (1098-1131) Mystic, philosopher.

Aladdin Ancient fairytale from Middle East.

Albedo Reflected light, incident radiation.

Alchemy Ancient philosophy and precursor of certain sciences linked to transmutation of material and magic.

Aldini, Giovanni (1762-1834) Physician from Bologna, interested in lighthouses, galvanism who performed famous demonstration of electro-stimulus on a criminal's dead body in London.

Aleixandre, Vincente (1898-1984) Spanish poet, winner of Nobel prize, author of Conocomiento de Rubin Darío.

Alexander, Eben Contemporary writer on his NDE who worked as a neurosurgeon.

Allusive Suggestive, indirect.

Alterity Otherness.

Alternative Reality Game Idea of immersive, interactive constructed online game with interventions into the reality thereof suggestive of a greater idea that reflects the Greek mythology of gods interfering in human affairs.

Alumbrados Group of heretical, mystical Christians who seemed to believe in individual illumination without external systems.

American Transcendentalism Movement in the US, influenced by Eastern thinking and Unitarianism, which stresses the individual, intuition, self-reliance and contact with nature, reflecting some of the Romantic movement. Thoreau and Emerson led the way.

Amida Buddhism associated with the Pure Land Buddhism.

Amplitudehedron A geometric structure used to simplify particle interactions, from Nima Arkani-Hamed.

An Claidheamh Soluis Irish meaning The Sword of Light which comes from Irish myth and also was used as the name for an Irish nationalist newspaper.

Anamnesis Implies a remembrance of the past, past lives or states.

Anathema Means excommunication but more commonly shunning.

Anchoress, anchorite A religious person who lived in a confined space to dedicate themselves to prayer and contemplation.

Angra Mainyu (Avestan) Ahriman, destructive Zoroastrian spirit.

Animism Belief of world and objects invested with spirits.

Anthropological Study of humans.

Antinomian A person who rejects existing moral systems or specifically in Christianity who believes in salvation by faith.

Apollo Greek and Roman god associated with many things such as sun and light. Apollian is used to describe ordered masculine, higher cortex functions by Paglia for example.

Apotheosis Raising an individual to godlike or divine status.

Apparition Appearances of Divine figures e.g. the Virgin Mary.

Apprehension Here, the act of understanding a concept.

Arche (Greek) Origin or source.

Archetypal Of original model or universal symbol used particularly by Jung in relation to the collective unconscious.

Archons Evil or demonic entities that rule the material world.

Ariel In *The Tempest* he was imprisoned by a witch until released and bound by Prospero. He acts as a benevolent force though he can cause thunder storms. His good actions allow him be released.

Aristotle (384-322 BC) Great Greek philosopher.

Ark of the Covenant Golden container/s that housed the ten commandments or some other sacred objects or force.

Armageddon Often conceived to be a final battleground or campaign based on Biblical extrapolation associated with Megiddo in Israel.

Ascetic Abstaining from pleasures of senses (like a glossary writer).

Astral Associated with the stars but having a specific meaning in many esoteric and magical disciplines.

Asunder Separate.

Athena, Despoina Atari, Dr. Article *'The Light of Hellenism,'* Paradigm Explorer, 2020/1.

Attire State of dress.

Atum (Egyptian) Solar god.

Aura Perceived atmosphere or emanation around people.

Aurobindo, Sri (1872-1950) Indian philosopher, spiritual leader, poet, yogi.

Aurora (Latin) The name of the Roman goddess of dawn is used for dawn as well as the polar lights.

Auto-da-fé Catholic ceremony of public penance.

AWOL Absent without leave.

Axion Hypothetical elementary particle.

Ayahuasca Traditional South American spiritual concoction derived from vines.

Aztecs Native Americans who had an empire in Mexico.

Ba (Egyptian) Various interpretation of bird symbol for spirit, usually after death, could be a manifestation of our true spirit.

Bacchus Another name for Dionysius, god of wine, fertility and ecstatic experience who liberates through possession, used in mystery traditions in Greece.

Bacon, Francis (1561-1626) Philosopher, statesman, empiricist. Associated with esoteric bodies. Wrote the *New Atlantis*.

Bacon, Francis (1909-1992) Irish born painter.

Bacon, Roger (1220-1292) 'Doctor Mirabilis,' friar, philosopher, scientist, magician. Interested in scientific experiment.

Bailey, Alice (1880-1949) Celebrated theosophist, esoteric writer.

Balder Norse god, son of Odin perhaps meaning shining one.

Ball and chain Heavy impediment tied to a prisoner's leg.

Ballard, Guy (1878-1939) Pen name Godfre Ray King inspired the I AM movement.

Bardo Tibetan idea of place between death and rebirth.

Barrett, William F. (1844-1925) Professor of Physics.

Batter In cooking a mixture of milk, eggs and flour.

Baudrillard, Jean (1929-2007) Cultural theorist.

Beamish Smiling radiantly, beaming.

Bechsgaard, Gitte *The Gift of Consciousness, Patanjali's Yoga Sutras*. Book 1, Cambridge Scholars.

Bécquer, Gustav Adolfo (1836-1870) Spanish Romantic writer.

Becquerel, Henri (1852-1908) Scientist, discovered radioactivity.

Behan, Brendan (1923-1964) Poet, writer, Republican.

Behaviourists Scientists who focus on studying how people behave and less of what is in their mind, often tending to suggest determinism it seems.

Bell, John Stewart (1928-1990) Physicist born in Belfast. Famous for Bell's Theorem.

Benedict XVI, Pope Joseph Ratzinger, *Jesus of Nazareth: Holy Week: From the Entrance into Jerusalem to the Resurrection.* 2011 particularly at pages 69 and 265.

Benediction Blessing.

Bennet, Edward Armstrong (1888-1977) Born in Ireland. Expert on Jung, who wrote about conversations.

Bentham, Jeremy (1748-1832) Philosopher.

Betide To happen.

Bhavacakra (Sanskrit) A wheel of life.

Binaural beats Beats created by different frequencies of sound entering the ears that are claimed to induce altered states by changing brainwave patterns.

Biologism The undue focus on determinism due to biology.

Bioluminescence Emission of light from living organisms.

Biophotons Photons of light produced by biological systems, manifested in biophotonics.

Bits A binary digit, basic unit of information.

Blake, William (1757-1827) Artist, poet, seer.

Blavatsky, Helena (1831-1891) Author, theosophist.

Blazing Lamp, Tantra of Important text in Tibetan Buddhism.

Blest Blessed.

Blight Plant disease of destructive force.

Blithe Happy, light-hearted.

Blue Lies September (2019) James Tunney. Dystopian novel.

Body-snatchers These were the people encouraged by the medical profession to collect corpses for the teaching of anatomy, which led at times to murder to facilitate fresh specimens.

Boehme, Jacob (1575-1624) Christian philosopher, mystic.

Bogdanov, Alexander (1873-1928) Russian Communist theorist.

Bogomil 10th century Bulgarian Christian Gnostic heresy.

Bohm, David (1917-1992) American physicist who developed ideas of the implicate order.

Bolshevik Party of Marxists founded by Lenin in 1912.

Bön Tibetan religion.

Booker, Christopher (1937-2019) Author of *The Seven Basic Plots: Why we Tell Stories*. Booker indicates how mysteries are a late type of story. He also uses light and dark to indicate bright and shadow sides of characters or types. Thus we have the light and dark feminine type for example.

Booty Plunder.

Bosch, Hieronymus (circa 1450-1516) Dutch painter who explored the archetypal and unconscious in visual form.

Boyle, Robert (1627-1691) Scientist, chemist and philosopher.

Bragg's Reflection This identifies the angles of reflection of rays from a crystal structure.

Brahman (Sanskrit) The ultimate reality essence or consciousness behind phenomena.

Brazen Head Magical, mechanical head made of brass. Brazen also means without shame and thus may refer to talking heads.

Brigid Pagan goddess in Ireland and the Celtic world.

Bruno, Giordano (1548-1600) Friar, magician, theologian.

Bucke, Richard Maurice (1837-1902) Psychiatrist.

Burgess, Anthony (1917-1993) Great writer from Manchester.

Burke, Edmund (1729-1797) Dublin born statesman, philosopher.

Burnished Highly polished by friction, lustrous, smooth and bright.

Bynum, Edward Bruce *Dark Light Consciousness: Melanin, Serpent Power, and the Luminous Matrix of Reality,* (2012).

Byrne, Lorna Spiritual teacher communicating with angels.

Byron, Lord (1788-1824) English poet, peer, politician, celebrated in Greece for his interest in independence.

Byzantine Relating to Byzantium (present Istanbul) or empire.

Caduceus Two serpents entwined on a stick, symbol of medicine and arising in Greek and Egyptian mythology.

Caliginous Dark, dim. From the Latin Caligo.

Caltech Californian Institute of Technology.

Calvino, Italo (1923-1985) Writer.

Camera lucida Optical device to enhance drawing.

Camera obscura Dark room or pinhole camera allowing outside image be projected within, used by some painters.

Campbell, Joseph (1904-1987) Professor of Literature.

Campbell, Tom Physicist, researcher in consciousness.

Candelabrum Unified holder for multiple candles.

Candle of Vision *Autobiography of a Mystic* (1918) AE Russell.

Carapace Shell.

Caravaggio, Michelangelo Merisi Da (1571-1610) One of the greatest painters ever.

Carnival Related to idea of flesh, putting away thereof, party before fasting. *Carnival of Light* was an avant-garde recording made by the Beatles near impossible to find.

Carr, Bernard Physicist, interested in psychic research.

Casement Window with hinges that open outwards.

Cat's Eyes Refers to the technology used to reflect light back to its source similar to actual cat's eyes based on *tapetum lucidum* cells or tissue at the back of their eyes. Jaguar eyes in the dark are significant symbols.

Category error A mistake associated with presenting one thing as if it belongs to another category.

Cathars A variant of Christianity, consistent with elements of Gnosticism, Buddhism and the Bogomils and reflecting some mystery school wisdom believing that we are spirits trapped in flesh by a lesser version of God. They were persecuted and exterminated by a Crusade and the Inquisition.

Celestial Heavenly, aerial, of the heavens.

Ceraunomancy Divination by thunder.

Chalice A cup often used in sacred or magical settings.

Chalmers, David Contemporary philosopher associated with the 'hard problem of consciousness.'

Champignon (French) A type of edible mushroom.

Champollion, Jean Francois (1790-1832) Great French innovator in interpretation of hieroglyphics.

Chaplin, Charlie (1889-1977) Great actor, director, composer.

Chardin, Teilhard de (1881-1955) Priest, palaeontologist and theologian.

Charism Gift of the Holy Spirit.

Charlatanism False or fraudulent practitioners or tricksters.

Cherenkov, Pavel (1904-1990) Soviet scientist who discovered the bluish glow of radioactive material under water.

Chomsky, Noam Contemporary historian, philosopher, linguist. He co-wrote *Manufacturing Consent: the Political Economy of the Mass Media* which put forward the 'propaganda model.'

Chromoluminarism Using optical effects of dots or bands of colour by Neo-Impressionists in painting to create luminosity.

Churchill, Winston (1874-1965) Prime Minister, writer.

Ciborium Cup or bowl for the communion in Catholicism.

Circumambulation Walking around holy objects or places.

Clairvoyance Clear seeing beyond the normal range of sensory perception, second sight.

Clare, Anthony (1942-2007) A celebrated professional and media psychiatrist and Professor from Ireland.

Cleave This is the word often used to describe the mystical tendency to reach for some kind of union with the Divine.

Cocoon Protective casing especially for insects to develop.

Cod Although a type of fish, here it means to fool.

Cold Light Light without heat.

Colditz Famous WWII German prisoner of war camp, used in a series of books by escapees.

Coleridge, Samuel Taylor (1772-1834) Poet, philosopher, Romantic.

Collegiants, Dutch Groups of Protestants without clerics.

Collider An accelerator which makes particles collide.

Comenius, John Amos (1592-1670) Philosopher, theologian, educator. See for example Howard Hotson, 'Via Lucis in tenebras. Comenius as prophet as the Age of Light,' in *Let There be Enlightenment. The Religious and Mystical Sources of Rationality,* eds. Matytsin and Edelstein, pg. 23.

Compass Instrument to find direction or to draw circles and arcs.

Confucianism Influential philosophy based on Confucius, emphasising value of secular, social conduct.

Conjecture Opinion without final or sufficient basis.

Conjure Generally means causing spirits to appear but it has another meaning of swearing an oath together.

Conscience Inner sense of right and wrong of the individual.

Consulate Where a consul or foreign representative operates from.

Copernicus, Nicolaus (1473-1543) Polish polymath, scientist.

Corbin, Henry (1903-1978) Philosopher, theologian.

Cordovero, Moses ben Jacob de (1522-1570) Kabbalist, writer of many works including *Ohr Yakar* (A Precious Light) and *Ohr Neerav* (A Pleasant Light).

Correspondences An elaborate or simple doctrine which seeks relationships within a whole or as with Swedenborg where the material world reflects a spiritual world.

Cosmic consciousness This is identified with Bucke and William James and suggests a higher consciousness more consistent with that regarded as fundamental in the universe by some.

Cosmology Study of origin and evolution of the universe.

Counterfeit False imitation.

Coven Gathering of witches.

Covenant Agreement. In spiritual terms it often refers to an agreement or promise between God and individuals.

Crick, Francis (1916-2004) Biologist, neuroscientist. Proponent of double helix DNA molecule with Watson.

Crookes, William (1832-1919) Chemist, physicist.

Crowley, Aleister (1875-1947) Writer, poet, painter, magician.

Crystallomancy Divination by crystals.

Cubism A style of painting, sculpture and architecture associated with Picasso and others that utilises multiple perspectives and planes to create a sense of dynamism.

Curie, Marie (1867-1934) Polish-French physicist. Double Nobel prize winner, discoverer or radium and polonium.

Curie, Pierre (1859-1906) French physicist.

Cybernetics Study of control and communications in human, animals and machines with particular emphasis on information and feedback, promoted by Norbert Weiner (1894-1964) and relevant to AI, robotics and unfortunately the control of humans.

Cymatics Study of the visible manifestations of sound.

Da Vinci, Leonardo (1452-1519) Great artist and polymath.

Daedulus (Greek) Mythic craftsman, architect, father of Icarus.

Daemonologie Book by King James (1599).

Daemons A guiding spirit, higher self or lesser god.

Dana or Danu Ancient Irish goddess.

Dante, Alighieri (1265-1321) Writer of the *Divine Comedy*.

Darby, John Nelson (1800-1882) Anglo-Irish Barrister, Bible teacher, member of the Plymouth Brethren. Seen to be the main promoter of Dispensationalism.

Darwinitis Term used by Tallis to suggest overuse of Darwin through biological reductionism.

Davy, Humphry (1778-1829) English inventor.

Dazzling darkness Recurrent description of mystical experiences indicating a darkness of inherent scintillating quality.

De Sade, Marquis (1740-1814) Revolutionary, writer, philosopher. Origin of term 'sadism.'

Dee, John (1527-1609) Polymath, magician to Elizabeth I, mystic, scientist, original 007.

Della Francesca, Piero (1416-1492) Celebrated Italian painter.

Della Porta, Giambattista (circa 1536-1615) Polymath and student of the esoteric who wrote Magia Naturalis.

Demain (French) Tomorrow.

Denkoroku (Record of the Transmission of Light) Zen book written in 1300 by Master Keizan Jokin Zenji.

Dermavision Claim that some people can see with their skin.

Descartes, René (1596-1650) Scientist, philosopher.

Determinism Idea that events are determined by existing causes.

Dick, Philip K. (1928-1982) Great Californian writer, philosopher and mystic.

Dickens, Charles (1812-1870) Great London writer.

Dionysius Greek god of wine, fertility and ecstasy, also known as Bacchus and involved in liberating people from their trapped potential. Dionysian represents this force in theory.

Dionysius the Areopagite First century Athenian who became a saint.

Dirac, Paul (1902-1984) English theoretical physicist who won the Nobel Prize and contributed to quantum electrodynamics.

Dispensationalism An idea of Biblical interpretation in accordance with unfolding ages with different features.

Disruptive Colouration A type of camouflage based on distortion of image perception through bands of light and dark colour.

Divination Indicated by 'mancy,' meaning seeking to know divine, foretell future or detect hidden. Predictive, prefigures psychology, prognosis. Francis Bacon distinguished artificial requiring signs and natural perceived within.

Divine With capitals indicates a specific idea of It but lower case is used in a more general sense.

Diwali (Sanskrit) Hindu festival of lights, row of lights.

DMT Dimethyltryptamine. Sometimes called the 'spirit molecule,' psychedelic substance available in certain plants that also occurs in the human body.

DNA Deoxyribonucleic acid, the double helix molecule that carries genetic information.

Dogon Ethnic group from Mali.

Don't immanentize the eschaton A phrase used to suggest the undesirability of hastening the end of the world.

Donoghue v. Stevenson [1932] AC 562.

Double slit Experiment showing dual nature of light.

Dragnet A comprehensive net to trap something.

Dragon Rouge International occult order based in Sweden.

Dross Worthless.

Dubuis, Jean (1919-2010) French scientist, esoteric leader.

Duck You Sucker! (1971) Film by Sergio Leone. Also named A Fistful of Dynamite and Once upon a Time the Revolution.

Duende (Spanish) Meaning a spirit or inspiration.

Dzogchen (Tibetan) Meaning great perfection. Path in Tibetan Buddhism to liberation.

Echolocation Use of soundwaves to locate and travel.

Eckankar Religion founded by Paul Twitchell in 1965.

Eckartshausen, Karl von (1752-1803) German mystic.

Ectoplasm Substance supposedly coming from mediums associated with spirit manifestations.

Eddington, Arthur (1882-1944) English scientist.

Edison, Thomas (1847-1931) Great American inventor who invented a light bulb and the motion picture camera.

Efflux Flowing out of substance.

Ehrman, Bart D. Contemporary professor of religious studies.

Ein Soph (Hebrew) In Kabbalah refers to source, infinity or God.

Einstein, Albert (1879-1955) Great German theoretical physicist.

Elcesaites Early-Jewish-Christian sect.

Electromagnetic Spectrum Entire range of light; radio-waves, microwaves, infrared, visible light, ultraviolet, X-rays and gamma rays that vary in frequency. Sound is left out because it needs a medium.

Elide To merge.

Eliminative Materialism Is a philosophical approach that uses materialism to eliminate certain mental elements of common sense as unreliable.

Empedocles (circa 494-434 BC) Greek pre-Socratic philosopher interested in many things including light and vision.

Empyrean Derived from Latin and Greek word for fire, its implication is misleading in spiritual terms in that it is rather light than physical fire.

Entheogenic Psychoactive substances which make the person 'full of god' through the feelings of awe induced.

Entoptic This refers to visual images that appear within the eye.

Entropy Usually associated with decline into disorder or lack of energy to create different types thereof.

Entryist Idea propounded by Leon Trotsky (1879-1940) and other Marxists like Gramsci involves the subversion of institutions to undermine their power to facilitate revolutionary change.

Epimetheus Forgotten brother of Prometheus.

Epiphany Manifestation, appearance or divine revelation.

Epistemology Study of the nature of knowledge.

Eriugena (circa 815-877) Irish theologian who wrote *The Division of Nature*.

Eschatology The doctrine of final causes.

Escheat Reversion of property to the lord or State.

Escrow Agreement involving a third party care of a bond, money or code.

Esoteric Meant for within a small group of people, specialised.

Ether Upper regions of the sky, formerly an invisible substance believed to permeate the universe, also an anaesthetic substance.

Etymology The history and linguistic origin of a word.

Euclid (circa 325 BC) Father of geometry.

Evans-Wentz, Walter (1878-1965) Wrote the *The Fairy Faith in Celtic Countries* based on his doctoral thesis and helped publish the *Tibetan Book of the Dead* in English.

Eviscerates To deprive of central elements, from the practice of removing central organs of humans or animals.

Exacerbate To make worse or more severe.

Exorcism Religious or spiritual attempt of removal of demonic forces from a possessed person.

Exoteric External and for the general public.

Expunge Remove completely.

Extant Still surviving or in existence.

Externalities Impacts on a third party often negative in economics.

Ezekiel Hebrew prophet.

Faraday, Michael (1791-1867) English scientist who explored electromagnetism.

Fatima Village in Portugal associated with the apparition of the Virgin Mary and the Miracle of the Sun in 1917 and the Three Secrets.

Faust Legends based on a German alchemist which were dramatised by Christopher Marlowe and Goethe.

Faustian Pact A pact with the devil.

Fenwick, Peter Neuropsychiatrist who has worked in particular on the dying process and the paradigm of science.

Fetch In Ireland and UK this was a supernatural double of a living person often at time of death.

Feynman, Richard (1918-1988) Theoretical physicist, wrote about light and matter, building on the work of Dirac and others.

Fibre-optics Transmission of data by light through cables.

Firefly A beetle whose body produces light.

Fission Separating into different parts.

FitzGerald, George Francis (1851-1901) Irish physicist.

Five Pure Lights Teaching of Dzogchen Buddhism.

Flotsam and Jetsam Materials floating from sinking ship.

Fluorescent Emitting light exposed to x-rays or visible light.

Fluoride Chemical substance added to the water supposedly to prevent tooth decay.

Fodder Food.

Ford, Debbie (1955-2013) *Dark Side of the Light Chasers* (1998).

Foreshore The inter-tidal zone, sea or land depending.

Fortune, Dion (1890-1946) Magician, author.

Forty Thieves Reference to the story of Ali Baba.

Fox, George (1624-1691) English Quaker founder.

Fractal A shape where the whole is made of same shaped parts.

Franklin, Benjamin (1706-1790) Scientist, statesman, polymath, inventor of the lightning rod amongst other things.

Frazer, George (1854-1941) Wrote *The Golden Bough* (1890).

Freemasons Fraternal, esoteric organisations with varying histories and rites that link back through working masons to Egypt and other places.

Freud, Sigmund (1856-1939) Great psychoanalyst.

Frost, Robert (1874-1963) American poet.

Fu (Chinese) Taoist concept meaning returning.

Fukuyama, Francis Contemporary political writer.

Fusion Joining together of small parts creating change or reaction.

Gabriel Archangel, significant to a number of religions.

Gaia (Greek) Mother earth goddess.

Galvani, Luigi (1737-1798) Doctor, philosopher who studied bioelectricity with experiments on animals.

Galvanisation Used to refer to the electro-stimulation of muscles.

Gamma rays Shortest wavelength on the electromagnetic spectrum resulting from radioactive decay and nuclear fission.

Ganzfeld Effect Perception and reactions caused by deprivation of diverse stimulus to brain as a result of unstructured uniform monostimulus causing unusual images, patterns or hallucinations. Possible origin of much Neolithic symbolism.

Gardner, Gerald (1884-1964) Witch, founder of Wiccanism.

Garuda (Hindu) Divine flying creature or sun-bird.

Gaslighting Manipulative use of a person's doubt to undermine accurate perceptions of reality by denial, misinformation and misdirection to promote an alternative, untrue version.

Gewacke, Marilyn Contemporary psychological explorer. See article in New Observations, Issue 132.

Ghostly Adjective of ghost which formerly referred to the spirit.

Gikatilla, Joseph ben Abraham 13th century Spanish Kabbalist.

Gilgamesh Hero of the ancient Sumerian epic poem.

Gita, Bhagavad (Sanskrit) Sacred, ancient text in long verse called the Song of God, involving a discussion between Arjuna and Krishna.

Gladiate Shaped like a sword.

Gnostic Gnosis. Relates to word knowledge in Greek and to certain groups two thousand years ago in early Christian and Jewish sects who focused on individual spiritual transformation.

Goethe, Johann Wolfgang von (1749-1832) One of the greatest minds.

Goetia (Greek) Sorcery, conjuration of demons.

Golem A magically created animated being from a shapeless mass of clay or earth in Hebrew folklore and mysticism.

Gothic May refer to Goths, ancient or modern, a type of architecture or a genre of novels with distinctive elements often about the supernatural.

Gráinne Irish legendary figure who may have reflected an earlier sun goddess.

Gramsci, Antonio (1891-1937) Italian Marxist.

Grand Unified Theory A model of an anticipated field in particle physics.

Great Chain of Being Developed from Plato to Plotinus and indicated a ladder of being from fullness to many manifestations from One to the Other, God to creatures, from spirit to matter, from humans down to animals and plants.

Great Luminary, The May represent the sun or a position in certain esoteric organisations or simply an individual such as Francis Bacon.

Great Spirit The Native American conception of the divine or celestial figure or God.

Grof, Stanislav Psychologist, developer of Holotropic breathing.

Gross Means flagrant or without deduction or awful.

Grosseteste, Robert (1175-1253) Bishop, philosopher, theologian.

Grosz, George (1893-1959) German Expressionist painter.

Hagiography The celebration of saints suggesting uncritical biography.

Hall, Manly P. (1901-1990) Canadian mystic, writer on esoterica.

Hallowed Holy, sacred from root word meaning whole.

Hallucinogen Substance that causes hallucinations.

Hard Problem of Consciousness Description of philosopher David Chalmers of issue materialists find difficult i.e. where does consciousness and phenomenal experience come from.

Harris, Sam Contemporary thinker, author of *Waking Up. A Guide to Spirituality without Religion* (2014).

Haven A safe place.

Hawking, Stephen (1942-2018) Among many things he conceived blackbody radiation predicted to come from black holes.

Hayman, Ronald (1932-2019) Wrote *A Life of Jung* (2001). The Jung quote is therefrom.

Heaney, Seamus (1939-2013) Irish poet.

Heard, Gerald (1889-1971) British writer, perennialist and leader of consciousness studies.

Heaven's Gate An infamous UFO religious group that led to a mass suicide.

Hecht, Anthony (1923-2004) US poet.

Hefty Heavy, forceful.

Heidegger, Martin (1889-1976) German philosopher.

Heisenberg, Werner Karl (1901-1976) Theoretical physicist who played a key role in the understanding of quantum physics. Known for the Uncertainty Principle.

Helios (Greek) God of the sun.

Heliotherapy Use of sunlight as therapy, especially for skin.

Heliotropism Turning towards the sun in plants.

Hellfire Clubs Series of clubs for aristocrats round Britain and Ireland in 18th century.

Helmholz, Herman von (1821-1894) German physicist.

Heresy Unorthodox position such as The Heresy of the Free Spirit.

Hermeticism Esoteric philosophy associated with Hermes Trismegistus expounded in the *Corpus Hermetica*.

Hermit, The This Tarot Card IX involves the person with the light to show the way. It suggests a unity of light.

Herophilos (circa 335-280 BC) Greek physician.

Hessdalen lights Recurrent lights seen in a valley in Norway.

Hildegard of Bingen (1098-1179) German Christian mystic.

Hitodama (Japanese) Balls of light that appear at night and may be believed to be souls of the dead.

Hockney, David Contemporary painter who has also studied the use of optical devices in art history.

Hoffman, Donald Cognitive psychologist who is developing a theory of conscious agents with books like *The Case against Reality: Why Evolution hid Reality from our Eyes*, 2019.

Holarchy System based on a number of whole, self-contained parts.

Holography The making of holograms.

Holon A part that is a whole. Term coined by Arthur Koestler.

Holy Ghost or Holy Spirit One aspect of God for Christians or the power of God for others.

Holy Grail Generally considered to be the cup from which Jesus drank from at the Last Supper, associated with Joseph of Arimathea and King Arthur, although other explanations exist.

Homunculus Artificial individual, form of a small human being.

Hoodwinked To be tricked.

Hooke, Robert (1635-1703) English scientist, polymath.

Hopkins, Gerard Manley (1844-1889) English Jesuit priest and poet who came to work in Ireland.

Horus, Eye of Protective Egyptian symbol.

Hubbard, L. Ron (1911-1986) Science fiction writer, founder of Scientology.

Hubris (Greek) Too much self-pride.

Hume David (1711-1776) Scottish philosopher.

Huygens, Christian (1629-1695) Scientist, inventor and astronomer particularly interested in light.

Hyde, Lewis Scholar who wrote *Tricksters Make this World* (1983).

Hydromancy Divination by water.

Hypnogogic State characterised by visions on falling asleep.

Hypnopompic State characterised by visions on waking up.

Hypnosis Refers to the concentration of attention such that a state of suggestibility arises generally for some purpose.

Hypotenuse Long side of a right-angled triangle, significant in esoteric lore, maybe mispresented at times.

Hypsistarians An obscure religion claimed to be a pagan offshoot of Judaism that flourished around the Black Sea and elsewhere in Russia for a couple of centuries before and after the birth of Christ that may have had an element of worship of light and fire.

I Ching *Book of Changes*. Ancient Chinese divination text.

Iamblichus (circa 242-325) Neo-Platonist particularly associated with interpretation of early texts and theurgy.

Ides Middle days of month in Roman times.

Ignatius of Loyola (1491-1556) Spanish founder of the Jesuits.

Ignus Fatus Mystic light of marshes maybe from released gases.

Illuminati May refer to the Bavarian Secret Sect of the later 18th century or be used to mean a shady controlling elite. The concept refers more to Enlightenment appropriation of spiritual light as something much narrower and instrumental.

Illuminatio (Latin) Illumination.

Illuminationism School of philosophy associated with Suhrawardi built on Neo-Platonism which uses light as central concept.

Illuminism This has various meanings and usually implies a scheme of illumination or enlightenment which have different emphases about how to obtain it.

Iluminismo Catalan mystical branch, enlightenment through grace.

Imaginal May relate to the imagination or the stage of transformation of an insect, by analogy to humans.

Immanent Pervasive in relation to divinity.

Imprimitura (Italian) Usually a dark layer underpainting.

Incarceration Imprisonment.

Incarnation Refers to spirit becoming flesh.

Ineffable Beyond expression.

Infancy Gospel of Thomas Non-canonical story of childhood of Jesus.

Inflection A slight change in voice or word to change state.

Inner light Used by some spiritual traditions, particularly Quakers who refer to light within. Also a Beatles song, refers to their Indian influence. Concept is part of perennial wisdom tradition.

Inscribe To write upon.

Inspiration From the Latin root which means to breathe in or take spirit in.

Instantaneity Done in an instant.

Instantiated Embodied, provide an example.

Intellectus (Latin) Understanding, sense.

Intelligentia (Latin) Christian sense of divine intelligence.

Introjection Various meanings but generally incorporating other views into your personality.

Intromitted This refers to theory of light coming in, also means introduction of male member.

Introspection Looking within.

Irish Triads Set of poetic lines or instructions from the 800's, translated from Irish by Kuno Meyer.

Isis (Egyptian) Goddess wife of Osiris, protector of Horus.

Iyengar, B.K.S. (1918-2014) Founder of Iyengar yoga.

Jack o' lantern Light in pumpkin, from Celtic light in a turnip based on stories of wandering spirits neither in heaven or hell. Also a type of poisonous mushroom that glows in the dark.

Jacklights A lantern used for hunting at night.

Jinn The demonic or supernatural beings of Arabia and Islam.

Job Prophet, subjected to great trials.

John of the Cross (1542-1591) Spanish mystic and saint.

Jones, Rufus (1863-1948) American Quaker.

Jorjani, Jason Reza Contemporary philosopher. See Prometheism.com for example.

Josephson, Brian Contemporary, Nobel laureate, pioneer in frontier of mind-matter studies.

Joyce, James (1882-1941) Great Irish writer (decent singer too).

Judas Apostle who betrayed Christ, subject of much artistic inspiration. Appears in a more favourable light in the Gnostic text The Gospel of Judas.

Judo (Japanese) The gentle way. Japanese martial art based on mastering throws, locks and chokes founded by Kano.

Jung, Carl (1875-1961) Great psychoanalyst, psychiatrist.

Jyotirlinga A sign or symbol associated with Shiva and an infinite pillar of light reflected in various temples in India.

Jyotisha (Sanskrit) Used for Indian astronomy and astrology.

Kabbalah (Hebrew) Meaning reception or tradition and describing a school of mysticism in Judaism.

Kaiser, David Contemporary historian of science. *How the Hippies Saved Physics; Science, Counterculture and the Quantum Revival* (2011).

Kalacakra (Sanskrit) Esoteric or tantric teachings in Buddhism.

Kaleidoscope Optical device which creates changing patterns through reflection and rotation.

Kali (Sanskrit) Generally a Hindu goddess but also may have a darker form.

Karma (Sanskrit) Idea of spiritual cause and effect.

Kavanagh, Patrick (1904-1967) Irish poet. Extract is from *Advent*.

Kennedy, David Author of *The Dark Sides of Virtue: Reassessing International Humanitarianism*, Princeton University Press (2004).

King, Stephen Contemporary horror writer.

Kingfisher Bird of beautiful plumage and often of sacred symbolic significance, sometimes of Christ, reversed is fisher king, keeper of the grail in Arthurian legend.

Kingsley, Peter Contemporary academic and mystic who resurrected certain of the pre-Socratic philosophers and has done remarkable work on Jung.

Kircher, Athanasius (1602-1680) German Jesuit polymath.

Kirk, Robert (1644-1692) Scottish Minister, Irish scholar and fairy historian. A man due re-visiting.

Klee, Paul (1879-1940) Swiss artist.

Know Thyself Inscribed on the Delphi Temple.

Kogi Native American people of Columbia.

Komorebi (Japanese) Light filtered through leaves.

Koresh, David (1959-1993) Real name Vernon Howell, head of the Branch Davidians involved in the tragic Waco Siege.

Krishna (Sanskrit) Hindu God associated with compassion.

Kundalini (Sanskrit) Coiled energy often conceived as a goddess or serpent lying at the base of the spine which when liberated creates a sense of spaciousness and spiritual enhancement.

Lampers Hunters and poachers who hunt at night with lamps.

Lao-Tzu Great Chinese Taoist philosopher.

Larmor, Joseph (1857-1942) Irish physicist.

LASER Light Activated by Stimulated Emission of Radiation produces 'coherent light.' The startling claim that a laser was used in ancient times was made in *Lost Secrets of the Sacred Ark* (2003) by Lawrence Gardner

Lattice Interlaced structure.

Lavoisier, Antoine (1743-1794) French chemist.

Lawrence, William (1783-1867) Distinguished English surgeon.

LCD Liquid crystal display.

Leary, Timothy (1920-1996) Explorer of consciousness and drugs.

LED Light-emitting diode.

Ledger Book of accounts.

Left brain Idea that the left is dominated with analytical thinking.

Left hand path An unhelpful term that suggests an individual, antinomian path based on will sometimes associated with black magic, which connection is disputed. Traceable back to India.

Legerdemain To be 'light' with the hands implying one was fooling someone else usually through diversion.

Lévi, Eliphas (1810-1875) Magician, occultist.

Leviathan Sea serpent in Bible.

Levity Often means humour but really means lightness.

Lewis, C.S. (1898-1963) Poet, writer, philosopher born in Belfast.

Lewis, Matthew (1775-1818) English writer.

Lichtdom (German) Cathedral of light concocted by Speer with Hitler's approval for some of the Nuremburg rallies.

Light year Distance light travels in a year.

Lightfast Resistant to colour loss when exposed to light.

Lightsaber Sword of light used in Star Wars.

Lightvessel Type of ship used as floating lighthouse.

Lilith Dark goddess figure in a number of traditions.

Lilly, John C. (1915-2001) Neurophysiologist, psychoanalyst, mystic, influential counter-cultural psychonaut from a Cold War background, wrote many things including *The Scientist*.

Limelight Stage illumination.

Limn To draw, detail or describe.

Lincoln Cathedral See for example *Bishop Robert Grosseteste and Lincoln Cathedral: Tracing Relationships between Medieval Concepts of Order and Built Form.* (ed. Temple et al.) 2014.

Linnet Small bird, sweet singer.

Lloyd, Seth Contemporary professor of Mechanical Engineering and Physics.

Lo Exclamation, bringing attention to something.

Lodge, Oliver (1851-1940) Physicist.

Logos (Greek) Elusive concept from Heraclitus through Christian theology indicating an ordering force usually divine in universe.

Loki A Norse god with three children.

Lommel, Pim van Contemporary Dutch surgeon studying NDEs.

Looking-pane Pane is a sheet of glass, thus looking-glass, mirror.

Lorca, Federico Garcia (1898-1936) Great Spanish poet.

LSD Lysergic acid diethylamide. Used for psychedelic experiences.

Lucid dreaming The state of being aware and controlling dreams.

Lucifer (Latin) Light-bringer stands sometimes for Venus or the Devil.

Luciferase Enzyme that produce bioluminescence.

Lugh Irish god believed to have a connection with light and sun.

Lumen naturae (Latin) Light of nature, a natural mystic force manifest in nature and humankind like proto-consciousness or consciousness, used by alchemists, Cicero.

Lumen naturale Natural light, or light of reason.

Lumière (French) Meaning light and name of the French brother pioneers of light.

Luminaries Bodies creating light or person of influence.

Luminosity The state of being luminous or emitting light or the amount thereof emitted particularly in astronomy.

Lunar Society of Birmingham The English Enlightenment society formed in 1775 with many notable industrialists and scientists.

Luria, Isaac (1534-1572) Rabbi, developed a school of Kabbalah.

Lux (Latin) Light.

Lux spiritualis (Latin) The light of the spirit, spiritual light.

Luxiduct I use this to describe a channel of light.

M Theory M stands for a number of possibilities but the theory seeks to represent a unified explanatory equations indicating an essence which combines the fundamental forces in physics.

Mach, Ernst (1838-1916) Austrian physicist and philosopher.

Machiavellianism Philosophy associated with Machiavelli particularly manifest in *The Prince*.

Macrocosm Whole of the universe or the totality of something.

MacSwiney, Terence (1879-1920) Revolutionary, Lord Mayor of Cork. Died after 74 days hunger strike in Brixton Prison.

Madonna The Virgin Mary and also a well know pop star.

Magic Lantern Projector from 17th century onwards.

Magic Utilisation of will, incantations or other methods to exert force on the physical domain.

Magick Magic as proposed by Crowley.

Magna Carta Great charter of rights agreed by King John.

Magnetoreception The biological sense of magnetic fields.

Magus, Magi (pl.) These were magicians often from the Iranian tradition originally and linked to Zoroastrianism.

Maltese Cross Esoteric symbol used by Christian warriors.

Mandean Mesopotamian gnostics probably pre-Christian in origin who have a concept of a supreme entity of light and a trapping of the soul in matter needing to be liberated.

Manhattan Project Source of nuclear weapons in WWII.

Manichaeism Persian religion established by Mani (circa 216-274) based on a light-darkness duality.

Manifold Meaning many or a set of points like that on a closed surface or a topological space locally resembles Euclidean one.

Mantra of light An ancient Buddhist mantra based on light.

Mao Zedong (1893-1976) Chinese Communist leader.

Marat, Jean Paul (1743-1793) Scientist, revolutionary.

Marley, Bob (1945-1981) Rastafari reggae singer.

Marlowe, Christopher (1564-1593) Elizabethan playwright, poet.

Martin, Malachi (1921-1999) Controversial Irish Jesuit, novelist, professor, polyglot, critic of the Vatican and reformers.

Mary Poppins Character in a series of books by P.L. Travers and films, with definite esoteric references.

Maslow, Abraham (1908-1970) American psychologist.

Massey, Gerald (1828-1907) Spiritualist, writer.

Masslessness State of being without mass.

Materialisation A process usually involving a medium who facilitates spiritual manifestations in matter.

Materiel This French word has been specifically adapted to refer to the military equipment necessary to fulfil a mission.

Matrix From the Latin word for womb or mother, the central meaning refers to the enclosure in which something happens with contemporary suggestions of falsehood.

Matterifestation My combination of matter and manifestation.

Mavromatis, Andreas *Hypnagogia: The Unique State of Consciousness between Wakefulness and Sleep,* Thyrsos Press London (2010).

Maximus the Confessor (circa 580-662) Monk, theologian.

Maya (Sanskrit) Concept of illusion.

Mazdean Linked to Ahura Mazda in Zoroastrianism.

McGilchrist, Iain Contemporary writer and psychiatrist who emphasises the significance of the two sides of the brain.

McLuhan, Marshall (1911-1980) Media theorist, conceived the concept of the global village. Wrote Understanding Media: The Extension of Man (1964).

Mechanistic Conceiving things as being machine like, determined, purely physical.

Meme An idea or picture in culture that spreads like a virus.

Mendeleev, Dmitri (1834-1907) Russian chemist, compiler of the Periodic Table.

Mensch (Yiddish) A good person.

Merkabah (Hebrew) Mystical school in Judaism associated with Ezekiel and riding in a heavenly cart or vehicle, which some see as inherently about ascension with light.

Metalanguage Language which describes other words.

Metanoia (Greek) In English means a transformation of spirit or conversion often after a difficult time, morphed into repentance.

Metaphysics Generally deals with nature of reality and often brings us into most fundamental types of meaning about nature, being and knowledge.

Meteor A meteor is the burning object falling into the earth's atmosphere. Meteorite is natural object from outer space that falls on the earth.

Michael Row the Boat Ashore American slavery spiritual song. I take this here to be St. Michael taking the souls to heaven.

Microcosm A little world that represents a bigger one.

Microtubules Argued to be significant for consciousness in the brain and perhaps through quantum functions, these thin cylinders play an important role in and between cells.

Midas King of Greek legend cursed by the realised wish of being able to transform everything into gold.

Midsommar The ancient Swedish summer solstice celebration.

Millenarianism Of which milenniumism is a form, focusing on the idea of a great catastrophe, often in religious contexts.

Milton, John (1608-1674) English poet, State official.

Mimesis Imitation. A complex theory based on the representation of reality in different form from Plato to Auerbach.

Minstrel Musician often with verses, from medieval times onwards.

Miranda Prospero's daughter in The Tempest.

Mirandola, Giovanni Pico Della (1463-1494) Renaissance philosopher, magician, perennialist. Wrote *Oration on the Dignity of Man*.

Miscreant A wrongdoer.

Mishlove, Jeffrey PhD, Eminent parapsychologist, celebrated communicator and author. Host of Thinking Allowed and New Thinking Allowed.

Mistleberger, P.T. Quote from *The Three Dangerous Magi: Osho, Gurdjieff,* Crowley (2010) pg. 206. On Crowley see pg. 390.

Mithraism Mystery cult associated with Roman Empire. Ancient god Mithras was worshipped. Emerged from Iran and elsewhere. Bull sacrifice was a feature of this secret, underground religion.

MLK, Martin Luther King (1929-1968) Great political and spiritual leader.

Mole The reference here is to *The Wind in the Willows* which begins with the Mole emerging from underground.

Monad A single unit.

Moriarty, Professor James Rival of Sherlock Holmes.

Morrigan Mythical Irish queen or goddess associated with war.

Mortal coil The burdens of life.

Mu Means a number of things in different oriental languages and is the 12th letter in Greek with a value of 40, used in many scientific contexts.

Mulla Sadra (circa 1571-1640) Iranian philosopher and theologian.

Mummery A ridiculous ceremony by mummers or mime actors.

Murugan Hindu deity.

Mushroom Cloud Form of gases after a large explosion involving flashes of light.

Musk, Elon Contemporary entrepreneur.

Muslin Thin cotton material.

Mysteries As in mystery school refers to initiations, acts, plays or doing something to experience a revelation usually in extraordinary, guided contexts by specialists and often intended to promote spiritual evolution. The common idea of a mystery is a story which has to be solved.

Nag Hammadi A place in Egypt where a collection of Christian and Gnostic texts were found in 1945.

Nagel, Thomas Philosopher who wrote *What is it Like to be a Bat?*

Narcissus Greek myth of proud, beautiful young man who fell in love with his reflection. Basis for a complex where a person is excessively enthralled to their own appearance.

Naturalist Philosophical approach which focuses on the natural as opposed to the supernatural or spiritual.

Nazis National Socialism evolved in Germany entranced with scientific racism, intending to create an empire.

NDE Near-Death Experience. Unique experience associated with death that often has profound spiritual consequences.

Negative theology Theology which emphasises denial of positive statements about God. Also known as apophatic.

Nemesis (Greek) Arch enemy, fatal rival.

Neon Chemical element in trace amounts in atmosphere, in gaseous state shines in electric current, used for signs.

Neo-Platonism This term is used to describe a loose school of philosophers from Plotinus onwards who sought to develop certain monist ideas related to The One. These ideas manifested within other Mediterranean philosophies and spiritual tradition.

Ness A headland.

Neuroendocrine Linking nerves and hormonal system.

Neuromania To distinguish between a necessary and a sufficient condition. Brain is necessary for a mind but not sufficient. Neural activity is not identical to the qualitative perception. Tallis uses this term.

Neuromelanin Dark pigment in the brain.

Neuroscience The study of the nervous system and especially the functions of the brain.

Neutralino Another hypothetical particle.

New Atlantis Utopian novel by Francis Bacon published in 1626.

New Thought Religiously based philosophy informed by Christianity and American Transcendentalism with heavy emphasis on the individual and intuition led by people like Phineas Quimby (1802-1866).

Newgrange Ancient Irish megalithic site, about 5,000 years old.

Newton, Isaac (1642-1727) Scientist, mathematician, astronomer, alchemist.

Nexus to Numinous This is a concept of mine advanced in *The Mystical Accord* that suggests that spiritual events or practices may create a channel to higher experience.

Nicholson, Philip Contemporary Author of *Meditation and Light Visions*. The article referred to in this book was presented in Beijing 2006 at the Conference on Comparative Mythology.

Nietzsche, Friedrich (1844-1900) German philosopher, author of *Thus Spake Zarathustra*.

Nightingale, Florence (1820-1910) Celebrated nurse of the Crimean War.

No Logo Book by Naomi Klein (1999).

Noetic Although it refers to the intellect, the usage through William James and others refers to a deeper level of knowledge or revelation consistent with mystical insight.

Non-locality While this has a constrained meaning within theoretical physicals it is often used to describe actions at a distance and hence seen by some to represent a ready explanation for much inexplicable phenomena incapable of explanations on a real, local basis.

Noosphere Concept of theologian, Jesuit and geologist Teilhard de Chardin (1881-1955) suggesting a zone of consciousness as part of evolution.

Northern Lights Aurora Borealis, solar wind on magnetosphere.

Novalis, Georg Philipp von Hardenberg (1772-1801) German Romantic, philosopher, mystic. mineralogist. Magic idealist.

Nth The last in a long series.

Numinous Spiritually uplifting, awe-inspiring.

O'Casey, Sean (1880-1964) Irish writer.

O'Reilly, John Boyle (1844-1890) Irish poet, revolutionary.

OBE Out-of-Body Experience. Such experiences may occur during traumatic events and altered states or be associated with certain medical conditions and can be induced in esoteric practices.

Obsequiousness Servile, fawning, obedient, humiliated attitude.

Occam's razor The principle of William of Ockham (1287-1347) to the effect that the simplest available answer is the better one or the one with fewest assumptions works best.

Occult Really means hidden and is used to refer to a whole range of activities dealing with the supernatural.

Ochorowicz, Julien (1850-1917) Polish Scientist.

Odin (Norse) Norse god.

One Flew Over the Cuckoo's Nest (1962) Book by Ken Kesey that became a celebrated film (1975) with Jack Nicholson.

Ong, Walter (1912-2003) Priest, philosopher, professor.

Ontology In philosophy and metaphysics the study of the nature of being and how things are.

Opalescence Optical effects usually from the scattering of light in opals although may refer to a more general iridescence.

Oppenheimer, Robert (1904-1967) Theoretical physicist. Head of Los Alamos, often called the father of the atomic bomb.

Optogenetics Refers to the use of light to control genetically modified neurons.

Or, Ora, Ohr (Hebrew) Light.

Orient The east. Journey to the east is often an internal one.

Orientation Guiding in a direction or attitude.

Orpheus Ancient Greek mystic, poet, prophet, musician founder of a mystery tradition of Orphism.

Orwell, George (1903-1950) Writer.

Oscillation Repetitive, rhythmic or co-ordinated movement around a central value or back and forth in rhythm.

Osiris Egyptian God of fertility and resurrection.

Osman Spare, Austin (1886-1956) English painter, occultist, chaos magician, sigil maker.

Our Lady of the Light A Mexican icon based on a mystical vision of the Virgin Mary in divine light.

Overtone singing Using various resonances in the body to create polyphonic sounds, a number of sounds at once.

Paganism & Neo-paganism Old and new paganism, from ancient practices to modern incarnations in Wicca and others.

Paglia, Camille Feminist who wrote *Sexual Personae: Art and Decadence from Nefertiti to Emily Dickinson* (1990).

Paine, Thomas (1737-1809) Great political activist and propagandist for the rights of man.

Palimpsest A re-used text that often allows elements of the scraped or erased text be examined.

Panentheism God is in everything and beyond. God is in the world and the world is in God.

Panopticon From the Greek meaning all-seeing. Prison type conceived by Jeremy Bentham. The panoptic effect was not always implemented as much as believed.

Panprotopsychism A refined idea of panpsychism where there are 'protophenomenal' properties.

Panpsychism Mind or proto-mind is everywhere or everything has a mind. Some further refine it to 'panexperientialism' where conscious experience is everywhere and a less common pancognitivism where thought is everywhere.

Pantheism Everything is God.

Paracelsus (1494-1541) Swiss doctor, philosopher, alchemist.

Parallax Effect produced when viewing from different angles.

Parapsychology Frontier of psychology and science suggesting need for a new paradigm in science or alternatively validating spiritual experience with scientific method against scientism.

Parmenides (circa 5th century BC) One of founders of Western philosophy, mere fragments of one poem *On Nature* remaining.

Paroxysmal Sudden outburst.

Parsons, Jack (1914-1952) Rocket engineer, occultist.

Patanjali Yoga Sutras Patanjali organised yoga knowledge therein well over two thousand years ago.

Peake, Anthony Contemporary, author of *The Out-Of-Body Experience: The History and Science of Astral Travel*, (2011) reference page 207.

Pearlescence Optical effects principally of a pearl.

Pelagius 4th century, Irish or British theologian.

Pelletier, Kenneth Contemporary author. See for example the New Thinking Allowed episode of May 2019, 'Consciousness Pioneer Arthur M. Young with Kenneth R. Pelletier.'

Pellucid Clear, translucent.

Pentecost Celebration of when Holy Spirit descended on the Apostles 50 days after Easter.

Penumbra Closed shadow around a light, lesser than the focus.

Per se (Latin) By or in itself.

Perennial Philosophy The idea advocated by Aldous Huxley and re-inforced by Huston Smith which can be found in Ficino and Mirandola suggesting one central idea of God or in a more modest form suggesting that there is one central idea of spiritual evolution.

Perennial Wisdom The idea that there is a commonality in structure or content within wisdom traditions that may even reflect an ancient unified theology or philosophy or alternatively that it is emergent and consistent because it is true.

Persephone (Greek) Daughter of Zeus and Demeter became goddess of the underworld and central in the mysteries.

Peyote Hallucinogenic or psychoactive substance from cactus.

Pha (Greek) Root meaning show or make visible.

Phantasm Generally a ghost or an illusion.

Phantasmagoria Sequence of confused images in mind.

Phenomenology This is the study of the structure of consciousness that concentrates on the reality of subjective experience associated with philosophers like Edmund Husserl.

Phos (Greek) Light, prefix indicating light.

Phosphenes Perception of light without light entering the eye.

Phosphorescence Emission of light without heat.

Photic Accessible or sensitive to light.

Photoaxis Where organisms move in response to light either towards or away.

Photobiology Study of light impact on organisms.

Photobiomodulation Using electromagnetic energy to create photochemical changes in cells that react to photons.

Photoluminescence Emission of light after absorption of photons.

Photonic Crystals An opal is a natural photonic crystal as are certain insects. Photonic crystals are structures which allow photons pass or not, depending on their wavelength. Cavities in such crystals may be used to trap light.

Photonic Levitation Refers to the use of light to levitate objects.

Photons Elementary particle of radiation, light particles.

Photosensitivity Sensitivity to light.

Photosynthesis Plant conversion of sunlight into chemical energy.

Phototropism Orientation of plants towards light.

Photuris Type of firefly.

Physicalist A person who focuses on the physical world as the exclusive reality, hence physicalism.

Picatrix A long book perhaps a thousand years old, originally in Arabic on magic and astrology.

Pick lint Picking pieces of dust from clothes and abnormally may be seen in certain states of disease, implication of being petty.

Piety Devout, devoted to religious duties, reverent.

Piezoluminescence Phenomenon of production of light through application of stress to certain stones.

Pineal gland Gland in the brain produces hormones but more particularly seen to be the seat of the soul or third eye.

Pinhole Camera Light proof box with a hole and not a lens to provide an inverted image inside of what is outside.

Pixelated Image broken up into small parts.

Pixie Mythical figures. Fairies.

Plasma Gas of ions that is a fundamental state of matter.

Plato (circa 427-347) Great Greek philosopher. Plato's Cave tells of people entranced by illusory flame shadows on a wall.

Pleroma (Greek) Meaning fullness and usually of divine powers.

Plight A difficult situation.

Plotinus (circa 204-270) Greek Roman who lived in Egypt and was identified with the Neo-Platonist school. Wrote the *Enneads* and sought to communicate Plato's ideas. Promoted idea of the One, that feels consistent with Indian thought for example.

Plymouth Brethren Offshoot of Anglicanism that grew up in Ireland that focused on the Bible as authority.

Poe, Edgar Allan (1809-1849) US writer.

Pointillism Style of painting based on use of points of paint.

Pol Pot (1925-1998) Cambodian communist tyrant.

Pope Leo XIII (1810-1903).

Portcullis Vertical gate in castle usually lattice structure.

Positivism In philosophy and other systems represents the focus on sense data, facts, empiricism, experience, experiment and evidence to implement a scientific method.

Postmodernism An increasingly diverse academic movement that distrusts every other theory but its own, seeks to destroy all certainties save itself, fragments grand theories to establish a new one, pick apart things so they cannot be put together again, applies incredulity with its own credulity, all the while ostensibly oblivious of destructiveness and discontent it unleashes and ideologies it may promote apart from itself consciously or not. But like a plunger, it may be useful at times.

Post-Structuralism You either know what it means or do not. If you do not you can study it yourself or take my word that ignorance is bliss but one always find good stuff somewhere. You might see Baudrillard or Derrida mentioned in passing here but even some of them had the good sense to reject the label.

Pound A place of confinement.

Prana (Sanskrit) Breath, vital, life force.

Prefecture Jurisdiction ruled by a prefect.

Prescience Sense of knowing what will happen in the future.

Pribram, Karl (1919-2015) Proponent of Holonomic brain model who studied the mind through psychiatry and psychology.

Primordial Original, from the beginning.

Prisca Theologia Ancient theology which suggests some ancient, actual theology but should probably be considered more as independent and inevitable outcome of intrinsic spiritual evolution deriving credibility through recurrence in different cultures and not wholly explicable through transmission.

Procrustean Based on the myth of Procrustes who stretched or cut people to make them fit an iron bed. Refers to a solution that is arbitrarily standard.

Project Y Lab that was the essence of the Manhattan Project.

Prometheanism The myth from Greece, left to us in two main forms from accounts by Hesiod and Aeschylus.

Proscription To ban something, usually with serious consequences.

Prospero Great magician in fiction. He can bind spirits, good or bad, control the weather. He seeks to control his world. However the conflict is with his heart and relinquishing power. Uses angelic inspiration of Ariel and heart of his daughter.

Protean Able to change quickly.

Providence Divine or spiritual ordering.

Pseudo-Dionysius the Areopagite (5th - 6th century) Mystical Neo-Platonist, Christian writings misleadingly under the name of a first century saint.

Pseudo-Science Literally means false science which suggests that the alleged science lacks scientific rigour and does not abide by standard methods or protocols but also may be used improperly itself in the context of anomalies or changing paradigms.

Psilocybin Psychedelic substance found in mushrooms.

Psychedelics Substances that cause profound mental states characterised by hallucinations and perceptual distortion.

Psychometry The name for the apparent ability to read or perceive objects or associations therewith through special perception.

Psychonaut A term used to indicate the exploration of spiritual states through altered consciousness that may work for some or represent the cart before the horse at times for others.

Ptolemy (circa 100-170) Mathematician, astronomer, geographer.

Puerpal Fever Infection of mothers following childbirth that became known as the doctor's plague due to their role in spreading it.

Puff Something that can rise in the air. A breath out.

Pullman, Philip Contemporary author.

Purce, Jill Contemporary author of *The Mystic Spiral*, pioneer in sound healing.

Pure Land Buddhist school and destination.

Purkinje Image Refers to a range of images visible on the eye of someone else on the cornea or lens.

Pyramid texts Inscribed on Egyptian walls of Pharaohs representing spiritual journey, being oldest such records.

Pyromancy Divination by fire.

Pythagoras (circa 570-495 BC) Philosopher, mathematician.

Qi (Chinese) Vital energy underpinning concepts of the body and earth in ancient Chinese worldview.

Quadragint (Latin) Prefix or word meaning Forty.

Quagmire Marshy land or a trap.

Quakers The Friends are an influential Protestant group that have widened their base in recent times, united by the idea of light within and dedicated to applications of practice to society. See *Quaker Epistemology* BRP (2019) Laura Rediehs for example.

Quantum A discrete quantity, relating to quantum physics.

Quantum Biology Applications of quantum theory to biology.

Quantum Electrodynamics - QED Deals with how light interacts with matter and particles with each other, quantum field theory of the electromagnetic force.

Quantum Physics Branch of physics evolved in relation to the atomic and subatomic scale, at strange domain of the very small.

Quasar The most remote celestial objects that emit a range of waves and were seen to be 'quasi-stellar.'

Quietism A type of abandonment of the will to contemplation but often means a non-engagement which is deeper and may be criticised by other mystics.

Quintessence The fifth element, essential elements, sought by certain esoteric traditions.

Quirt A short whip.

Ra Ancient Egyptian sun god.

Rabelais, Francois (1494-1553) French writer, monk.

Radiance Light emitted, brightness.

Radiation Electromagnetic emission of energy as waves.

Radin, Dean Contemporary parapsychological researcher.

Rainbow Body A phenomenon in Tibetan Buddhism involving the transformation in life or at death into a light body on attainment of a very high state of spiritual evolution.

Ramanujan, Srinivasa (1887-1920) Great Indian mathematician.

Rand, Ayn (1905-1982) Hugely influential author and objectivist. Championed individuality of the few through dominance and materialism as the only spirituality she tolerated.

Rastafarianism Religious and political movement from Jamaica in the 1930's which combines a number of influences and locates Zion in Africa and Ethiopia with reverence for Haile Selassie.

Reality tunnel Concept used by Robert Anton Wilson.

Realty Personal property, real property.

Reductionist Someone who seeks to find answers to questions by reducing to smallest elements thereby risking losing some element of the whole.

Refection Refreshment with food and drink.

Reformation, The The Protestant division from the Catholic church as a protest against institutional abuse associated with the growth of nations states, religious civil war and the rise of science.

Refraction Change in the direction of a wave by its speed moving through the interface of a medium, bending a wave.

Regardie, Israel (1907-1985) Magician, occultist, writer.

Reich, Wilhelm (1897-1957) Radical psychiatrist.

Reign of Terror Time of massacres and executions in the 1790's during the French Revolution, before Robespierre's death.

Religion The word is believed to be based on the Latin verb to bind.

Renaissance Meaning rebirth focused in the 15th and 16th century associated with a rise in humanism.

Rennet Enzyme of stomachs of ruminant animals.

Requiem Catholic mass for the dead.

Resonant Hyperspectral Imaging See PNAS, Dec, 2018. Juan Colás et al. *'Quantifying single-cell secretion in real time using resonant hyperspectral imaging.'*

Resurrection Men Bodysnatchers. Name for grave robbers who served anatomists and surgeons and others no doubt.

Retro-reflection Where light reflects back to its source.

Reuther, Rosemary Contemporary Catholic theologian and feminist. The quote is from *Sexism and God Talk*, Boston, Beacon Press, 1983.

Rhenium (Re) Rare chemical element from the Latin for Rhine.

Rheum Mucus discharged by eyes during sleep.

Right Brain Linked to unitive thinking, imagination, intuition.

Roberts, Jane (1929-1984) Author, medium who channelled Seth.

Robertson, Morgan (1861-1915) Author of the prophetic novel *Futility*. Also anticipated Pearl Harbour with a short story in 1914 which involves a weapon based on ultraviolet light.

Robespierre, Maximilien (1758-1794) Lawyer, revolutionary.

Rod of Asklepios Snake on a stick. Some trace it to Moses in Bible but associated most with Greek god of healing and medicine.

Roerich, Nicholas (1874-1947) Painter, mystic, writer, advocate of protection of spiritual and cultural heritage.

Romanticism Description of an attitude and movement from end of the 17th century in philosophy, art and music that means different things. At times it stood against organised religion, elements of science, rationalism in favour of the sublime, nature, individuals and intuition. Focus on the individual outside social convention often meant a quest for the unusual and occult. Argued to have mutated into techno-romanticism and cyber-romanticism. See the work of Mark Coeckelbergh for example.

Rookery In London rookeries were slums so named because they looked like places where animals or birds bred.

Roosevelt, Eleanor (1884-1962) Human rights advocate and First Lady of the United States.

Rosicrucianism Diverse, influential but elusive esoteric and sometimes exoteric movement indicated by a combination of a cross and rose symbol to promote spiritual evolution.

Rotten, Johnny John Joseph Lydon, formerly of The Sex Pistols. English son of Irish emigrants.

Round Table The legendary meeting place of King Arthur and his knights, who may represent parts of the whole.

Rousseau, Jean Jacques (1712-1778) He was crucial in ideas of Romanticism. He argued for simplicity and openness not necessarily a return to wilderness.

Rubicon River between Italy and Gaul which Caesar crossed and is synonymous with an irrevocable course of action.

Rubidium Element with chemical symbol Rb, number 37. Alkali metal.

Rubin, Vera (1928-2016) Astronomer, confirmed existence of dark matter.

Rudderless Without direction.

Rumi (circa 1207-1273) Mystic, poet, scholar, theologian.

Rushlight An ancient source of light by burning rushes.

Russell, Bertrand (1872-1970) British philosopher, polymath.

Sacks, Oliver (1933-2015) British neuroscientist and author.

Sacristy A place in or adjacent to a church where sacred vestments and objects are kept.

Sadhguru, Jaggi Vasudev Contemporary Indian guru.

Sage A wise person.

Sai Baba, Sathya (1926-2011) Indian guru.

Saint-Martin, **Louis Claude de** (1743-1803) Influential French mystic, inspiration for Martinism.

Sankaracharya Title of teacher based on Shankara.

Sant Mat Indian spiritual tradition of teaching of saints.

Santa Lucia A festival originally celebrating the Italian martyr who used lights to navigate the catacombs which probably reflected a pagan pre-Christian solstice celebration.

Sapientia (Latin) Wisdom with discernment.

Satanism The use or promotion of Satan sometimes by people who believe the figure does not exist to oppose people who do, apparently ranging from those who conceive it as merely symbolic, artistic or Romantic play to seriously nasty and destructive forces manifested in evil or attempting to be.

Savile, Jimmy (1926-2011) BBC star accused of horrendous crimes after his death (which is always too late).

Savoy, Gene (1927-2007) Explorer, founder of Cosolargy.

Scarface Film from 1983 about a Cuban drug boss in Miami.

Scarify To make shallow cuts or incisions.

Scholem, Gershom (1897-1982) The quote on the Torah is from *On the Kabbalah and its Symbolism*, 1965.

Schopenhauer, Arthur (1788-1860) German philosopher.

Schrödinger, Erwin (1887-1961) Great theoretical physicist from Austria, who lived in Ireland for a substantial period.

Scientia (Latin) Knowledge.

Scientism Approach which elevates science beyond the domain of its method, scope and claims to be able to answer all questions of knowledge or discredit other ways of attaining knowledge.

Scientocracy Rule by an elite group of scientists and experts substituting scientism and objectives over all. Technocracy.

Scientology Church founded by Hubbard.

Scintilla (Latin) Spark, glittering speck used for very small amount.

Scriabin, Alexander (1872-1915) Russian composer.

Scrooge, Ebenezer Main character in Dickens, *A Christmas Carol*.

Scry To scry is to use some reflective surface in divination like a crystal ball or a blue bottle by the Irish healer Biddy Early.

Second Sight Could include a range of powers such as remote-viewing, premonitions, visions of the future.

Sensorimotor Sensory and motor functions of nerves.

Sentinel Soldier who keeps watch or an indicator of disease.

Sergius (1314-1392) Russian saint.

Seurat, Georges (1859-1891) French post-Impressionist painter know for pointillism.

Sextant Device for taking angles in navigation and surveying.

Sfumato (Italian) Refers to a smoky effect in painting.

Shakti (Sanskrit) Cosmic force often manifest as a goddess.

Shamanism Practice associated with a Siberian origin but fairly universal which involves initiates accessing altered states of consciousness for the benefit of the group. See 'Brain changes during a shamanic trance. Altered modes of consciousness, hemispheric laterality and systemic psychobiology,' in Flor-Henry (et al.) *Cogent Psychology,* 2017, Vol.4, Issue 1.

Shamash Sumerian Sun God. In (Hebrew) Shammash is the candle used to light other lights.

Shantedeva One or more individuals of that name, of the 8th century who wrote texts celebrated in Mahayana Buddhism.

Shekinah (Hebrew) Meaning dwelling and referring to the presence of God often in a female form.

Sheldrake, Rupert Contemporary biologist, critic of materialism proponent of morphogenetic fields.

Shelley, Mary Wollstonecraft (1797-1851) Author of *Frankenstein. The Modern Prometheus*, married to Percy Bysshe Shelley.

Shen Kuo (1031-1095) Chinese polymath, scientist author of the Dream Pool Essays.

Sherlock Holmes Character created by Arthur Conan Doyle (1859-1930) in his classic series.

Shine, Betty (1929-2002) Famous medium, spiritualist.

Shorn Cut away, as with hair or wool from sheep.

Shrine A place or object of worship.

Siddhis (Sanskrit) Powers developed by yogis.

Signature The doctrine of signatures looks for correspondences in nature to signal deeper truths.

Simulacrum Imitation of something or someone.

Singularity Generally indicates a point of technological development usually associated with AI which represents a point of no return, particularly for humans.

Siri, Giuseppe (1906-1989) Cardinal believed by some to have been elected pope, a conspiracy theory if you like.

Smith, Huston (1919-2016) Religious scholar, perennialist.

Smith, Joseph (1805-1844) Founder of Mormonism.

Smithereens From Irish, meaning small pieces.

Socrates (470-399 BC) Great Athenian philosopher.

Sojourn A temporary stay or a holiday. Hence sojourners. Sojourner Truth was a famous abolitionist, women's right activist (1797-1893), Isabella Baumfree.

Sorcery Means different things at different times, usually meant in terms of black magic.

Sorokin, Pitirim (1889-1968) Russian-American sociologist.

Sovereignty State of power of control, make final decision, be independent.

Spectroscopy Looks at the interaction of matter and radiation.

Spinthariscope A device for seeing nuclear disintegration.

Spiritescence My application of suffix of light to spirit.

Spiritscape My word indicating vista of the spiritually aware.

Spooks Ghosts or spies.

Spooky action at a distance Phrase used by Einstein to indicate one necessary result of the nature of quantum mechanics.

Sprite Phenomenon of light occurring above storms as well as being a type of small spirit.

St. Anthony (251-356) One of the earliest Christian monks in Egypt. Also known as Anthony the Great.

St. Augustine (354-430) Amongst other things developed ideas of spiritual light or divine illumination.

St. Bridget (circa 451-525) Irish saint who had characteristics of a Celtic pagan goddess. Known as Bride.

St. Clare (1194-1253) Or Santa Clara is the patron saint of tv because of her ability to remote view.

St. Joseph of Cupertino (1603-1663) Known for levitation.

St. Malachy (1094-1148) Visionary Irish saint.

St. Pancras (circa 289-304) Roman saint associated with two churches in North London and also name of a railway station.

Stalin, Josef (1878-1953) Premier of Soviet Union, Dictator.

Stambha In Hindu systems, a column linking heaven and earth.

Star Trek Celebrated US TV series.

Star Wars Famous movie series by George Lucas.

Steiner, Rudolf (1861-1925) Austrian philosopher, spiritual seeker.

Stockholm Syndrome Where the captive identifies with the captor.

Stoker, Bram (1847-1912) Born in Dublin, author of *Dracula*.

Stradivarius The celebrated violins produced by the Stradivari family in the 17th and 18th century, whose few remaining examples are incredibly expensive reflecting their quality.

Straw men An argument refuted that is not the one presented or relevant is setting up a straw man.

Strieber, Whitley Contemporary writer of books such as *The Wolfen*, *Communion* and *The Hunger*, famous for his encounters with extraordinary or non-human consciousnesses.

Strobe Lighting of a particular flashing type.

Stroboscopic effect Changes in perception by different speeds of viewing or recording images as the 'wagon wheel' effect.

Strutt, John William (1842-1919) Title Baron Rayleigh. British scientist awarded the Nobel Prize.

Subjective Refers to the unique experience of the particular person.

Sublimation Changing from one form to another such as a solid to a gas, letting off steam.

Substantia Nigra (Latin) Black substance, part of brain controlling movement and reward.

Succour Help.

Sufi An adherent of the mystical school of Islam seen to reflect the perennial wisdom and associated with great flowerings of mystical literature and poetry.

Suhrawardi (circa 1154-1191) Associated with the foundation of Illuminationist school and known as the Master of Illumination. Wrote *Philosophy of Illumination* and *Flashes of Light.*

Sullied To damage or dirty.

Sullivan, Neil J. Author of *A Prometheus Bomb: The Manhattan Project and Government in the Dark* (2016).

Sum (Latin) I am. English meaning amount or total.

Sunflowers Flowers, notably painted by Vincent van Gogh.

Sunwind Solar wind. A plasma streaming from the sun's corona.

Supercelestial Divine domain above the power of stars.

Superconductivity State characterised by absence of electrical resistance with low temperatures save in relation to DNA.

Superconscious Conscious above the normal.

Supermundane Above this world.

Supernal Celestial, above or high.

Supernatural Relating to forces beyond the observable universe.

Supersensory While suggesting something above or beyond the senses, the distinction between what is sensory and not is very difficult, when senses vary and new ones are discovered.

Supersymmetry A theory which seeks to provide a solution to some fundamental conundrums in particle physics.

Surjection Mathematical mapping.

Swedenborg, Emanuel (1688-1722) Great Swedish scientist and mystic, reputed to be one of the most intelligent people ever. He wrote about communicating with all types of spirits and presented visions of heaven and hell.

Swift, Jonathan (1667-1745) Dublin writer, Dean Swift.

Sword in the Stone A sword embedded in stone that will only yield to the genuine king.

Symeon The New Theologian (949-1022). Byzantine mystic monk.

Sympathetic magic Looks to correspondence, similarities and likenesses to exert a force or power or to have participation.

Synaesthesia A condition whereby stimulation of one sense has manifestations in another.

Tagore, Rabindranath (1861-1941) Bengali writer, artist.

Talbot, Michael (1953-1992) Writer of *The Holographic Universe.*

Tallis, Raymond Contemporary writer, neuroscientist.

Talos Bronze automaton in Greek legend.

Tammuz Babylonian god. Used for an ancient Babylonian festival believed by some to have been taken over by other religions. Also a Jewish month.

Tanizaki, Junichiro (1886-1965) Japanese writer.

Tantra (Sanskrit) Meaning loom or weave, it means different things from certain exoteric practices associated with Hindu and Buddhism to esoteric practices that are often related to physical paths to higher consciousness.

Taoism The great philosophy and religion of China that emphasises the way or Tao and derives many profound insight through observation of natural forces.

Tatty-bogler (Scots) Scarecrow.

Taylor, Thomas (1758-1835) Writer and translator, Neo-Platonist.

Technocracy The ideology or goal of exclusive, elite governance or control by experts, technocrats or scientists.

Technoromantics A term which has acquired different meanings, positive or negative depending on your position. I use it to refer to the mixture of romanticism and technology.

Templeton, Kirk Author of dissertation on *Suhrawardi, Abhinavgupta and the Metaphysics of Light* (2013).

Tesla, Nikola (1856-1943) Great inventor interested in light.

Tether To tie.

The Chalice and the Blade: Our History Our Future Riane Eisler (1987).

The Cloud of Unknowing Great Christian mystical book by an unknown author. Late 14th century.

The Cloud Upon the Sanctuary Book by Eckartshausen.

The Crest Jewel of Wisdom Vivekachudamani (Sanskrit) Eight century text of Advaita Vedanta often seen as one of Shankara's work, but contested.

The Divine Comedy Epic poem by Dante.

The Emerald Tablet Important Hermetic text relevant to many esoteric bodies.

The Ghent Altarpiece See *The Ghent Altarpiece: Art, History, Science and Religion. Eds. Praet and Martens*. In particular Marc De Mey 'Perception. De Vision Dei: Optics, Theology and Philosophy in the Ghent Altarpiece.'

The Gnosis of the Light (1918) A translation by Rev. F. Lamplugh.

The Light of Asia A book published in 1879 by the poet Edwin Arnold about the Buddha who also published *The Light of The World* about Jesus.

The Light upon the Candlestick (1662) published in Holland known in Latin as *Lucerna Super Candelabrum.*

The Monk (1796) Matthew Lewis.

The PK Man: A True Story of Mind Over Matter Jeffrey Mishlove (2000) Fascinating investigation of an incredible individual raising profound issues about the nature of humanity.

The Red Book This was a collection of works by Jung in relation to his own explorations and experiments for a few years after 1913 that were not published until a decade ago.

The Secret Commonwealth While it now refers to a novel by Philip Pullman, it was used by Robert Kirk in 1691 to refer to the domains of fairies and other supernatural beings.

The Secret of the Golden Flower Ancient Taoist text that provides a classic breathing technique for meditation and spiritual development with light as a concept therein.

The Selfish Gene Richard Dawkins book (1976), also uses the idea of the meme to spread culture. This is an influential book which seems to have convinced a generation with its battering ram to the construct of the spiritual universe.

The Signature of All Things Jacob Boehme's book based on the doctrine of signatures indicated a suggestiveness of significance related to the shape of things. Boehme (1575-1624) was one of the most influential mystics in Europe.

The Society of the Spectacle Guy Debord (1931-1994) Marxist philosopher, influenced Situationist movement with 1967 text.

The Stripping of the Altars: *Traditional Religion in England 1400-1580* Eamon Duffy (1992) Yale University Press.

The Tempest Play by Shakespeare circa 1610.

The Twilight Zone US tv series.

The Unbearable Lightness of Being Book (1984) by the Czech writer Milan Kundera, (b. 1929). Also filmed (1988).

The Wreck of the Titan Book by Morgan Robertson (1912) based on *Futility* (1898) which anticipated the Titanic sinking.

Thelema Philosophy, practice or religion promoted by Aleister Crowley after channelled messages in Egypt.

Thence From there.

Theoria (Greek) Contemplation.

Theosophy Refers to a philosophy or religion of Blavatsky or more generally an approach to God based on mystical experience.

Theurgy Practice of establishing connection with deities that may evolve to some perceived union or contact with an emanation or sense of presence thereof though mystical or magical practices.

They Live (1988) Film based on the idea of a false reality of control discovered with the use of special sunglasses.

Thiel, Peter Contemporary entrepreneur.

Third Eye An eye of perception located in the pineal gland believed to be the seat of the soul by some.

Thralldom State of slavery, being a thrall. Hence enthralled.

Tiffany, Louis Comfort (1848-1933) Created beautiful art nouveau vases and especially lamps.

Tiso, Father Catholic priest interested in inter-faith work.

TMA In *2001: A Space Odyssey* it was the monolith called the Tycho Magnetic Anomaly.

Toland, Gregg (1904-1948) US cinematographer.

Tolkien, J.R.R. (1892-1973) Great writer, teacher of language.

Tononi, Giulio Neuroscientist. Proponent of integrated information theory of consciousness.

Topography Surface features including on semiconductors.

TQM Total Quality Management. System of management based on the work of people like W. Edwards Deming (1900-1993).

Traherne, Thomas (circa 1636-1674) English metaphysical poet.

Transcranial magnetic stimulation Using magnetic fields to stimulate nerve cells in the brain.

Transducer A technology that converts energy from one form to another.

Transfiguration Christian term refers to transformation of Jesus as a demonstration to three apostles, characterised by radiance. Used in a wider sense to indicate profound states of change.

Transhumanism Trend to merge human beings and technology.

Transient Luminous Events Light sights from atmosphere.

Transient Lunar Phenomena Used to describe recurrent, inexplicable phenomena often associated with light on the moon.

Transjection Injection through layer such as skin.

Translucence Phenomenon of light passing through a medium and allowing form be perceived still.

Trappist Branch of Cistercians of Catholic Church cloistered monks whose origin was in La Trappe Abbey. Also a star.

Travers, P.L. (1899-1996) Author of Mary Poppins.

Trotsky, Leon (1879-1940) Marxist, Bolshevik, writer.

Tulpa A thought-created entity claimed to be capable of independent existence.

Tumbril Type of cart used during the French Revolution.

Turing Test Test to find out whether a computer can be passed off as a human. From Alan Turing (1912-1954) the great scientist.

Twilight of the Gods Work by Wagner.

Twilight of the Idols Book from 1888 by Nietzsche.

Tyndall, John (1820-1893) Irish physicist interested in sunlight, the separation of religion and science.

Tzitzum Kabbalist concept of the contraction of God's infinite light to allow creation.

UAP Unidentified aerial phenomenon.

Über Here the suffix to 'mensch' means above, beyond, super to perhaps supra and refers to Nietzsche's idea of the ideal person, a concept borrowed by the Nazis.

Ubiquity Pervasiveness, state of being everywhere.

UFO Unidentified Flying Object.

Unbeknownst That which is not known but suggested or claimed perhaps to exist and existing beyond comprehension.

Underhill, Evelyn (1875-1941) Great writer on Mysticism as well as novelist writing *The Column of Dust* and *The Grey World*.

Unencumbered Unburdened, without restrictions.

Unquenchable Cannot be put out, cannot be quenched.

Upanishads Great Indian, Hindu religious or Vedanta spiritual texts that marshal many familiar concepts such as Brahman and Atman.

Utilitarian Philosophy seeking to maximise utility or happiness and minimise pain.

Utu Mesopotamian sun god.

Vajrayana A type of Buddhism based on the Buddhist tantra.

Van Gogh, Vincent (1853-1890) Post-impressionist painter.

Vaughan, Henry (1621-1695) Twin of Thomas. Metaphysical poet.

Vaughan, Thomas (1621-1666) Welsh philosopher, alchemist, mystic who wrote also under the name Eugenius Philalethes.

Vedic The Vedas represent a series of religious, sacred and mythological texts in Sanskrit.

Vestments Clothing usually wore in Christian ceremonies.

Vishnu Hindu god who may manifest in various avatars.

Vivisection Surgery for experiments on living animals.

VLA Very Large Array of radio telescopes in New Mexico.

Voldemort Lord Voldemort, Tom Marvolo Riddle. The dark force in *Harry Potter*.

Von Franz, Marie Louise (1915-1998) Jungian who worked on alchemy and fairy tales.

Wagner, Richard (1813-1883) German composer of Ring cycle.

Wake (Noun) Vigil over a dead person. (Verb) To come out of a sleep state. *Finnegans Wake* is different from Finnegan's Wake.

Wald, George (1906-1997) Nobel prize winner who studied pigments in the retina.

Wallace, Alfred Russel (1823-1913) Jointly conceived the theory of evolution but the emphasis on a spiritual dimension did not fit the needs of the class wanting to employ it as a weapon.

Warpn'weft The warp and weft are the down and across threads of the loom in weaving.

Watchers The non-canonical Book of Enoch describes Watchers as the fallen angels who fathered the Nephilim.

Wells, H.G. (1866-1946) Great writer of science fiction and tireless advocate of an open conspiracy for world government in the form of a scientocracy that displaces religion.

Wheeler, John (1911-2008) US theoretical physicist who worked on the Manhattan Project.

Whistler, James Abbott McNeill (1834-1903) American artist.

Wild goose chase A frantic pursuit of the unobtainable.

Wilde, **Oscar** (1854-1900) Irish poet, playwright, novelist.

Will o' wisp Ghost light seen in marshy areas often at night.

Williams, Charlie 'On 'modified human agents:' John Lilly and the paranoid style in American Neuroscience,' *History of the Human Sciences,* Oct 9, 2019.

Wilson, Colin (1931-2013) Writer, philosopher.

Wilson, Robert Anton (1932-2007) Writer of *The Illuminatus Trilogy* and *Cosmic Trigger: The Final Secret of the Illuminati.*

WIMP The hypothetical weakly interacting massive particles.

Wittgenstein, Ludwig (1889-1951) Austrian philosopher.

Wolf, Fred Alan Contemporary US theoretical physicist interested in consciousness.

Wolfe, Tom (1930-2018) Writer. See 'McLuhan's 'New World',' The Wilson Quarterly, Spring 2004, Vol. 28, No.2, 18-25.

Wollstonecraft, Mary (1759-1797) Great writer, philosopher and advocate for rights of women. Mother of Mary Shelley. The quote *'The silken wings..'* comes from an essay entitled *'On Poetry and our Relish for the Beauties of Nature.'*

Yak Butter Lamp Traditional lamp of Tibetan Buddhism.

Yang Active, male principle of the universe associated with light.

Yeats, William Butler (1865-1939) Senator. Magician. Playwright. Poet. Extract here is from *He Wishes for the Clothes of Heaven*.

Yin Passive female principles associated with earth and dark.

Yogis (Sanskrit) Practitioners of yoga, but especially evolved spiritual ones.

Yoke Used to attach animals, from the words to join. Like yoga.

Yonder Over there, more distant.

Young, Arthur M. (1905-1995) Inventor, scientist, philosopher.

Zamyatin, Yevgeny (1884-1937) Russian science fiction writer.

Zen Form of Buddhism perfected in Japan, China, Korea emphasising intuition, meditation as a path to enlightenment.

Zero Sum Game A game where one's gain is at another's expense.

Zest Energy.

Zohar (Hebrew) Meaning radiance, splendour or even light. This text is foundational in Kabbalah.

Zooplankton Category of plankton that drift in water.

Zoroastrianism Iranian religion from before Islam, set up by Zoroaster (Zarathustra) which tended towards monotheism though not fully and had rituals associated with fire and purification in particular. Magic is linked to it but is most likely divine light magic.

Zuboff, Shoshana Contemporary writer of *The Age of Surveillance Capitalism: The Fight for a Human Future at the New Frontier of Power* (2018).

Zwicky, Fritz (1898-1974) Bulgarian-Swiss Astronomer famous for suggesting dark matter.

About the Author

James Tunney obtained an honours degree in law from Trinity College Dublin, qualified as a Barrister at the Honorable Society of the King's Inn, Dublin and obtained an LLM from Queen Mary College, University of London.

Since then he worked as a Lecturer and Senior Lecturer in UK universities. He has been a Visiting Professor in Germany and France, lecturer around the world and worked as an international legal consultant in places such as Lesotho and Moldova for bodies such as the UNDP. He talked in many countries and published regularly on issues associated with globalisation. He has taught, written and talked about subjects such as indigenous rights, travel and tourism law, culture and heritage, IP, communications technology law, competition law, China and World Trade.

He decided to leave the academic world behind to concentrate on artistic and spiritual development. He has exhibited paintings in a number of countries and has continued his writing.

This book is the second in a series on Mysticism, and Spiritual Consciousness.

If you have enjoyed this book, please leave a review on Amazon.

MYSTICISM & SPIRITUAL CONSIOUSNESS

The Mystical Accord – Sutras to Suit Our Times,
Lines for Spiritual Evolution

FICTION

Blue Lies September

Ireland I Don't Recognise Who She Is